KURDS AND YEZIDIS IN THE MIDDLE EAST

KURDS AND YEZIDIS IN THE MIDDLE EAST

Shifting Identities, Borders, and the Experience of Minority Communities

Edited by
Güneş Murat Tezcür

I.B.TAURIS
LONDON • NEW YORK • OXFORD • NEW DELHI • SYDNEY

I.B. TAURIS

Bloomsbury Publishing Plc

50 Bedford Square, London, WC1B 3DP, UK

1385 Broadway, New York, NY 10018, USA

29 Earlsfort Terrace, Dublin 2, Ireland

BLOOMSBURY, I.B. TAURIS and the I.B. Tauris logo are trademarks of
Bloomsbury Publishing Plc

First published in Great Britain 2021
This paperback edition published in 2022

Cover design: Adriana Brioso
Cover image: Yezidis in the Sinjar mountains in Mosul, Iraq, 2014. (© Emrah Yorulmaz/
Anadolu Agency/Getty Images)

A catalogue record for this book is available from the British Library.

A catalog record for this book is available from the Library of Congress.

ISBN: HB: 978-0-7556-0119-6
           PB: 978-0-7556-3992-2
       ePDF: 978-0-7556-0121-9
      eBook: 978-0-7556-0120-2

Series: Kurdish Studies

Typeset by Integra Software Services Pvt. Ltd.

To find out more about our authors and books visit www.bloomsbury.com
and sign up for our newsletters.

CONTENTS

LIST OF ILLUSTRATIONS

Figures

Tables

LIST OF CONTRIBUTORS

Majid Hassan Ali (PhD, University of Bamberg) is Associate Member of the Department of Yezidi Studies at the Giorgi Tsereteli Institute of Oriental Studies, Ilia State University, Tbilisi, Georgia.

Tutku Ayhan is a PhD candidate of Security Studies at the University of Central Florida, USA.

Mücahit Bilici is Associate Professor of Sociology at John Jay College and CUNY Graduate Center, USA.

Ekrem Karakoç (PhD, Penn State University) is Associate Professor of Political Science at Binghamton University, USA.

Zeynep Kaya (PhD, London School of Economics) is Senior Teaching Fellow at SOAS, University of London, UK.

Bahadin H. Kerborani is a PhD student at the Department of Near Eastern Languages and Civilizations at the University of Chicago, USA.

Ohannes Kılıçdağı (PhD, Boğaziçi University) was the Nikit and Eleanora Ordjanian Visiting Professor at Columbia University in spring 2020.

Ege Özen (PhD, Binghamton University) is Assistant Professor of Political Science at College of Staten Island, CUNY, USA.

Bayar Mustafa Sevdeen (PhD, University of Mosul) is Dean of School of Social Sciences at the University of Kurdistan, Hewlêr, Iraq.

Güneş Murat Tezcür (PhD, University of Michigan) is Jalal Talabani Chair and Professor at the University of Central Florida, USA.

Arzu Yılmaz (PhD, Ankara University) is a visiting scholar at the University of Hamburg, Germany.

ACKNOWLEDGMENTS

The tragedy of August 2014 put the Yezidi, a community hitherto on the margins of Iraqi society and politics, under international limelight. While the Yezidis have developed a unique historical resiliency due to their experiences as a historically marginalized minority, the audacity and brutality of the assault has pushed the community to the brink of survival. At the same time the visceral visibility of the community's suffering has diminished Yezidis' obscurity and generated global sympathy. In this sense, the Yezidi experience has some resemblances to the Kurdish experience: being victims of mass violence leading to greater international recognition.

In this historical context, this volume aims to offer the first comparative study about the formations and intersubjective perceptions characterizing Kurdish and Yezidi political identities. It aims to facilitate greater dialogue between these Kurdish and Yezidi studies and explore the common and distinctive factors shaping Kurdish and Yezidi politics in both historical and contemporary times. In doing so, it also aims to reach broader audiences who are interested in minority relations, ethnic and religious identities in the Middle East.

The idea for this book emerged at an event organized by Kurdish Political Studies Program (KPSP) at the University of Central Florida (UCF), the first and only academic entity dedicated to the study of Kurdish issues in North America. Dr. Naj Karim's vision was central to the founding of the KPSP. In Kurdish Studies, his legacy will live on through the KPSP. Kerstin Hamann has played a pivotal leadership role that has helped KPSP flourish at UCF since 2015. Most of the chapters of this book were initially presented at the conference titled "Borders, Identities and Refugees: The Kurdish Experience in the Middle East" at UCF on March 1, 2019. Firat Bozcali, Hakan Özoğlu, Haidar Khezri, Tyler Fisher, and Hille Hanso enriched the conference with their presentations. UCF and Global Religion Research Initiative (GRRI) based at the University of Notre Dame provided financial support for the conference and parts of research that inform the analyses in this book.

As typical of her, Doreen Horschig provided meticulous assistance during the preparation of this book for publication. Fırat Esmer of Bremen, Germany (originally from Diyarbakir), and Jeen Maltayi of Duhok were marvelous companions and offered valuable support during the fieldwork in Iraqi Kurdistan in May and June 2018. The resourcefulness and kindness of Dr. Gazi Zibari of Shreveport, Louisiana, and the hospitality of Dr. Nizar Ismet, the director of Duhok Health, made the fieldwork a smooth experience. It was a pleasure to work with Sophie Rudland of I.B. Tauris who has been very supportive of the project from the beginning.

Developing an appreciation of the experiences of ordinary people who often find themselves in extraordinary situations has been an indicator of my own scholarly maturity. I am personally grateful to many Yezidis and Kurds who generously shared their often agonizing stories with me and my colleagues.

In order to make the book more accessible, diacritical marks and long vowel markers are mostly avoided. Accordingly, transliterations of Arabic and Kurdish names of locations, people, and entities typically follow the most common English forms throughout the chapters (e.g., Sinjar rather than Shingal, which is used by Yezidis). At the same time, original acronyms of organizations, such as YNK instead of PUK or AKP instead of JDP, are used. The spelling "Yezidi" is preferred over "Yazidi" as the former is closer to the self-descriptions of the community in Kurdish, Êzîdî.

ABBREVIATIONS

AKP	(*Adalet ve Kalkınma Partisi*—Justice and Development Party), the ruling political party in Turkey since 2002
BBP	(*Büyük Birlik Partisi*—Great Union Party), a minor far-right political party in Turkey
CGI	Central Government of Iraq
CHP	(*Cumhuriyet Halk Partisi*—Republican People's Party), the main opposition political party in Turkey since 2002
ENKS	(*Encûmena Niştimanî ya Kurdî li Sûriyê*—Kurdish National Council in Syria), the Syrian Kurdish political party affiliated with KDP in Iraq
HDP	(*Halkların Demokratik Partisi*—Peoples' Democratic Party), the main Kurdish political party in Turkey
HPÊ	(*Hêza Parastina Êzîdxan*—Yezidi Defense Forces), a Yezidi militia
ICC	International Criminal Court
IS	(Islamic State—*ad-Dawlah al-Islāmiyah fī 'l-ʿIrāq wa-sh-Shām*), a transitional Salafi-jihadist group primarily based in Iraq and Syria
ISI	(Islamic State of Iraq—*Dawlat al-ʿIrāq al-ʿIslāmiyyah*), a Salafi-jihadist group in post-Saddam Iraq
KDP	(*Partiya Demokrat a Kurdistanê*—Kurdistan Democratic Party), one of the main Kurdish political parties in Iraq, based in Erbil
KRG/KRI	Kurdistan Regional Government/Kurdistan Region of Iraq
MHP	(*Milliyetçi Hareket Partisi*—Nationalistic Action Party), a far-right political party in Turkey
PKK	Kurdistan Workers' Party (*Partiya Karkerên Kurdistan*), a transitional armed Kurdish organization
PYD	(*Partiya Yekîtiya Demokrat*—Democratic Union Party), the main Kurdish political party in Syria
Saadet	(*Saadet Partisi*—Felicity Party), a minor Islamist political party in Turkey
TEVDA	(Yezidi Free Democratic Movement), a Yezidi social movement based in Iraq
UNHCR	United Nations High Commission for Refugees
YNK	(*Yekîtiya Niştimanî ya Kurdistanê*—Patriotic Union of Kurdistan), one of the main Kurdish political parties in Iraq, based in Sulaymaniyah
YPŞ	(*Yekîneyên Berxwedana Şingal*—Resistance Units of Shingal), a Yezidi militia affiliated with PKK

1

INTRODUCTION: TOWARD A CROSS-FERTILIZATION BETWEEN KURDISH AND YEZIDI STUDIES

Güneş Murat Tezcür

Introduction

The experience of victimhood has been a core aspect of both Kurdish and Yezidi political self-identifications and narratives in modern times. Kurds are a paradigmatic persecuted ethnic minority; Yezidis are a paradigmatic persecuted religious minority. Kurdish victimhood primarily derives from the experience of being a suppressed ethnic minority by four Middle Eastern states, for example, Saddam's genocidal Anfal campaign involving massive usage of chemical weapons. Yezidi victimhood, which has a longer lineage, primarily derives from the experience of persecution at the hand of Muslim rulers and neighbors based on a code of religious difference, for example, the genocidal campaign involving sexual slavery by the self-styled Islamic State (IS). The Kurdish politics of memory is an unbroken history of state violence, lack of political unity, and frustrated national ambitions. The Yezidi politics of memory is an unbroken history of violent *firmans* (i.e., military campaigns) by Ottoman pashas, Kurdish amirs, and Muslim clerics. Consequently, the Kurdish and Yezidi remembrance is primarily the memory of wounds. To paraphrase Milan Kundera's famous quote, the Kurdish and Yezidi struggle against hegemonic states and religious entities is the struggle of memory against forgetting.

It is tempting to take these distinctive but overlapping visceral experiences and memories of victimhood as the basis of a comparative study of Kurds and Yezidis. Such a study could start with the premise of how ethnic and religious persecution and violence have shaped the basic contours of these two communities' daily experiences and political struggles. While such a premise would be promising, it could also be misleading without a systematic attention to the agency of Kurdish and Yezidi actors in effectively challenging hegemonic projects through various forms of physical and symbolic resistance. It would also ignore how the politics of memory inevitably tends to be highly selective and entails the politics of forgetting.[1] The sharp distinction between victim and aggressor is not sustainable in certain historical contexts characterized by shifting alliances, porous identities, and contentious politics.[2]

This book transcends victimization narratives and offers a comparative study of Kurdish and Yezidi experiences with each other and other groups in the Middle East in both historical and contemporary times. It aims to offer fresh and nuanced perspectives about multidimensional identities and shifting borders characterizing these dynamic experiences. In doing so, it focuses on historical processes shaping the evolution of political identities and discusses the centrality of intersubjective perceptions, which are informed by power asymmetries, to these processes. It includes contributions from both established and emerging scholars that speak to multiple disciplines including political science, sociology, history, and cultural and area studies. The contributors, coming from different geographical and institutional settings, engage with similar themes from distinctive scholarly traditions.[3] All chapters are based on original empirical research, including fieldwork (primarily in Iraqi Kurdistan), archival study, or survey data.

The book has three distinguishing characteristics. First, it is the first systematic study covering Kurdish and Yezidi experiences in a comparative and integrated way. Yezidis are a primarily Kurdish-speaking group with a distinctive religious belief system. A group historically lacking an established intellectual class and written record, they have attracted the interest of travelers, soldiers, scholars, and statesmen since the early nineteenth century. At the same time, there has been limited engagement with the large field of Kurdish studies.[4] Yezidis remained on the margins of scholarly works about Kurds before the tragedy in August 2014 generated significant public and academic interest in the Yezidis.

The long-lasting marginality of Kurdish studies in the Western academia further aggravated the isolation of Yezidi studies. Most of the extant work focused on Kurdish interactions with more hegemonic actors, the Iranian, Iraqi, Syrian, and Turkish states that hindered Kurdish aspirations for greater rights and power with repression and violence since the early twentieth century. As a result, the intra-Kurdish relations and minorities in Kurdistan, such as Armenians and Yezidis, received much less systematic attention—until very recently. This book aims to facilitate a greater degree of communication and integration between Kurdish and Yezidi studies. As I elaborate further below, the book engages with two overarching and interrelated themes to facilitate greater dialogue between Kurdish and Yezidi studies: (a) *formations* of Kurdish and Yezidi political identities in different historical settings and (b) intersubjective *perceptions* of Kurds and Yezidis by their neighbors and hegemonic powers. As several chapters in this book demonstrate, studying how both more powerful societal groups such as ethnic Turks in contemporary Turkey and less powerful groups such as the Armenians in the early twentieth-century eastern Anatolia and the Yezidis in the early twenty-first century perceived Kurds opens up new avenues of promising research and valuable insights about peace and conflict characterizing intergroup relations.

Second, the book presents novel interpretations based on original empirical research with a truly interdisciplinary approach. Chapters employ both quantitative and qualitative methods to address similar questions about identity formation and intersubjective perceptions. Several chapters utilize in-depth interviews with a wide range of ordinary people ranging from Kurdish refugees who fled from Turkish counterinsurgency operations to the relative safety of Iraqi Kurdistan in the 1990s to Yezidi survivors of the 2014 genocidal attacks. Other chapters utilize historical material, including a canonical Kurdish text from the late seventeenth century, writings of Western travelers to Kurdistan from the nineteenth century, and local Armenian newspapers from the early twentieth, and Arabic sources from the mid-twentieth-century Iraq. Another chapter utilizes a nationally representative survey conducted in Turkey. This methodological diversity and richness of empirical sources in primary languages, including Kurdish, Armenian, Arabic, and Turkish, reflect the increasing maturity of scholarship on Kurdish and Yezidi issues.

Finally, the book develops innovative conceptual approaches exploring shifts in the majority-minority relations characterized by both dominance-subordination and coexistence-cooperation. It engages with broader scholarly literature such as minority rights and democratization, politics of identity, nationalism, political violence, and refugees. In particular, various chapters suggest how the notion of victimhood is a historically contingent process. An ethnic or religious group may be the victims of stronger neighbors or colonial powers while appearing as a repressive force in the eyes of an even weaker minority. This dualistic dynamic is particularly insightful in exploring the contemporary evolution of Kurdish-Yezidi relations in Iraq characterized by patterns of solidarity in the face of common enemies but also mutual suspicions and tensions.

I now offer a brief overview of the evolution of Kurdish and Yezidi studies in the last several decades. Building on this overview, I then present a thematic road map that summarizes the main arguments of the chapters organized along two sections.

Renaissance in Kurdish Studies and Revival of Yezidi Studies

One of the negative implications of Kurds lacking a state of their own is the fragmentation and marginalization of Kurdish studies.[5] Among other reasons, the division of the Kurdish homeland among four states controlled by three dominant linguistic groups (Arabic, Persian, and Turkish), the suspicion and hostility of these states to any work deviating from their ruling ideologies, and the lack of resources available to and continuing restrictions on Kurdish language hampered scholarly studies on Kurdish people for a long time.[6] In comparison, Yezidi studies remained an even more insulated and smaller field of inquiry despite a number of notable contributions on the origins, evolution, and nature of Yezidism since the early 1990s.[7] As Christine Allison noted, Yezidis, practicing a set of religious beliefs transmitted primarily orally, were a subaltern group even among Kurds.[8] The historical marginality of Yezidis has inevitably limited scholarly and public interest about the group.

The geopolitical developments and popular struggles in Kurdish lands in the last two decades have led to some sea changes, including unprecedented forms of Kurdish nationalist mobilization and governance. While Kurdish aspirations for secession from Iraq resulted in a bitter failure in the fall of 2017, the widespread image of the Kurdistan Regional Government (KRG) as an island of stability in a country of chaos has remained well-anchored.[9] Meanwhile, the diversification and popularization of Kurdish nationalist movement in Turkey, despite major setbacks in the post-2015 period, have introduced an unprecedented element of democratic struggle to Kurdish activism. More recently, the formation of Kurdish self-rule in northern Syria and the rise of the Kurdish armed groups as the most important local ally of the Western coalition in the fight against the IS enhanced the global visibility and prominence of Kurdish politics. Besides, the technological revolutions, including rapid growth in social media, greatly expanded the interconnectedness and awareness of a Kurdish public sphere. All these macro-level dynamics have had positive implications for the academic study of Kurdish issues that attract a large number of talented, ambitious, and well-trained young scholars in many disciplines.

Figure 1.1 shows the number of English-language doctoral dissertations that focus on Kurds and Yezidis (i.e., mentioning the terms *Kurds*, *Kurdish*, *Kurdistan*,

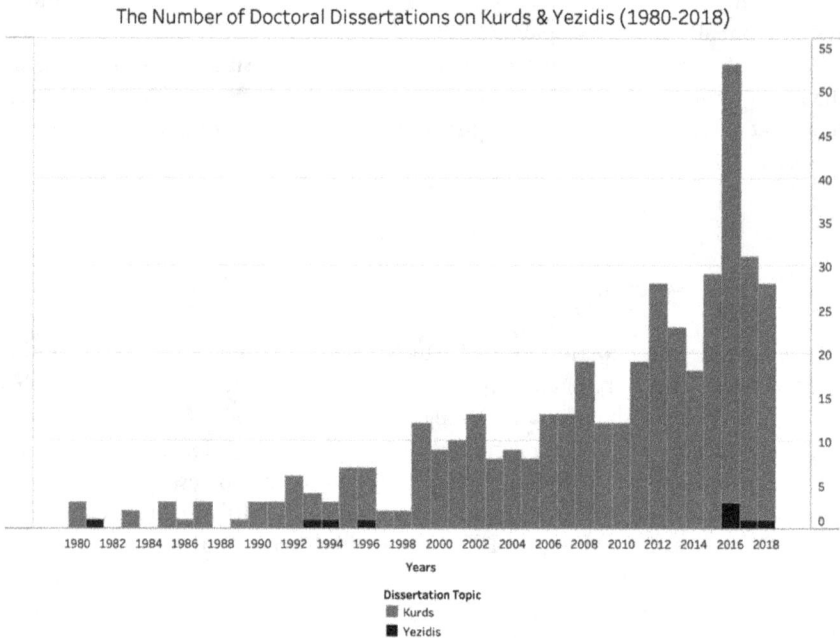

Figure 1.1 The Number of Doctoral Dissertations on Kurds and Yezidis
Source: Proquest Dissertations & Theses (compiled in October 2019). The graph shows only English-language dissertations.

Kurd, or *Yezidi, Yazidi,* or *Ezidi*) from 1980 to 2018. An overwhelming majority of these dissertations were completed either in British or American universities. While there are 418 dissertations on Kurds, there are only nine dissertations on Yezidis.[10] There has been a steady increase in scholarly interest in Kurdish issue especially after 2005. It is not coincidental that this current period has seen the consolidation of Kurdish self-rule in Iraq, the rise of Kurdish sociopolitical activism in Turkey, the growing influence of the Kurdish diaspora in Europe, and, most recently, the formation of de facto Kurdish autonomy in Syria. This rise has a convex shape suggesting that the last few years saw a more rapid increase. For instance, there were more than fifty dissertations studying various aspects of Kurdish issues in 2016 alone. Overall, the proliferation of publications, including articles in leading social science journals and books published by top university presses, indicates the growing vibrancy of Kurdish studies as an academic field that attracts greater scholarly and public attention than ever.[11]

Figure 1.2 shows the disciplinary subjects of doctoral dissertations on Kurds. Not surprisingly, a plurality of dissertations are classified under the subject of "Middle Eastern Studies." Interestingly, there are also a large number of dissertations in political science, international relations, and international law. This pattern suggests that scholarly interest in Kurdish issues parallels the growing importance and visibility of Kurdish political actors in domestic, regional, and international arenas, as mentioned above. At the same time, the fact that many other disciplines, such as cultural anthropology, history, and sociology, are well represented in the dissertations shows the growing breadth and scope of Kurdish studies.

In comparison, scholarly interest in Yezidis continues to remain very limited. It is clear that the tragic events in August 2014 have triggered scholarly interest in the group. Five dissertations were completed on the community from 2016 to 2018.[12] Yet there were only four English-language doctoral dissertations dealing with any aspects of Yezidi people from 1980 to 2000.[13] Even more strikingly, there

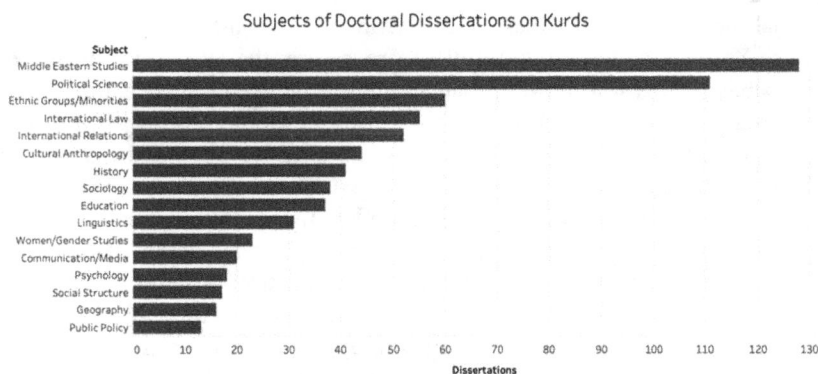

Figure 1.2 Subjects of Doctoral Dissertations on Kurds
Source: Proquest Dissertations & Theses (compiled in October 2019). The graph shows only English-language dissertations.

was not a single dissertation on the community for twenty years, from 1996 to 2016.[14] Major books on Iraqi and Kurdish politics published during this period barely mention Yezidis at all.[15] This lack of scholarly attention partially reflects the fact that Yezidis were a relatively small demographic group that lacked strong international connections and remained on the margins of politics in modern Iraq. Yet Yezidis' perceived heterodoxy and the lack of a written tradition are also likely to play a role in their invisibility in such works. Even the conventional description of Yezidism as a "syncretistic" religion implies its lack of originality and reflects its marginality.[16] After all, all religions evolve in close interaction with and often incorporate beliefs and practices from each other. Only with the rise of orthodox interpretations often backed by political power, a homogenous and puritan stance imposes itself.

Overall, the upward trend in both Kurdish and, to a limited extent, Yezidi studies is likely to accelerate in the upcoming years given the continuing saliency of Middle Eastern geopolitics and the rise of a new generation of scholars. Research on Kurdish and Yezidi society and politics will also strongly benefit from comparative studies informed by broader scholarly perspectives and discussions. With this premise, a central contention of this book is that cross-fertilization between the studies of Kurdish and Yezidi people would be mutually beneficial and lead to unique conceptual insights and original empirical findings.

A Thematic Overview: Formations of and Perceptions of Group Identities

This book brings together nine chapters providing conceptually insightful and empirically rich studies about the formation and perceptions of Kurdish and Yezidi political identities. The first thematic section includes four chapters and concerns the *formations* of Kurdish and Yezidi political identities in various historical settings. The second theme is about intergroup relations and revolves around five chapters discussing *perceptions* of Kurds and Yezidis by their neighbors and external actors (i.e., Ottoman-Yezidi, Armenian-Kurdish, Western-Kurdish, Turkish-Kurdish, and Kurdish-Yezidi). In each case, the asymmetric nature of these perceptions reflects power dynamics underlying intergroup relations. While extant scholarship has dealt with the state-Kurdish relations extensively, the topic of intergroup relations in Kurdish lands has attracted less attention. Chapters in this book aim to address this gap and operate under the analytical assumption that the emergence and evolution of group identities are historically contingent (not deterministic) processes that are conditioned by interactions among groups, states, and external powers. This approach is an antidote against "groupism,"[17] the tendency to treat social entities as being monolithic, homogenous, and externally closed, as it focuses on the *process* of identifications through which such entities come into existence and gain widespread acceptance, typically as a result of political struggles.

In particular, the boundaries between Kurdish and Yezidi identities have never been fixed and have been a primary source of historical contestation. On the one hand, the rise of secular Kurdish nationalism in the second half of the twentieth century allowed Kurdish leaders to aim to transcend religious differences and represent Yezidis under a nationalist framework, hence the hyphenated identity of Yezidi-Kurds.[18] The promise of secular Kurdish nationalism has been the reconfiguration and recognition of Yezidism as the original religion of Kurds.[19] In fact, secular Kurdish leaders portray Yezidis as the defenders of the Kurdish national identity, language, and culture.[20] These attempts have appealed to some Yezidis living in Iraqi Kurdistan. On the other hand, the late twentieth century and early twenty-first century saw the rise of autonomous Yezidi actors both in Iraq and Europe that aim to carve out a distinctive and narrower political identity based on the unique historical experience of the community. These attempts have gained a new impetus in the aftermath of the 2014 genocidal attacks that traumatized the society. The attacks led to greater geographical and political fragmentation of the Yezidi community while bringing unprecedented global attention to its plight. The tension between these two tendencies is likely to be central to the evolution of Yezidi political identity in the foreseeable future.

The first section on formations of Kurdish and Yezidi political identities is composed of four chapters. The two chapters, embodying distinctive methodological and chronological styles, approach the question of Kurdish political identity (*Kurdiyatî*) from opposite directions. While Mücahit Bilici offers an incisive interpretation of a canonical text that has been central to Kurdish nationalist discourses in contemporary times, Arzu Yılmaz focuses on a paradoxical situation, the subaltern experience of Kurdish refugees who seek a national homeland beyond their land of birth. In comparison, the chapter by Majid Hassan Ali and the chapter by Güneş Murat Tezcür, Zeynep Kaya, and Bayar Sevdeen offer rich discussions of the evolution of Yezidi political aspirations and movements since the mid-twentieth century with a focus on the experience of the community in Iraq. Both chapters argue that the genocidal attacks in August 2014 were a critical juncture[21] with lasting implications for the internal dynamics of the Yezidi community and its relations with other communities in Iraq.[22] While the IS violence exacerbated fragmentation and precariousness of the community, it also had the unintended consequence of making the community internally more pluralistic and open and globally more visible. All these four chapters suggest the formation of political identities is a highly contested process characterized by unexpected twists and turns.

The second set of chapters in the book shifts the focus to the intergroup relations involving Kurds and Yezidis in both historical and contemporary times. The chapters by Bahadin Kerborani and Zeynep Kaya explore how powerful actors with imperialist agendas developed stereotypical views of Yezidis and Kurds, respectively. For the Ottomans of the sixteenth and seventeenth centuries, Yezidis were "uncivilized" "devil worshippers" who remained outside of the imperial moral order. For the Europeans of the nineteenth and early twentieth centuries, Kurds were uncivilized indigenous people with weak claims to nationhood. In both cases, asymmetric and stereotypical views played a lasting role in shaping collective aspirations for greater recognition and legitimacy.

The following two chapters focus on how the Kurds were perceived by a vulnerable minority (ethnic Armenians) and a dominant majority (ethnic Turks). As Ohannes Kılıçdağı demonstrates the conflict over land became a major wedge issue between Armenians and Kurds in eastern Anatolia by the turn of the twentieth century. While the Armenian intellectuals were fearful of Kurdish tribes and viewed them as uncivilized, they also sought avenues of cohabitation up until the First World War. In a similar vein, Ekrem Karakoç and Ege Özen, using an original public opinion survey, address the issue of Turkish views of the Kurds in contemporary Turkey. Their findings are not encouraging. While these views exhibit some diversity, they tend to be highly dismissive of Kurdish demands for greater rights and liberties. In Tutku Ayhan's chapter that focuses on contemporary Yezidi-Kurdish relations, the positions are reversed. She suggests that the Yezidis, as a religious minority, are often portrayed as less civilized in majoritarian Kurdish discourses and continue to have a precarious existence in the aftermath of the IS attacks of 2014, what they call the last *firman*. Overall, these three chapters point out the pitfalls and challenges characterizing ethnic and religious pluralism. In the light of these comparative remarks, I now offer more detailed summaries of each chapter.

Formations: Kurdish and Yezidi Identities

Mem û Zîn, a love story written by Ehmedê Xanî (1651–1707) in Kurdish, is a canonical text for successive generations of intellectuals searching for a historical anchor of a distinctive Kurdish national identity. At the same time, more critical scholarship questions the tendency to assign nationalist tones and motives to Xanî. Bilici makes a critical intervention into this debate. In his original interpretation, Xanî is portrayed as a scholar of contract theory, which has been the foundational idea to liberalism and republicanism in the Western political thought. According to Bilici, Xanî expresses uncannily modern political ideas such as peoplehood and sovereignty while adopting a secular understanding of the origins and dynamics of earthly power. He identifies similarities between Xanî, on the one hand, and realism of Niccolo Machiavelli, and social contract theory of Thomas Hobbes, on the other. He also compares Xanî to Enlightenment thinkers in terms of the secularity of his analysis and his rational theology and argues that his modernity in a premodern age is an anomaly.

Bilici explains Xanî's anomaly in geopolitical terms. He argues that the Kurdish experience of being in the midst of an ongoing clash between two powerful Muslim empires, the Ottomans and the Safavids, in the early modern age, generated an inter-imperial fault line conducive to self-reflexivity and search for an alternative mode of political governance. In this historical context where Kurds occupy a liminal and precarious state, Xanî developed his ideas about a new form of sovereignty that exhibited a shift from the kingship to the people as agents of history. Such a shift is captured by the Xanî's strong preference for vernacularization associated with popular demands and power. In Bilici's interpretation, the fact that Kurds lacked a powerful sovereign paved the way for Xanî's engagement with the notion of popular sovereignty. He also makes some critical reflections about Xanî's modern ideas and political projects pursued by Kurdish organizations, PKK, PYD, and HDP in Turkey, Syria, and beyond. The implication is that the pursuit of a Kurdish polity remains an uncompleted, contested, and ongoing process across centuries.

In comparison to the Kurdish experience, the emergence of an independent Yezidi political identity is a more recent process, as discussed by Ali in his chapter. The genocidal attacks of 2014 have contributed to a proliferation of voices and platforms about distinctive Yezidi identity at multiple levels. It is now possible to talk about a Yezidi politics of recognition that entails increasing assertiveness by various Yezidi actors and represents a major transformation given Yezidis' long history of isolation, marginalization, and persecution. For the first time, crimes committed against Yezidi people are internationally recognized even if the pursuit of justice remains elusive. At the same time, Yezidis who remain in Iraq are now subject to the authority of multiple political actors with conflicting and opposing agendas. This situation aggravates political fragmentation among Yezidis and complicates the formation of a unified stance within the community. Ironically, demographic, economic, and political weaknesses of the community reinforce its political fragmentation, as a variety of local and international entities aim to co-opt Yezidi groups into their larger agendas. Given ongoing political tensions and economic deprivation in Yezidi homelands in Iraq and Kurdistan, the Yezidi diaspora is likely to play a decisive role in the future of Yezidism more than ever.

The chapter by Ali helps us better understand these developments and offers a comprehensive discussion of the transformations of the Yezidi identity since the early twentieth century in Iraq, the Caucasus, and the diaspora. Ali's historical survey shows that both Kurdish and Arab nationalists in Iraq tried to incorporate Yezidis into their political agendas since the 1960s. In contrast, Yezidis in the Caucasus, especially in Armenia, developed a more independent identity under the Soviet system. The rivalry between Kurdish and Arab nationalisms produced competing claims over the origins and nature of Yezidism, while independent Yezidi voices remained mostly silent. The Ba'th regime tried to incorporate Yezidis into Sunni Arab nationalism while the Barzani movement solicited Yezidi participation into the Kurdish nationalist struggle. This pattern continued until the US invasion of Iraq in 2003. The invasion enabled greater Kurdish influence over Yezidis but also facilitated the rise of autonomous ethno-nationalist political tendencies among Yezidis. The latter propagate the idea that Yezidis are distinct from both Kurds and Arabs and challenge the Kurdish nationalist discourse emphasizing common historical and cultural bonds between Kurds and Yezidis.

Ali argues that the inability and unwillingness of both the Iraqi army and Peshmerga to protect Yezidis from the IS in August 2014 greatly undermined the credibility of Iraqi and Kurdish systems in the eyes of Yezidis. Furthermore, similar to the observations made in both Tezcür, Kaya, and Sevdeen, and Ayhan chapters, Ali suggests that the 2014 debacle has undermined Yezidis' relations with their Sunni Muslim neighbors. In particular, he notes that many Yezidis believed that the Peshmerga did not care about them enough because of their distinctive religious faith. Consequently, a distinctive flag (red and white with a yellow sun in the middle) symbolizing an independent Yezidi identity became more popular in many different settings. Furthermore, an increasing number of Yezidi organizations in Western countries, such as Yazda and Free Yezidi Foundation, emerged. These developments generated conflict with Yezidis with a more pro-Kurdish stance and exacerbated internal divisions. Overall, experiences of discrimination, marginalization, and violence have heightened Yezidi self-awareness of their separate ethnoreligious identity.

Similar to Bilici, Yılmaz also explores the notion of Kurdish political agency, albeit in a dramatically different context. She focuses on the experiences of Kurdish refugees who fled to the Kurdistan Region of Iraq (KRI) from Turkey in the 1990s. The Turkish counterinsurgency campaigns aiming to depopulate the countryside in an effort to cut civilian support for the PKK had brutal consequences for the local population. Villagers in mountainous border zones were especially adversely affected by the armed conflict. A large number of them moved to the newly established KRI. Yılmaz offers a well-researched analysis of the precarious experiences of these Kurdish refugees in Kurdistan, an autonomous entity lacking sovereignty. She argues that they gradually developed their own political agency that occasionally put them at odds with both the KDP, one of the dominant political forces in the KRI, and the PKK. They tried to develop an autonomous stance during the power struggle between these two Kurdish nationalistic parties. She describes them as "refugee warriors" who engaged in political struggles via armed means. Their experience challenges the conventional descriptions of refugees as being passive victims of forces beyond their control.

An ironic aspect of the experience of these refugees was that they had more cultural freedoms (i.e., education in Kurdish) in exile. As "exiled Kurds in Kurdistan," they engaged in constructing a collective Kurdish identity rather than sought a temporary shelter and a permanent return to their villages. In this regard, their experience transcended the distinction between home and exile and generated ambivalent forms of Kurdish political identity. While they refused to be labeled as refugees, they continued to have a precarious existence given the ongoing tensions between the KDP and PKK. They sought a new home and developed a sense of national belonging in the KRI while lacking citizenship rights and opportunities to engage in democratic politics. In a sense, this experience of liminality reflects a longer historical trajectory of Kurdish people of being on the margins since the times of Ehmedê Xanî.

The last chapter in this section switches back to the Yezidis. Tezcür, Kaya, and Sevdeen argue how the IS' attacks in 2014, which have some similarities to the previous anti-Yezidi campaigns, have had some unique implications for Yezidi people. For the first time, the plight of Yezidis attracted global interest and contributed to the reputation of the community as a persecuted religious minority par excellence. In particular, tragic experiences of captured Yezidi women and children have shaped the international image of the community. An increasing number of Yezidi women survivors has emerged as prominent representatives of the community at the international scene and facilitated progressive change regarding women's societal roles among the Yezidis. Given the long history of entrenched patriarchal practices among Yezidis, this represents a paradoxical outcome of the IS brutality. Nonetheless, the traumatic experience accelerated the fragmentation of Yezidi in multiple ways. As also noted by Ali, a significant cleavage among Yezidis concerns their attitudes toward Kurdish leadership in the post-2014 era. While the hyphenated identity, Yezidi-Kurds, promoted by both the KDP and PKK involves some symbolic gains as well as various opportunities for the community, the rise of more independent-minded Yezidi organizations and activists with international connections shows its limits. In an ironic twist, Yezidi politics have started to resemble Kurdish politics, as the small size and political weakness of the community have facilitated its fragmentation as different members of the community sought the support of a variety of local, regional, and international actors.

Perceptions: Kurds and Yezidis in the Eyes of Others

The five chapters in this section pursue a cognitive approach and document intersubjective perceptions central to power relations among ethnic and religious groups. Kerborani explores the depiction of Yezidis in the Ottoman and Kurdish sources between the sixteenth and the eighteenth centuries. As the Ottomans prevailed over the Safavids and established their rule over upper Mesopotamia in the early sixteenth centuries, Yezidi notables and tribes became part of the Ottoman political landscape. Kerborani challenges the narratives of victimhood (i.e., Ottoman persecution of Yezidis) as being too simplistic and argues that Yezidis were active participants in the imperial order. At the same time, he also demonstrates that how historical and religious prejudices (e.g., the claim that Yezidis were followers of the Umayyad Caliph Yazid who ordered the execution of Hussein, grandson of Prophet Muhammad, at the Battle of Karbala) colored the Ottoman perceptions of the community and facilitated their dehumanization. Evliya Çelebi's *Seyahatname* exemplifies such pejorative views of Yezidis during the earlier centuries of the Ottoman rule. Kerborani's discussion suggests that there is an element of historical continuity in how Yezidis have been constructed as the "religious other" by certain Muslim actors, whether the Ottoman and Kurdish notables and clerics in the early modern era or the IS ideologues in the twenty-first century.

Stereotypical views have also characterized Western views of the Kurds. Kaya discusses how Western colonial constructions of Kurds evolved between the nineteenth and twentieth centuries. These parochial constructions, based on preconceived notions of nationhood and civilization, were generally dismissive of Kurds as being "uncivilized," "tribalistic," and "underdeveloped." From the Western perspective, Kurds were perceived to lack a unified leadership, a sense of collective identity, and high levels of development. Interestingly, such views have some parallels to how Turks continue to perceive Kurds in the twenty-first century, as discussed by Karakoç and Özen in their own chapter.

Western travelers and military officers also produced a series of maps of Kurdistan and Kurdish lands. Ironically, these maps subsequently informed nationalistic demands articulated by Kurdish nationalists in the twentieth century. Kaya documents how European cartographic depictions and ethnographic studies of the Kurds and other groups in eastern Anatolia and Mesopotamia had a decisive influence over the nature of Kurdish territorial claims. With the collapse of the Ottoman Empire in the aftermath of the First World War, these depictions informed how Kurdish nationalist leaders constructed a Kurdish homeland and made political demands. While the rise of Turkish nationalism and the colonial designs ultimately left these demands unrealized, the notion of a Kurdish homeland has proved to be long-lasting. In sharp contrast to condescending attitudes of Western travelers and officers of earlier times who viewed Kurds lacking requirements of nationhood, the idea of national unity continues to animate political imaginations of Kurds across borders.

In the absence of a sovereign Kurdish state, the boundaries of such a homeland, which challenges and transcends existing state boundaries, also remain a source of ongoing contestation. For instance, official and unofficial maps depicting Kurdistan exhibited significant differences during the Kurdish independence referendum in fall 2017. The official maps produced by the KDP only included the KRI and disputed territories, such as Sinjar and Kirkuk. Unofficial maps, produced by ordinary people and often posted on billboards and commercial buildings, often depict a greater Kurdistan, extending from the Mediterranean to the Persian Gulf.

Before the Armenian Genocide, Kurds, Armenians, Assyrians, and Yezidis coexisted in many different parts of eastern Anatolia and upper Mesopotamia. Westerners visiting the region before the First World War typically depicted Armenians as being more developed and civilized than Kurds, as Kaya noted. Adopting a more indigenous perspective, Kılıçdağı discusses how Armenians viewed Kurds around the time of the 1908 Constitutional Revolution in the Ottoman Empire, with its promise of religious equality. Utilizing a rich array of Armenian documents, including local newspapers from the period, he shows how Armenians perceived themselves as being culturally and morally superior to Kurds, just like Westerners. At the same time, Armenians were politically and militarily weaker than Kurds. In particular, Armenian lands and properties were vulnerable to attacks by local Kurdish chieftains. Consequently, Armenian leaders and intellectuals explored ways to contain these attacks and coexist with their Kurdish neighbors. Intriguingly, some of them espoused a "civilizing mission" to be enacted by Armenians among Kurds.

Armenians did not develop a victimhood complex vis-à-vis Kurds despite their vulnerabilities, as their main concern was the policies of the Ottoman authorities. Nor did they pursue an agenda of domination, unlike Westerners during the colonial times or Turks after the foundation of the Turkish Republic. As indigenous people facing more powerful neighbors, they sought compromises as a strategy of survival while being confident of their more advanced level of civilization. Kılıçdağı captures the Armenian tragedy in a dramatic fashion. To paraphrase him, while Armenians had behaved like white men, they would soon realize that they were the "Indians" in the scene. The genocidal campaign pursued by the Ottoman state against Armenians during the First World War and mobilized local Kurdish actors destroyed centuries-old religious plurality in eastern Anatolia.

Coexistence continues to be fragile in Anatolia in the twenty-first century. Karakoç and Özen go beyond perspectives that primarily conceptualize the Kurdish question in Turkey as a conflict between the Turkish state elites and Kurdish nationalist leaders. They argue that Turkish public opinion has a significant influence over the eventual resolution of the conflict. It may be infeasible for a Turkish leader to make compromises and recognize Kurdish rights without support from broad segments of Turkish society. Yet the authors depict a pessimistic picture about Turkish views of Kurds on the basis of an original public opinion survey conducted in 2015, several months before the collapse of the so-called peace process between the Turkish state and the PKK leadership. The findings demonstrate that heavy majorities exhibit categorial opposition to all forms of Kurdish demands, including both cultural and political rights.

Karakoç and Özen make a compelling argument that Turks perceive Kurds as their subordinates who need to be content with the status quo. Political differences among Turks do not necessarily lead to different views of Kurdish demands. Major Turkish political parties have dramatically different positions on the role of religion in sociopolitical life, foreign policy, and allocation of public resources. At the same time, supporters of these parties seem to have a widespread consensus that Kurds are not entitled to basic linguistic and cultural rights. Neither religiosity nor party affiliation has a significant influence on how Turks perceive Kurdish rights. Turks who are willing to consider constitutional recognition of Kurds or Kurdish autonomy make very small minorities. Ironically, there is more support for Kurdish independence, indicating that a considerable number of Turks prefer Kurdish citizens of Turkey seeking more rights to leave the country and have a state of their own somewhere else. The only exception to this general pattern is the attitudes of Turks living in areas with a significant Kurdish population. They tend to have more accommodative views of Kurdish rights and demands. This may reflect their status as a local minority, similar to Armenians a century ago, who perceive compromise as being essential to sustainable and peaceful coexistence.

Last but not least, Tutku Ayhan explores how Yezidi perceptions of Kurds are being transformed in the aftermath of the 2014 genocide. The general atmosphere of insecurity and religious extremism characterizing the post-Saddam Iraq further aggravated the precariousness of Yezidis who also became pawns in the Arab-Kurdish struggle over disputed territories. Yezidis who mostly speak the Kurmanji dialect of Kurdish and have many cultural affinities with Kurds became central to Kurdish national aspirations given both their demographic presence in disputed territories and symbolic importance representing religious tolerance of Kurdistan.

Accordingly, Kurdish forces expanded their control over the Yezidis lands following the fall of the Saddam regime in 2003. Before the IS onslaught, the Sinjar area, the historical homeland of Yezidi people, was under the control of Peshmerga. The abrupt withdrawal of Peshmerga without any significant resistance immediately after the IS initiated its attacks left entire Yezidi communities defenseless. This development, which seemed to vindicate historical Yezidi mistrust of Muslims, drove a wedge between Yezidis and Kurds, despite the Iraqi Kurdish leaders' depictions of Yezidis as the "original Kurds." As also argued in the previous chapters, this sense of betrayal was a major impetus to the crystallization of an independent ethnoreligious identity among some Yezidis who felt alienated from the hyphenated identity of Yezidi-Kurds promoted by the KRG leadership. Even if some Yezidis embrace the idea that they are the original Kurds (i.e., all Kurds were once Yezidis), they also emphasize the distinctive nature of Yezidi identity.

Ayhan conducted extensive fieldwork among Yezidi communities in both Iraqi Kurdistan and Germany and let Yezidis speak in their own voices. Her study incorporates but also goes beyond the impacts of sexual violence on the community. She argues that many Yezidis now perceive Kurds from a religious prism and disregard ethnic differences among Muslims who were perceived to persecute Yezidis for centuries. This perception is associated with the construction of a separate ethnoreligious Yezidi identity. Interestingly, Kurds, who have been characterized as being "backward" by Westerners, Armenians, and Turks, often perceive Yezidis as being less civilized, given the relative high levels of illiteracy, poverty, and rurality among the latter. In demographic, political, and symbolic ways, Yezidis remain a minority of a minority. The Yezidi self-perception of history as a cycle of persecution sustains the reconstruction and popular appeal of a separate ethnoreligious Yezidi identity.

Notes

1   Lewis Hyde (2019).
2   From a normative point of view, discourses of victimhood may continue to inform collective anxieties, reinforce exclusionary identity constructions, and foster aggression and mass violence. For a critical view of such discourses at the eve of the Armenian genocide, see Türkyılmaz (2011).
3   Six of the contributors obtained from or are pursuing their doctorates at US universities; two of them have PhDs from Turkish universities, and the remaining three from British, German, and Iraqi universities.
4   An important exception is the special issue of the now defunct *Journal of Kurdish Issues* (vol. 6, 2008). https://poj.peeters-leuven.be/content.php?url=issue. php&journal_code=JKS&issue=0&vol=6
5   An extensive and critical review of Kurdish studies is provided by Scalbert-Yücel and Le Ray (2006). As they note, works produced in Russia and the Soviet Union since the nineteenth century were central to the formation of Kurdology as a domain of knowledge. For a survey of the evolution of Kurdish studies in the United States, see Gunter (2018).
6   An important indicator of the marginality of Kurdish studies was the dearth of scholarship utilizing Kurdish language sources (either published material or interviews) until very recently. Many scholars who dealt with Kurdish issues spoke Turkish, Arabic, or Persian, but not Kurdish. This situation is obviously a product of policies of linguistic homogeneity aggressively by the regional states. For a critical reflection on linguistic power relations, see Soleimani and Mohammadpour (2019).

7   In the Western academia, these contributions include Guest (1993); Kreyenbroek (1995, 2009); Fuccaro (1999b); Allison (2001); Spät (2005); Açıkyıldız (2010); Maisel (2016); Omarkhali (2017). In the former Soviet Union, Celîlê Celîlʹand Ordîxanê Celîl compiled an extremely rich source on Kurdish and Yezidi oral literature (Celîl and Celîl 2014).

8   Allison (2008).

9   For the referendum, see Kaplan (2019). The KRG, especially after 2007, has generated significant institutional and financial resources for academic work. At the same time, patron-client relations prevalent in sociopolitical life in the KRG remain a major hurdle for the autonomy and institutionalization of scholarship in social sciences and humanities.

10 While there were eleven theses mentioning Yezidis in their abstract, two of these theses actually focused on Kurds.

11 For instance, see Aslan (2014); Belge (2016); Hakyemez (2017); Jamison (2016); Tezcür (2016).

12 Not surprisingly, all these five theses focus on Yezidi experiences of genocide, sexual violence, or displacement.

13 Three of these dissertations were completed in British universities. One of them later, which was based on extensive fieldwork in Iraq, was published as a book (Allison 2001) that remains a central source of reference.

14 An important exception to this trend is doctoral dissertation of Birgül Açıkyıldız completed in the Institute of Art and Archaeology at the University of Paris I Panthéon-Sorbonne in 2006. The dissertation was later published as a book (Açıkyıldız 2010).

15 Romano (2006); Tripp (2002).

16 For instance, McDowall (2004: 11) defines Yezidism as "a synthesis of old pagan elements, Zoroastrian dualist elements, and Manichean gnosis overlaid with Jewish, Muslim and Christian elements." For a critical discussion of the view that Yezidism is a derivative of Zoroastrianism and lacks an original religious structure, see Gökçen (2014: 58–60).

17 Brubaker (2004).

18 To use terminology of Andreas Wimmer (2008: 1032), this strategy could be characterized as "incorporation."

19 Like the Turkish nation-building process of the 1930s, the Kurdish national-building process also seeks national origins in pre-Islamic sources in an effort to emphasize the Kurdish distinctiveness from their dominating neighbors who happen to be Muslims. Kurdish elites also claimed Zoroastrianism as an original religion of Kurdish people. For the appeal of Zoroastrianism among ordinary Kurds, especially in the aftermath of the IS attacks, see Szanto (2018).

20 For instance, "Barzanî: Kurdên êzîdî nasnameya netewî ya kurdî parastine," 2015. This stance is also shared by the PKK that increased its presence and appeal among the Yezidis since August 2014.

21 I rely on the definition of Capoccia and Kelemen (2017: 348) who emphasize that critical junctures are short periods of time when political agents face a broader range of options than typical and the choices they make "among these options are likely to have a significant impact on subsequent outcomes."

22 The four chapters about the Yezidis primarily focus on Iraq. For Yezidi communities in Syria, see Maisel (2016), in Europe, see Kreyenbroek (2009), and in the Caucasus, see Six-Hohenbalken (2019).

Section I

FORMATIONS: KURDISH AND YEZIDI POLITICAL IDENTITIES

2

EHMEDÊ XANÎ'S POLITICAL PHILOSOPHY IN
MEM Û ZÎN

Mücahit Bilici

Introduction

Ehmedê Xanî's (1650–1707) *Mem û Zîn* has rightly been called "the national epic of the Kurds."[1] A work whose significance exceeds its literary attainments, *Mem û Zîn*'s prominent status within Kurdish classical literature continues to generate controversy. This is due not only to the fact that the text stands at the intersection of literature and politics, but also to the work's place as a recurrent touchstone for Kurdish intellectuals interested in articulating a national narrative. *Mem û Zîn*'s rediscovery in the post–First World War era of ethnic or national "revivals" is no coincidence. Like their contemporaries, the late-Ottoman-era Kurdish elites were interested in the ideas of self-determination and nationhood and deployed a national movement of their own to retrieve, imagine, and construct a collective identity for their people.

To the dubious relationship between historiography and nation-building, the Kurds provide no exception.[2] Nations require origins, traditions, historical depth—and nationalists have not been shy about inventing them.[3] A range of scholars[4] have traced the shifting perceptions and reception of *Mem û Zîn* as a piece of literature and shown how it came to occupy such a central place in Kurdish consciousness over the course of the past century. In doing so, the scholarship has been vigilant against nationalists' attempts to conscript Xanî as an instrument of nation-building. This salutary caution has, however, meant that Xanî's ideas (as opposed to their literary expression) have yet to receive serious attention and engagement. In this chapter, I engage with Xanî's ideas as expressions of political theory and highlight his political philosophy as an early modern thinker.

Xanî's Novelty

Xanî's towering status within Kurdish literature is universally recognized. Xanî completed *Mem û Zîn* in 1695 at the age of forty-four. He was able to engage in such literary-intellectual production because his was an era of relative political stability in the Kurdish lands due to a recent peace accord, the Treaty of Zuhab or Qasr-e Shirin (1639), between the Ottomans and the Safavids. At the same time, the aftereffects of the prolonged conflict between the two empires—which had devastated Kurdish social, economic, and cultural life—still lingered.[5] The subjugated Kurdish principalities were always fragile and precarious political entities. The landscape was calm enough to allow Xanî to think, but brimming with memories still raw enough to pose radical questions.

Xanî was, by all accounts, a frontier figure. Like all Kurdish littérateurs of the classical era, he emerged out of the *medrese* tradition and had strong Sufi affinities. Yet with him a whole range of novelties enters the Kurdish imagination. To describe the novelty of his literary materials he used the language of (religious) deviance, *bid'a*, which implies innovation both in the sense of new beginnings and in the sense of departure from convention.[6]

Xanî ji kemalê bêkemal î	Xanî, though lacking in perfection,
Meydanê kemalê dîti xalî	You found unoccupied the arena of excellence
Ye'nî ne ji qabil û xebîrî	And stepped forward not because of skill or knowledge
Belkî bi te'essub û 'eşirî	But rather out of loyalty and noble love for the people.
Hasil ji 'inad eger ji bêdad	In short – call it stubbornness or impudence –
Ev bid'ete kir xilafê mu'tad	He enacted this novelty, contravening convention

His literary output was a work of deliberate design, not just an aesthetic outgrowth of his life. He did not simply produce literature. Very much like a contemporary anthropologist who reflects on her own subjectivity as she pursues her work, Xanî explained why and how he engaged in such literary "engineering" (his word of choice would have been *alchemy*). He was not the first to write in Kurdish but, as far as we know, everything he wrote, he wrote in Kurdish at a time when men of letters were expected to show off their accomplishment in Persian, Arabic, or Turkish. Arguably, Melayê Jizîrî is the greater poet; Xanî's uniqueness lies in his cultural politics and his vision for the Kurdish people.

Safî şemirand vexwari durdî	He refused to drink the fine wine and chose, instead, the cloudy one
Manendê durrê lîsanê Kurdî	That is, he preferred the pearl-like Kurdish language over others
Înaye nîzam û întîzamê	He gave order and regularity to this language
Kêşaye cefa ji boyi 'amê	He suffered, laboring for the benefit of the people

A common assumption in the scholarly literature is that Xanî wrote for the court and educated elite only. That this is not, in fact, the case is made clear by Xanî's own words: in both *Mem û Zîn* and *Nûbihara Bicûkan* he explicitly states that he has engaged in his projects for the benefit of the people (*ji boyi amê*). Xanî's "populism" (if not patriotism) is an obvious and direct result of the interest in vernacularization that underlies all his works. Here are the opening lines of *Nûbihara Bicûkan* (1683):

Ev çend kelime ne, ji luxatan	Here are a few words from lexicons.
Vêk êxistin Ehmedê Xanî	Ehmedê Xanî put them together
Navê "Nûbihara Biçûkan" lê danî	And named it *Nûbihara Biçûkan*
Ne ji bo sahib rewacan	Not for the elite ones,
Belkî ji bo biçûkên Kurmancan	But rather for the Kurds' little ones

A similar move can be seen in the lines where he explains his motivation for writing *Mem û Zîn*:

De xelq-i nebêjitin ku Ekrad	So that people do not say that the Kurds
Bê me'rifet in, bê 'esl û bunyad	Lack education, origin, and foundations
Enwaên milel xudan kitêb in	Various nations have their classics
Kurmanc-i tenê di bê hisêb in	Only the Kurds lack them

Xanî is a vernacularizer not only in language, but also in theology. He authored the first Kurdish dictionary, *Nûbihara Bicûkan*, and the first Kurdish-language text laying out the basics of Islamic belief, *Aqîdeya Îmanê*. The ideas and claims with respect to Kurdish identity that appear in *Mem û Zîn*—claims that, encountered there, might strike the reader as exceptional—are reiterated in his other works. His poetry, theology, and political philosophy all seem to converge.

Let us consider an example for our immediate purposes. Below is a poem from Xanî's *Diwan*,[7] also published in *Jin* magazine's twelfth issue in 1918:

Zahidê xelwetnişîn pabendê kirdarê xwe ye
Tacirê rîhletguzîn dilnarê dînarê xwe ye
Aşîqe dîlberhebîn dildarê dîdarê xwe ye
Da bizanî her kesek bê şubhe xemxwarê xwe ye

Bê amel tu j'kes meke hêvî ata û himmetê
Bê xerez nakêşitin qet kes ji bo kes zehmetê
Kes nehin qet hilgiritin barê te ew bê ucretê
Gerçi Îsa bit ewî vêk rakirê barê xwe ye

Hoşîyar bî, da nekî umrê xwe bê hasil telef
Ku nedaye faîde mal, genc û ewlad û xelef
Macerayê Xidr û dîwarê yetîmî bû selef
Vî zemanî her kesek mî'marê dîwarê xwe ye

If I were to summarize the poem, it goes something like this: From the ascetic hermit who focuses on his prayers to the traveling merchant who pursues his profits to the lover who is eager to see the face of his beloved, everyone is worried about themselves and busy with their own affairs. Those who do not work hard have no right to expect help from others. No one helps anyone for no reason. Nobody carries another's burden for nothing. Even if you were Jesus, all you could do would be to carry your own burden. Wake up, O Xanî, so you do not waste your time in this world. Know that family, children, and posterity are of no use unless you work. The wall of the orphans mentioned in the story of Khidr now belongs to the past. *In this age, everyone is the architect of their own wall.*

Here, Xanî makes two, by and large modern, moves. He stresses secularity and human subjectivity and autonomy. He transcends religious excuses and emphasizes human agency. The most striking part is neither his disburdening Jesus of his responsibilities nor his pointing out the expiration date on the wonders worked by Khidr, the Qur'anic companion of Moses. Rather it is the line: "In this age, everyone is the architect of their own wall." I must admit, when I first heard this poem as an audio recording. I was under the impression that it was a poem written by Cegerxwîn, the twentieth-century Kurdish poet who was reading it on the recording. So modern-sounding was it that I was quite startled to learn that the lines belonged to Ehmedê Xanî.

No student of Kurdish history can fail to be genuinely amazed at the intensity and novelty of Xanî's ideas. One aspect of his work that resonates particularly for contemporary ears is that he appears to be a harbinger of Kurdish nationalism. Given the imagined or real presence of strong elements of nationalist sentiment in his magnum opus, *Mem û Zîn*, it comes as no surprise that controversy has arisen around his relationship to nationalism. Was he so ahead of his time that he should be called a premodern nationalist, a nationalist *avant la lettre*? Or—his modern-sounding ideas notwithstanding—is this image simply a mirage, because nationalism is a modern phenomenon and Xanî surely belongs to a premodern age?

The sentiment expressed below by one of the doyens of Kurdish Studies, Martin van Bruinessen, represents a common experience, shared by many contemporary academics upon encountering Xanî's political writing in *Mem û Zîn*:

> Certain passages in the *dibace* (introduction) of *Mem û Zîn* certainly have a modern ring to them, as if they were spoken by nationalists of the early 20th century instead of three centuries ago. It is as if Xanî was calling for a Kurdish national state. In fact, I myself have for a while suspected that these words were not by Xanî but were inserted into his work by a much later copyist, so modern they sounded to me. But these words also occur in the critical edition by M. A. Rudenko, which is based on nine different manuscripts, the oldest of which was written in 1731–32, i.e. well before the appearance of modern nationalism in the Middle East. So it must have been Ehmedê Xanî himself who wrote them.[8]

If we were to accept that the modern-sounding elements in Xanî's writings were indeed later additions to the text, that would offer a satisfying solution to the problem. So long as we are not able to make such a claim, however, engagement with Xanî's ideas remains an intellectual challenge and a responsibility. Major scholars in the field have tried to thread their way through this challenge without tripping the landmines of anachronism, without giving way to retrospective nationalism. As a consequence, they chose to downplay Xanî's modernity and assimilate him back to the medieval milieu.[9] Following a point made by Izzeddin Mustafa Rasul and perpetuated by Farhad Shakely and others, Maria O'Shea, for example, says, "[D]espite claims that Khani was an early advocate of national self-determination, he appears to have been a supporter of a Platonic system of rule by a philosopher King, not necessarily a Kurdish one, but one wise, cultured and benign."[10]

For Kurds, who lack a state of their own in this age of nation-states, it is hard to imagine that a seventeenth-century Kurdish thinker espoused nationalism before its appearance in Europe. There is neither consensus on the origins of the Kurds as a people nor an agreed-upon date for the beginnings of Kurdish nationalism in the literature. A claim of premodern nationalism sounds simply unacceptable. It is for this reason that many scholars cling to Anthony Smith's *ethnie* in order to speak of premodern Kurdish existence, even as they overwhelmingly submit to the hegemonic appeal of Anderson or Hobsbawm-style modernism.[11]

As much as refusing to attribute nationalism to Xanî is the expected course of action for progressive scholars rightly suspicious of nationalism and its historiographic traps, leaving untouched Xanî's modern dimension for fear of seeing nationalism where there is none has not been helpful, either. The question remains: How are we to explain the uncannily modern character of Xanî's political ideas?

The Question of Nationalism

Nationalism, as a political commitment or guiding spirit, is typically superficial, lazy, and selective when it comes to historiography. As such it can easily become a refuge for intellectual flaccidity and an excuse for avoiding critical confrontation. Identity politics should not block, let alone replace, intellectual scrutiny, but intellectual scrutiny, too, should rise above identity politics when it comes to deciding what qualifies as philosophy. I argue that Xanî deserves to be taken seriously as a political philosopher, and the existing literature seems not to have done so. What is the philosophical merit of Xanî?

I ultimately argue that Xanî should be seen as a social contract theorist. His diagnosis of the problem of disunity[12] among the Kurds, though succinct and in poetic form, contains all the parts of a social contract theory. Completed in 1695, roughly half a century after Thomas Hobbes's *Leviathan* (1651),[13] Xanî's brief discussion implies a concise yet robust conception of the social contract. Kurds' failure to establish unity and achieve political success is due, according to Xanî, to the fact that they do not want to leave the state of nature and enter a commonwealth. Kurds enjoy a liberty without civility. Fear of being beholden to others leads to the failure of the civilizational project among them. By civilizational project, I mean efforts toward political solidarity, which are not necessarily to be identified with the form of nation. This discussion needs to be carried out independent of the narrow debate on nationalism. By doing so, we can release Xanî's response to the predicament of Kurdish civility from the confines of nationalist discourse, foregrounding the striking modernity of his approach without risking the anachronistic appropriation of Xanî as a nationalist.

In the prefatory essay to his English translation of *Mem û Zîn*, Salah Saadalla[14] characterizes Xanî in the following way: "The Kurds consider Xanî not only as their greatest poet but also as their unrivalled pioneer of the Kurdish national ideology, who formulated clearly its goals and defined the means to attain them."[15] Kurdish intellectual Nureddin Zaza (1919–1988), in his preface to the story of "Memê Alan," describes Xanî as a thinker of the dialectic and a precursor of Hegel and Marx.[16] As noted by others,[17] a leading figure of Kurdish nationalism, Mîr Celadet Bedirxan, has gone so far as to praise Xanî as the prophet of the Kurds[18] or consecrate his status as the "third teacher"[19]—a reference to Farabi who, for his commentary on Aristotle, is famously known as "the second teacher." Similar enthusiasm is found in Faik Bulut's sensational Turkish book, *The Unknown World of the Kurds in Ehmedê Xanî's Writings*, where the desire to depict a simultaneously "exotic" and "progressive" Kurdish culture readily generates anachronisms and exaggerations.[20]

Given nationalism's tendency to invent tradition and assert the primacy of all things "ours," one has to be very cautious about such nation-building activities. Yet while caution against such overreach is commendable, some of those "excessive interpretations"[21] contain a grain of truth. Some scholars, whose primary focus is the literary character of Xanî's work, consider it a mistake to devote much attention to *Mem û Zîn*'s political commentary (which occurs largely in a separate, introductory section). They argue that the text should be read primarily as a literary work within the classical *mesnevi* tradition and not as a philosophical text.[22] However, treating Xanî as merely a poet who produced literature using existing forms in his native idiom in order to elevate the status of the Kurdish language does not do him justice, either. To argue for the multivalence of Xanî's work is one thing; to depoliticize a fundamentally political text is another thing entirely.

I suggest that approaches that tend to depoliticize Xanî do a disservice to his proper understanding on two accounts. First, the relevant passages are indeed political commentary. That they are introduced in a book of literature or in the form of poetry does not make them less philosophical or unworthy of philosophical attention. Second, if we were to choose to understand one in terms of the other, we would do better to understand the literary main part of the work in light of those introductory comments, for the prior work is what defines and situates the latter. If Xanî himself, with an astounding degree of self-reflexivity, describes his literary venture as a political act, we cannot simply ignore the political character of the enterprise.

Explaining Xanî as an Anomaly

While, as we have seen, Xanî ought not to be hijacked by the nationalist narrative, his anomalous status as a thinker cannot be ignored, either. I believe Xanî can be compared philosophically to Niccolo Machiavelli on the question of politics and to Hobbes on the question of social contract. He can be compared to Enlightenment thinkers in terms of the secularity of his analysis and his rational theology. Xanî is anomalous because he is modern in a premodern age. Of course Xanî sounds anachronistic, because we see him in relation to a destitute Kurdish society and the absent modernity of the so-called Muslim world. We assume that what seems unlikely for a society at a given time must be unlikely for individuals within it, as well. But if we think of Xanî as a coeval of Enlightenment thought and early modern Europe, he no longer appears so anomalous. It becomes palatable, even, to consider Xanî in many ways a unique figure in history, a man ahead of his time. We should not deny the philosophical respect we show for Anaximander's fragments in the Ancient Greek tradition to the political and philosophical fragments of Xanî in the Introduction of Mem û Zîn. If we had no part of Mem û Zîn but the *dibace*, Xanî would still be as important intellectually.

The early modern period is seen as a time when philosophical thought has one foot in the middle ages and one foot in modernity. Science, reason, natural law, and human agency are in the ascendant, while belief in God still dominates, religious dogmas are being questioned, and aristocratic culture is still prevalent. It is an era of transitions and vernacularizations of various kinds. It is worth remembering, though, that before the concept of popular sovereignty burst into the open with mass movements like the French Revolution, it already permeated the literate classes. And as sovereignty gained traction as a concept, it underwent a transition from divine and royal to secular and popular.

Is it possible that a particular—and unusual—spatio-temporal conjuncture generated a unique combination of stimuli (comparable to, say, the English Civil War) and that that stimulus interacted with Xanî's native genius to produce a set of untimely ideas? If we were to entertain this possibility, then we could begin to ask at least two questions: First, what was the historical context that bequeathed Xanî his political consciousness? Second, if not nationalism, what would be a more legitimate explanatory framework for expressing Xanî's location in history and his intellectual contribution?

In what follows, I will first answer these two questions by visiting the historical context of Xanî's political ideas and situating him in the early modern framework. Then I will bring to light his political philosophy as it is expressed in sections 5–6 of *Mem û Zîn*. I hope to present Xanî's political philosophy and make it visible with resort to three interrelated concepts: peoplehood, sovereignty, and social contract.

Historical Context of His Political Consciousness

The fifteenth and sixteenth centuries that shaped Ehmedê Xanî were characterized by the rise and fall of Kurdish emirates during a time of inter-imperial competition. The geographic character of the lands where the Kurds lived seems to have always conditioned the politics and prospects of the Kurds. One popular expression of this fact is the famous mantra, "Kurds have no friends but the mountains." Much as they are celebrated, the mountains have been a mixed blessing for the Kurds:

they allowed the Kurds to escape the control of the empires surrounding them but also made it difficult for them to create a central authority of their own.

With the rise of the Safavid dynasty, the Kurds became sandwiched between two of the three Muslim empires[23] of the day. Kurdish lands became an arena of "evolving identities, competing loyalties, and shifting boundaries," as the subtitle of a book[24] nicely captures. Kurdistan acted as a buffer zone between the Ottomans and the Safavids. It turned into a space of conflict and battleground for recurrent wars. Caught in a centuries-long crossfire of two empires, the Kurds always found themselves "awash in blood," as Xanî writes:

Bif'kir ji 'ereb heta ve gurcan	Look, from the Arabs to the Georgians
Kirmanc ci bûye şubhê burcan	Kurds have become like fortresses
Ev rûm û 'ecem bi wan hisar in	Turks and Persians are shielded by them
Kirmanc hemî li çar kinar in	It is all Kurds on all sides
Herdu terefan qebîlê kirmanc	Both parties have turned the Kurdish clans
Bo tîrê qeda kirine amanc	Into targets for their fatal arrows
Goya ko li serhedan kilîd in	Assumed to be locks at the frontier
Her ta'ife seddek in sedîd in	Each community is a solid barrier
Ev qulzimê rûm û behrê tacîk	The ocean-like Turks and Tajiks
Hindî ko bikin xurûc û tehrîk	Whenever they rise and move
Kirmanc dibin bi xwîn mulettex	The Kurds become awash in blood
Wan jêk ve dikin misalê berzex	As, like a buffer, they keep the two sides apart

The Ottoman-Safavid struggle was "the central international conflict in the Muslim world"[25] and Kurdish participation in those conflicts—on one side or both—was the price to be paid for living on the frontiers of these two empires. From the Battle of Chaldiran[26] in 1514 to the Qasr-e Shirin treaty in 1639, the two states, according to Sabri Ateş, "fought over the borderlands extending from the Persian Gulf to Mount Ararat and the transformation of this indeterminate borderland into a clearly defined and increasingly monitored border took almost four centuries."[27]

What gave some unity to the residual identity of these borderland inhabitants was not only local religious and kinship networks but also a shared "frontier ethos."[28] Kurds came to see themselves in contradistinction to the powers that surrounded them. It is important to remember "that the external classification of the Kurds" played an important role in Kurds' own self-perception.[29] This residual character of Kurdish identity can be seen as something emerging out of an inter-imperial space, a product of subjection to integration. If nothing else succeeded in giving a relative coherence to Kurdishness, the double limits placed on them by these two empires did.

And that is why "Kurdistan's peripherality"[30] or its "borderland"[31] status is key to its political and intellectual development. Frontier ethos, borderland experience, and peripheral precariousness all contributed to the formation of Kurdish identity as articulated in both *Sharafnama* (1597) and *Mem û Zîn* (1695). Kurdish liminality and the tectonic friction between the Ottoman and Safavid military-cultural powerhouses resulted in an intensified "border" experience among the Kurds, especially their intellectuals. This heightened condition of liminality forced a heightened consciousness of the self by generating frequent reminders of otherness. Dwelling on shifting borders, between contending armies, the Kurds (or, at least, their scholars) were ironically forced into a premature "modernity" marked by intensified self-awareness and a critical spirit, due to multiple, forced comparisons (*mahkum*) and consciousness of relative deprivations (*mahrum*). Xanî flourished on the fertile post-volcanic ashland of the Ottoman-Safavid conflict that had flowed over the Kurdish lands. Kurdistan gained a modern territorial meaning first and foremost by becoming the main theater of Ottoman-Persian rivalry. This rivalry gave local Kurdish rulers some leverage but at the same time kept them in an uncertain, precarious position. Kurds' status with respect to the confrontation of two empires was, in Xanî's own terms, one of *berzah* (a passage, a buffer zone between the two powers, a limbo).

From Evliya Çelebi to Sharaf Khan and Ehmedê Xanî, all contemporary literary and political writings perceived the Kurdish principalities as strategic spots or "solid barriers" scattered across a region of "incessant power struggle."[32] This continuous scramble between the Ottomans and the Safavids sharpened the political sensibilities of the Kurdish dynasties with respect to rulership, diplomacy, kingship, and sovereignty. Divided and oscillating between the Ottomans and the Safavids, the elites of the prominent Kurdish principalities were sharply aware of the need for administrative expertise (as in the case of Sharaf Khan) and of the importance of political legitimacy and courtly space for literary production (as in the case of Ehmedê Xanî).

Kurdish Identity and Territoriality

Evliya Çelebi's map of Kurdistan more or less corresponds to our contemporary understanding of the Kurdish lands. Similarly, Xanî's own reference to the plight of the Kurds in the lands stretching "from Arabs to Georgians" (*bifikir ji Ereb heta va Gurcan*) implies an emergent conception of territoriality and peoplehood.

The territoriality and identity of the Kurdish lands emerged out of the in-between-ness of the Kurds vis-à-vis the two empires. It was not an internally bounded territory but an externally demarcated one. Although political elites could limit their concerns to their immediate locality and their relationship to the imperial centers, Kurdish *ulama*, who were more widely traveled and less tied to a local political unit, were in a better position to imagine the larger populace and broader experience of borderlands. The equilibrium between the two empires created a relative stability in Kurdistan's history, paving the way for the flourishing of art and culture. "It is not surprising that the literary use of Kurdish coincides with the rise of Kurdish political power in the fifteenth and sixteenth centuries."[33]

One might wonder, at this point, if it is not anachronistic to use the word *Kurd* to describe the people of the land at that time. The use of the word *Kurd* is justified since Xanî himself spoke in terms of peoples when he referred to others and conceived of the "people" as his unit of analysis. He appears to use *Kurd*, *akrad*, and *Kurmanji* interchangeably. Whenever he says *me* (us) as in *derdê me* (our plight), he seems to mean all the Kurdish populace. When he addresses the elite he says so. Otherwise, there is reason to believe that by "us" or "Kurds" he means the people and not just the courtly class. He blames the elite for their failures in leadership; when he speaks of suffering, he typically has ordinary people (including poets like himself) in mind.

Tebi'iyyetê wan eger ci 'ar e	If subordination to them be shameful
Ew 'are li xelqê namidar e	The disgrace of it falls to the elite
Namus e li hakim û emîran	It is a matter of honor for the rulers and princes
Tawan ci ye şai'r û feqîran	What are the poet and the poor to do?

He does not mention dynastic names (Ottomans or Safavids) or imperial titles (sultans and shahs) or countries but instead identifies the dominant ethno-political category (Turk, Ajam) or neighboring ethnic categories (Rom/Turk, Ajam/Tajik, Arabs, Georgians). Moreover, in an extremely fragmented tribal society, he does not mention Botis, Rojikis, etc. but calls his own people either *Kurmanj* or *Kurd*. I think we can safely assume that Xanî is referring to the people rather than the ruling class exclusively when he says Kurds.

Having established the existence of Kurdishness, at least as a residual and liminal category, we move on to the second component: is there any reason to think that Xanî was intellectually on par with early modern European thought? Here a slightly unexpected fact about the state of Kurdish scholarship in the seventeenth century comes into play.

According to Khaled El-Rouayheb, the works of fifteenth- and sixteenth-century Persian and Kurdish scholars were suffused with the call for *tahqiq* (the verification of truth). While elsewhere there might have been an eclipse of the philosophical sciences, Kurdish scholars were a notable exception; they played a major role in the "reinvigoration of the rational sciences" in the Muslim world.[34] The seventeenth-century Kurdish scholars in Istanbul and Damascus were simultaneously introducing the rational sciences to Ottoman scholarly circles. Historian, geographer, and encyclopedist Katip Çelebi (d.1657) notes, for example, that after the eclipse of the philosophical sciences (*felsefiyat*) in the Ottoman capital it was only thanks to "the novices of scholars … in the lands of the Kurds [who] came to Rum" and taught rational sciences that seventeenth-century intellectual life was revitalized in Istanbul and elsewhere (quoted in El-Rouayheb[35]). Mulla Mahmud Kurdî (d. 1663), according to the seventeenth-century Damascene historian Muhammad Amin al-Muhibbî (d.1699), "was the first to teach the books of the Persians" in Damascus and he "opened the gate of verification [*tahqîq*] in that city. Similarly Mulla Chelebi Amidi (d. 1656), according to al-Muhibbi, counted as his students almost all prominent Ottoman scholars active in the last quarter of the seventeenth century."[36]

The scholarly climate out of which Xanî emerged was intellectually sophisticated and rationalist in orientation. It provides us with a strong ground for conceiving of Xanî as an early modern thinker at the intersection of medieval (Muslim) civilization and emerging (European) modernity.

Xanî's Early Modernity

The Ottoman defeat of the Safavids with the help of the Kurdish emirates allowed for both political autonomy and cultural growth in Kurdish lands. Ottoman domination also triggered a linguistic shift and opened room for a comparative assessment of the merit and status of languages. The relative weakening of Persianate literary hegemony had consequences both in the Kurdish princely courts and Kurdish scholarly institutions. Turkish became the dominant language of translation and communication in the Kurdish princely courts, while Kurdish became an aspiring language of literature and education in Kurdish *medreses*.[37] Both *Sharafnama* and *Mem û Zîn* are products of this intensified political experience. If *Sharafnama* reflects the moment of "the flourishing of the system of principalities in the late sixteenth century," *Mem û Zîn* is an elegy over the ruins of that system.

Could it be that Xanî's political awakening and his futuristic ideas were simply the result of a historical accident? Whatever conditions generated political modernity in Europe (and elsewhere) might have made an earlier appearance in the life and times of Xanî. Two cases that come to mind here as potentially comparable are Ibn Khaldun and Machiavelli, both of them scholars who served as court secretaries. One was premodern and witnessed in his journeys the rise and fall of many states; the other was an early modern courtier, in whose day Italy was a patchwork of principalities harried by the French and the Habsburgs. Such a concatenation of events cannot be simply dismissed; it stands as a challenge for historians and philosophers to find structural reasons for Xanî's untimely modernity.

My own explanation is that the inter-imperial fault line[38] on which the Kurds found themselves created a zone of tectonic shifts that invited an intellect like Xanî to make sense of the "plight" of the Kurds. This in-between zone opened up a space of reflection and posed a rare demand for self-reflexivity, encouraging a genius like Xanî to see and think, so to say, beyond his time. Here I am employing a structural-historical explanation in the manner of Montesquieu. Montesquieu believed in the social genesis of ideas and drew attention to both social and physical factors. For example, his classification of societies (republic, monarchy, despotism) was based on the size and population density of the society. Large empires were likely to be despotic, while very small city-states were likely to become republics. What sort of political structure would a buffer zone like Kurdistan generate? Whether we call the Kurdish emirates or mini-states feudal or anarchic, they always remained fragmentary and always lacked the conditions of kingship. Their distance from the Ottoman capital created local autonomy and confederative potential at the horizontal level. Yet, as Xanî notes, the stiff-necked independence among the Kurdish people prevented them from forming a union or a civil compact.

It is helpful to think of Xanî as a frontier figure of his Muslim scholarly milieu. He represents a peak moment of Muslim thought as it was appropriated and circulated within the Kurdish cultural domain, even as it had already gone into decline elsewhere. In other words, Xanî can be seen as a fruit of Kurdish *hikmah* (philosophy or learned tradition) at its most mature moment, before the Kurds, too, began to participate in the broader decline of Islamic civilization. Hence he was a late fruit of the Islamic intellectual tradition, protected by geographic-cultural factors and left to ripen in the final days before Muslim civilization decisively passed the torch of intellectual leadership to Western civilization. Though he casts it in narrow Marxist terms, Amir Hassanpour makes a similar argument when he writes, "[I]f European Renaissance was the budding of the capitalist era, the 'renaissance' of seventeenth century Kurdistan was the climax of its feudal order."[39] To summarize, what is new/pioneering in the West overlaps intellectually with what was old/disappearing in the Muslim world. We can understand early modernity, as a milieu, as the transition between the end of Muslim civilization and the rise of Western civilization.

If we set these two trends side by side, Xanî might appear too modern for the Muslim tradition and too Muslim for our sense of modernity as a novel Western phenomenon. There are, however, a number of compelling reasons to see Xanî as an early modern thinker. I argue that Xanî is not only early modern but also *an* early modern, for at least eight reasons:

1. The secularity of his ideas. In this regard, Xanî shows similarities to Ibn Khaldun, whose analysis of *umran* gave autonomy to causal/scientific explanations, as opposed to fate or divine predestination. There are abundant mystical tales and supernatural stories about Jizîrî and Feqîyê Teyran, but none about Xanî.[40] Similarly, *Mem û Zîn* has no room for fairies and supernatural beings. Xanî's world is relatively secular, purged of spirits and jinn.

2. His understanding of state and power is based on "realism," not theology. Xanî demystifies political power and explains statehood in terms of seizing power with determination. In this he bears a strong similarity to Machiavelli.

3. In his search for an answer to the puzzle of Kurdish misfortune, Xanî takes his audiences through a step-by-step divestment or gradual transition from the supernatural forces of fate to the agency of human beings (and not of the elites only).

4. In locating sovereignty, we see a gradual shift in his discourse from the authority of kingship (divine or otherwise) to the people as actors of history. Xanî rejects the *corpus mysticum* of kingship.

5. Xanî is a vernacularizer par excellence. Vernacularization of language (an early modern phenomenon) represents the demand, needs, and growing power of publics—the necessity of disseminating knowledge among the people. For Xanî such empowerment is a burning issue.

6. In Xanî's universe, we discover modern subjectivity. Every individual has to take responsibility for him-/herself. This is not only found in *Mem û Zîn* but also in his poetry, the *Diwan*, as well: *vi zemani her kesek mi'marê diwarê xwe ye* (In this age, everybody is the architect of their own wall).

7. An important distinction that has gone unnoticed or been lost in most English translations and interpretations of the text is the fact that Xanî often juxtaposes—while carefully distinguishing between—*mîr* (princes) and *mêr* (people). This distinction prefigures the emergence of people as autonomous political actors.

8. Xanî's self-reflexivity. As an author he has a plan; he has engineered a literary text with a very modern political agenda. When it comes to self-reflexivity, he is more like an anthropologist.

Xanî's Political Philosophy: Sovereignty, Peoplehood, Social Contract

We can now turn our attention to some of the conceptual strands Xanî weaves together in his political philosophy. My discussion here is limited to three concepts that are particularly relevant for our present purposes: sovereignty, peoplehood, and social contract.

Sovereignty

According to Xanî, the *production of poetry* and the *exercise of sovereignty* are twin processes. The aesthetic and the political domains are symbolized by verse and coin. He sees literature as dependent on sovereignty for its validation. Here literature or poetry stands for "value" in general. He conveys the notion of value without validity through the image of coins that, although real, cannot be used in the marketplace. Recognition of value is possible only through the validation provided by sovereignty. One of the central points of Xanî's political writing is that the validity of a given society's literature is dependent on the recognition garnered by the sovereignty of its people. The image of the king in Xanî is entirely instrumental. To the extent that a king may be the form and vessel of sovereignty, kingship is desirable to him. But should such a figure prove unavailable to the Kurds, he is prepared to move on to other means in pursuit of his goal. It is the very absence of a king among the Kurds that pushes Xanî's thinking beyond the classical and into an early modern possibility: sovereignty without a king. This is precisely why Xanî's conception of sovereignty, as it moves from princely sovereignty toward the sovereignty of the people—albeit a virtue made of necessity—is truly modern.

In this, Xanî's heirs are contemporary Kurdish militant and political parties like the PKK, PYD, and HDP. Eschewing the goal of a Kurdish state, they have turned toward the postmodern ecological-anarcho-libertarian-municipal imagination of post-Marxist leftist thinkers. PKK's imprisoned leader's almost religious adherence to the ideas of Murray Bookchin, a relatively obscure American thinker, is an obvious case in point. It could be understood as a mere intellectual vagary, were it not that Bookchin-inspired ecological communitarian ideas have been put into practice, to the dismay of some Kurdish people and the delight of metropolitan Marxist intellectuals, in Rojava (Western Kurdistan or Northern Syria).

Returning to Xanî's political ideas, we should note that he does not merely raise them in passing in the preface. It is my contention that as much as *Mem û Zîn* is a literary project, it is a political project. More specifically, if Xanî's own self-presentation is taken seriously, *Mem û Zîn* appears to have been devised as a political tool, if not an outright subaltern weapon.

Consider the flow of the *Dibace* (Introduction). After a few segments laying out the plight of the Kurds (despair, current reality, and hope for change), it soon offers a remedy: a king appears. The king represents sovereignty; our currency becomes minted coinage, as Xanî puts it, no longer doubtful and worthless exchange. If we had a king our fortune would have brightened.

Qet mumkin e ev ji çerxê lewleb	Is it possible that the wheel of fortune favor us
Tali' bibitin ji bo me kewkeb	That a star shine over us
Bexte me ji bo me ra bibit yar	That our luck become amicable to us
Carek bibitin ji xwabê hisyar	That it awaken once from slumber
Rabit ji me jî cihanpenahek	That a world refuge emerge for us
Peyda bibitin me padişahek	And a king appear
Şîrê hunera me bête danîn	That the power of our art be established
Qedrê qelema me bêta zanîn	The value of our pen acknowledged
Derdê me bibînitin ilacê	Our plight remedied
'Ilmê me bibînitin rewacê	Our learning sought after
Ger dê hebuya me serfirazek	If we had a proud leader
Sahipkeremek, suxennewazek	Generous and a patron of literature
Neqdê me dibû bi sikke meskûk	Our currency would be minted coinage
Ned'ma wehe bêrewac û meşkûk	Not such doubtful and worthless exchange
Herçend ko xalis û temîz in	Even when pure and distinct
Neqdên bi sikkeyê 'ezîz in	Coins gain their value when stamped at a mint
Ger dê hebuya me padişahek	If we had a king
Layiq bidiya Xwedê kulahek	If God had deemed him worthy of a crown
Te'yîn bibuwa ji bo wî tacek	And a throne had been established for him
Elbette dibû me jî rewacek.	Our fortune would have brightened
Xemxwarî dikir li me yetîman	He would have cared for us compassionately
Tinane dere ji dest leîman	He would have saved us from the accursed ones
Xalib nedibu li ser me ev Rom	Rum would not be victorious over us
Nedbûna xerabe ê di dest bûm	We would not be the ruins where the owl perches

Xanî starts his disquisition on the plight of the Kurds by asking a cupbearer to pour wine so the glass (in a species of fortune-telling) can reveal the situation. At this stage, the source of history is fate (Fortuna) and a king merely appears. The king has no prior justification; he is simply dispensed by destiny. Responsibility lies with *felek*, which is at once the sky (and by extension, the zodiac) and destiny. Here Xanî fantasizes about what such a king could do. His king is the ideal-type of a sovereign who looks after the orphans and defends them from the attacks of the Turks and Persians. While emphasizing the role of the sovereign in pulling the Kurds out of their misery, Xanî realizes that this is simply wishful thinking. For a moment, he plunges back into despair. In what will prove to be a transitional gesture, the poet resigns himself to the divine decree.

Emma ji ezel Xwedê wisa kir	But God from eternity so willed that
Ev Rum u 'Ecem li ser me rakir	These Turks and Persians be unleashed against us

Then he begins to assign responsibility for the Kurds' plight, turning first to the elite:

Tebi'iyyetê wan eger ci 'ar e	If subordination to them be shameful
Ew 'are li xelqê namidar e	The disgrace of it falls to the elite
Namus e li hakim û emîran	It is a matter of honor for the rulers and princes
Tawan ci ye şai'r û feqîran	What are the poet and the poor to do?

Criticizing the elite or nobility for their failure to effectively lead the Kurds, he goes on as if to imply that there is no magic to the job. It is significant to note that nowhere in *Mem û Zîn* does Xanî mention *farr*, the royal glory customarily invoked in texts praising kings.[41] When he writes about the *mîr*s (princes)—again going against convention—Xanî subjects them to criticism.[42] He warns against bad rulers and the harm they cause. Even so, some interpreters describe him as having written *Mem û Zîn* to please the mîr of Botan (O'Shea and Leezenberg) or even seeking "a royalty" (*telif ücreti*).[43] Yet this tendency to reduce Xanî's diagnosis of social ills to a play for princely patronage goes against the spirit of the text. The misunderstanding is driven, of course, by Xanî's invocation of a king. But what many commentators have failed to appreciate is that both kingship and currency are symbols of the sovereignty of a people, which gives validity to its literary currency.

Her çi bire şîrî destê himmet	Anyone who raised the sword resolutely
Zebt kir ji bo xwe bi mêrî dewlet	Would seize the state for himself with virility
Lewra ku cîhan wekî 'erûs e	That is why the world is like a bride
Wê hukmi di destê şîrê rus e	Falling to the hand that draws the sword
Lê 'eqd û sîdaq û mehr û kabin	The bride's contract and dowry
Lutf û kerem û 'eta û bexşîn	Are kindness and generosity
Pirsî ji dinê min ev bi hikmet	With wisdom I asked the world
Mehra te ci? Gote min ku himmet	What is your dowry? She answered: determination

Hasil ku dinê bi şîr û îhsan	Thus by sword and benevolence the world
Tesxîri dibit ji boyi însan	Surrenders to such a man

Here kingship is demystified and the state-founding act is explained in terms of power. It almost implies that anybody could do the job of becoming the sovereign. Readers familiar with Machiavelli should immediately recognize that Xanî's Prince here is almost identical to Machiavelli's. A quote from *The Prince* will refresh our memory:

> I conclude, therefore, that since Fortuna changes and men remain set in their ways, they will prosper as long as the two are in accord with one another, but they will not prosper, when the two are not in accord. I certainly think this: that it is better to be impetuous than cautious, because Fortuna is a woman and it is necessary, in order to keep her under, to beat and knock her about. And one sees that she lets herself be conquered by men of this sort more than by those who proceed coldly. And therefore, like a woman, she is always the friend of the young, because they are less cautious, fiercer, and master her with more audacity.[44]

The similarities are many. Both have a vision of political rule that is free from moralizing influences. Both of them rely on the notion of virility (*virtù* in Machiavelli and *mêrînî* in Xanî). A ruler should be someone who can be resolute in the application of power (by the sword) but should also be capable of employing kindness. Machiavelli agrees with Xanî, though in a slightly pessimistic register: "a ruler who wants to remain in power should not always be good." The two share a conception of Fortuna as a woman (Machiavelli) and a bride (Xanî)—though Xanî's approach is more sharia-compliant—who ultimately demands to be mastered and gives herself only to those men who court her with determination. Like Machiavelli, Xanî was an early modern thinker whose ideas included elements of both the medieval (traditional) and modern (innovative) worlds. Both were well aware of the novelty of their ideas. And like Xanî, Machiavelli too was a transitional figure.[45] The pair are caught between two cosmologies, in an encounter between fate (*fortuna*) and will (*virtù*).

Peoplehood

Xanî's analysis is not romantic nationalism but a prescient philosophical perspective on sovereignty and the liberation of a people. If not for nationalism, then certainly for modernity, Xanî was a prophet whose audience was the future. Of course Xanî did not have an industrial, mass society that would fulfill the conditions of modern nationalism. But we should keep in mind that incipient nationalism was always an elite phenomenon. Elites first contrived and then invited the masses into a newly fashioned identity and a vernacular body politic. That is precisely what Xanî does. Scholars of nationalism are vigilant about its retrospective attribution, but they might do well to devote more attention to the forward-thinking character of national movements. From Xanî to Koyî to Nursi, most Kurdish intellectuals have complained about the lack of receptivity on the part of their contemporaries and chosen, instead, to speak to the future.[46] Whether the Kurds of Xanî's time saw themselves as Kurds is much less the question than whether Xanî saw them as such. The poet is not only reporting to us about the existence of Kurdish identity, he is an author and performer of it.

According to neo-perennialist scholars of nationalism like Steven Grosby, a certain form of premodern national community emerged in the past on the basis of "the native land" versus "the foreigner." In the case of Japanese society, collective national consciousness was encapsulated in two samurai slogans: "revere the emperor" and "expel the barbarian."[47] From this perspective, Kurds are, for Xanî, a people caught between the two empires and stretching from the land of the Arabs to that of the Georgians. The people that enter Xanî's imagination as Kurds are constituted not by some essential quality or even self-conscious choice, but by external forces. Even when an in-group lacks solidarity, it may be forced into it by an out-group. As Hobbes puts it, "[T]he multitude sufficient to confide in for our security is not determined by any number but by comparison with the enemy we fear."[48] Besides, John Lie, who uses the notion of peoplehood as a supra-notion that captures ethnicity, nation, and race all at once, defines it as "a self-reflexive identity."[49] Peoplehood, defined accordingly, becomes possible when what was once restricted to the elite becomes an attribute of the populace.

At the next turning point in the *dibace*, Xanî begins to question the divine wisdom in the condition of his people:

Ez mame di hikmeta Xwedê da	I wonder at the wisdom of the Lord
Kurmanc-i di dewleta dinê da	With regard to a temporal state
Aya bi çi wechî mane mehrûm	Why is it that the Kurds remain deprived?
Bilcumle ji bo çi bûne mehkûm	For what reason are they all condemned?

Here Xanî turns his face away from the heavens and down to earth, looking to the people themselves as the source of needed agency. There, however, he sees their miserable condition and describes it as a paradox to be resolved. They are generous and brave but occupy an unfortunate position between the two empires. Their liminality and victimhood leave them in chaos, relegated to object status. Xanî appeals to their "honor" as a mode of motivation and speaks of their bravery. At this point the shift of focus from the elite (*mîrs*, princes) to the people (*mêrs*, men) is made visible by pairing them. The transition from *mîr* to *mêr* functions as a transfer of agency:

Her mîreke *wan bi bezlê Hatem*	Each *prince* of them is generous like Hatem
Her mêreke *wan bi rezme Rustem*	Every *man* of them is brave like Rustem

In the absence of a king and having called into question the power of fate, the new task for Xanî is to encourage people to pull themselves out of their current condition. Here we reach the point where the very absence of a king pulls Xanî's imagination toward a modern conception of sovereignty, one that demands a popular body politic. After discussing how Kurds are victimized at the hands of the Turkish and Persian empires, Xanî tries to awaken his people by praising them:

Cuwamêrî û himmet û sexawet	Resolution, bravery and generosity
Mêrînî û xîret û celadet	Courage, princeliness and endurance
Ew xetm e jibo qebîlê ekrad	That is the mettle of the Kurds
Wan dane bi şîrê himmetê dad	Who gain their rights with the sword of zeal

Once Xanî conceives of the possibility of people as autonomous actors in the making of history, he has to come up with mechanisms for coordinating their collective behavior. That is precisely where the question of a commonwealth arises. And that question assumes urgency in places where there is chaos or civil war.

Social Contract

While examples of Xani's 'people'ism abound, a particularly early one is *Mem û Zîn*'s dedication (section 5). In the dedication, which by *mesnevi* convention is typically addressed to a ruler, Xanî's addressee is not an individual person, but the Kurdish communities—that is, the Kurds as a people:[50]

Îş'ara medîheta tewaifê di Kurdan e	In praise of the brave and eager
bi şeca'et û xîretê	Kurdish peoples [communities]
izhara bedbextî û bêtali'iya wan e	To demonstrate how unlucky and
digel hinde semahet û hemiyyetê	unfortunate they are
	Despite their generosity and devotion

Kurds' lack of solidarity, problematized so emphatically in Xanî, has long been echoed by various Kurdish figures, from sixteenth-century Sharaf Khan to twentieth-century Said Nursi. Nursi's famous tripartite diagnosis of late-Ottoman malaise was originally conceived in a specifically Kurdish context (only later was it detached from its Kurdish origins and applied to Turkish society). He believed that there were three major problems in Kurdish society: ignorance, poverty, and disunity. Against these three enemies, his weapons of choice were education, industry, and union. The question of Kurdish disunity is a problem that persists to this day and includes the "organizational rivalries" of contemporary Kurdish political groups.[51]

Xanî continues with the observation that the Kurds seem not to want to leave the state of nature and enter the commonwealth. In the natural state they are brave and generous but their pride and aversion to indebtedness prevent them from entering the civil state.

Hindî ji şeca'etê xeyûr in	Great as is their zeal for deeds of bravery
Ew çend ji minnetê nefûr in	Even so is their aversion to indebtedness
Ev xîret û ev uluwwê himmet	This courage and high-mindedness
Bû maniĕ hemlê barê minnet	Became a hindrance to their carrying the burden of obligation
Lew pêkve hemîşe bêtifaq in	That is why they are always disunited
Daîm bi temerrud û şiqaq in	They are always rebellious and divided

Rather than surrender to a social contract, they prefer the liberty enjoyed in the state of nature. Xanî depicts the Kurds as anarchically democratic and fond of "autonomy," a form of liberty without civility. If commonwealth or civil state (notice, it is no longer a king but some form of "establishment") is created, their subordination will end. It is due to the failure of the Kurds to pursue the greater common good that they remain subordinate.

Ger dê hebûya me ittifaqek	If we could form a union by agreement
Vêk ra bikira me inqiyadek	And to that union we all submitted
Rum û 'Ereb û 'Ecem temamî	It would force the Turks, Arabs and Persians all together
Hemiyan ji me ra dikir xulamî	To show deference to us
Tekmîl dikir me dîn û dewlet	Then we would perfect religion and State
Tehsîl dikir me 'ilm û hikmet	We would be able to cultivate knowledge and wisdom
Temyîz dibûn ji hev meqalat	Then the hodgepodge would be sorted
Mumtaz dibûn xwedankemalat	Those with excellence would become distinguished

If only we were to have unity among us, Xanî writes, and submit or bind ourselves to one another, then all of the Ottomans and Arabs and Persians would recognize and respect us, we would reach excellence in religion and state, and we would become producers of knowledge and wisdom.

Submission to the common good seems to be the key to the legitimacy of a commonwealth. It thus makes sense to compare the greater good with an entity above the individual and below God. In section 17 of *Leviathan*, Hobbes writes thus of the agreement by which commonwealth is created:

[A] real unity of them all in one and the same person, made with the covenant of every man with every man, in such a manner as if every man should say to every man: I authorize and give up my right of governing myself to this man, or to this assembly of men, on this condition; that thou give up thy right to his,

and authorize all his actions in like manner. This done, the multitude so united
in one person is called a Commonwealth; in Latin, *Civitas*. This is the generation
of that great Leviathan, or rather, to speak more reverently, of that mortal god to
which we owe, under the immortal God, our peace and defense.[52]

In the figure of Xanî, Kurdish intellectual liminality generated consciousness not
only in the domain of politics but also in the domain of language. The power of
Farsi as a literary language encouraged competition among its linguistic neighbors
and a desire for promoting one's own language.[53] Political liminality and linguistic
liminality opened up a space in which proving the capaciousness and precision of
the Kurdish language became an imperative.

Xanî ji kemalê bêkemal î	Xanî, though lacking in perfection
Meydanê kemalê dîti xalî	You found unoccupied the arena of excellence
Ye'nî ne ji qabil û xebîrî	And stepped forward not because of skill or
Belkî bi te'essub û 'eşirî	knowledge
	But rather out of loyalty and noble love for the people
Hasil ji 'înad eger ji bêdad	In short- call it stubbornness or impudence-
Ev bid'ete kir xilafê mu'tad	He enacted this novelty, contravening convention
De xelq-i nebêjitin ku Ekrad	So that people do not say that the Kurds
Bê me'rifet in, bê 'esl û bunyad	Lack education, origin, and foundations
Enwa'ên milel xudan kitêb in	Various nations have their classics
Kurmanc-i tenê di bê hisêb in	Only the Kurds lack them

In this section, Xanî explains his project and notes its "unusual novelty." He wants
to refine and raise up Kurdish as a language of art and literature. The Kurds, Xanî
believes, do ultimately have the potential as a people; what they lack is leadership.

I believe there is something more to the emphasis on Kurdish as a language in
Xanî's project. He is not simply using language, he is fashioning it as a member of
a pair: Word and Coin, Literature and Sovereignty. His insistent pairing of the two
implies that he has in mind something beyond the mere use of the Kurdish language
for literary purposes. For him, literature, too, is a gesture of sovereignty. The role
of speech in the process of liberation has been noted by scholars of subordinate
groups: movement from object (mass) status to subject status (peoplehood)
involves a stage where the deployment of "speech" functions both as a weapon
and a means of restoring humanity to the subject/ed.[54] Speech (in this case, the
composition of literature) makes visible that which is invisible and gives validity
to the humanity of the subject. Xanî's aesthetics can thus be seen as politics by
other means. The sovereignty of a people is conceived in Xanî's self-presentation
as having both literary and political dimensions.

This becomes clear when, in the absence of sovereign Kurdish power to mint
coins—a symbol of authority—Xanî describes *himself* as minting coins. In a
section where he explicates his purpose in writing this book *in Kurdish*, he claims

that in his poetry he is minting pure coins and draws attention to the relationship between sovereignty, legitimacy, and recognition.

Ev pol gerçi bêbeha ne	These coins may be worthless
Yekrû ne û saf û bêbaha ne	Yet they are refined, pure and priceless
Bêhile û xurde û temam in	With no defect, small and quite perfect
Meqbûle mu'amela 'awam in	As general tender they are valid
Kirmancî ye sirf e, beguman e	Pure Kurdish, not suspect
Zêr nîne bibin sipîderman e	Not gold, perhaps, but not tinsel

Xanî's modernity and his location in relation to nationalism can be understood with close attention to the nexus of sovereignty, peoplehood, and social contract in his methodological reflections in the Introduction to *Mem û Zîn*.

Already in the sixteenth and seventeenth centuries in Europe, many thinkers were concerned with developing new principles for understanding society. "The aim," as Sofia Nasstrom has observed,

> was to separate the rule of society from both the sacred authority of God and its representative on earth, the king. The state of nature was an important device in this break from the theological-political logic. By commencing from a state of nature it was possible to hold a place between past and future, to circumvent the authority of the existing regime and to begin anew. [55]

The social contract theorists Hobbes, Locke, and Rousseau shared this common concern. Breaking with the past was important. Yet even in their day, contract theory had not completely decapitated the king. For example, Hobbes's *Leviathan* imagined the sovereign who would rule over the people to be either "one man" or an "assembly of men to bear their person." Thus the people's contract with either their representative (a king) or with each other (a form of union) becomes the basis for the constitution of a new society. A government is constructed out of a multitude of free, more or less equal, and conflicting wills. In a commonwealth obedience to the government is understood as the equivalent of obedience to one's self. Locke, unlike Hobbes, is not happy with a person as sovereign and seeks to rely instead on the consent of the majority.

Xanî in his analysis of sovereignty begins with God and destiny as potential sources of change for the Kurds. Then he moves on to the possibility of a king (the Hobbesian moment) and from there transitions to *mîrs* (princes, elites) and further to *mêrs* (men, people) as respective loci of sovereignty. Finally he arrives at a Lockean moment where he calls the Kurds to unite into a community by entering into a contract with one another (*vêkra me bikira inqiyadek*).

Here it is important to highlight two words with which Xanî reaches bedrock in his search for the source and locus of sovereignty: *ittifaq* (union) and *inqiyad* (to tie oneself to, to make a covenant with). He combines the two in an interesting way; he proposes that the people make *inqiyad* to an *ittifaq*. The impersonal and abstract sovereign thus emerges as a result of agreement among a stubborn, conflicting, and atomized multitude.

Xanî's body politic is so virtuous, it seems, that it manages to skip the step of regicide and arrive directly at a popular/democratic notion of sovereignty. This, however, is no real virtue, simply a necessity: the Kurds did not have a king to behead. In Europe, the transition from royal to popular sovereignty happened much later, during the age of democratic revolutions (1776–1848). Replacing the personal rule of a king with the impersonal self-rule of a people was not easy. It required the birth of the people as the legitimate foundation of public authority. What others only after much time and struggle could imagine (at least theoretically)—a political body without a head—was for Xanî and the Kurds, whose desire for a king of their own was never fulfilled, not quite so difficult to imagine. Xanî had to imagine a form of unity for a people without a king. The kingless body politic Xanî, *faute de mieux*, imagined for the Kurds generated a modern-seeming theory of social contract.

In short, whether it was the person of Leviathan (Hobbes), the principle of majority rule (Locke), or the general will (Rousseau), all social contract theorists tried to generate a device or mechanism for the exercise of sovereignty by the people. Though Xanî's analysis is by no means as detailed or philosophically presented, it does have all the key components of a social contract theory.

Conclusion

For Anthony Giddens, a key feature of modernity is reflexivity.[56] Reflexivity, which is an essential part of all human activity, undergoes a radical intensification in modern times. As a seventeenth-century thinker, Ehmedê Xanî appears unexpectedly modern in the way he understands and speaks of politics. In his poetic self-reflections, one can trace the birth of a Kurdish political subjectivity that has not yet acquired the form of "nation"—which requires certain preconditions that were lacking among the Kurds—but approaches the concept of "peoplehood." In Xanî, the lack of a king as sovereign and other factors that keep Kurds in their state of nature open the possibility of conceiving a union (Hobbes's "mortal god"). This form in Xanî's discourse, which has the semblance of nation yet is not, can be accommodated under the broader notion of "peoplehood." Stuck in between a not-yet-nation and a body politic that lacks a head, Xanî's search for a new form of sovereignty took him to the threshold of social contract theory. Notwithstanding their compactness of expression, Xanî's ideas on sovereignty, peoplehood, and commonwealth are rich enough to grant him the status of a not-yet-recognized social contract theorist for the Kurds.

In terms of historical period, Xanî belongs to the early modern era, but intellectually he is ahead of his time: properly modern. That nationalism in the nineteenth-century sense may not, as many others have argued, be attributed to him should not diminish our appreciation of Xanî's contemporary relevance as a thinker.

Notes

1 Kurdo (2010).
2 Vali (2003).
3 Hobsbawm and Ranger (1983).
4 Bruinessen (2003); Chyet (1991); Leezenberg (2019a); Yildirim (2011).
5 Ateş (2019).
6 The Kurdish text reproduced here is from Arif Zerevan's transcription published as Xanî (2004). The English translation is mine. In preparing my translation I often consulted the admirable translations into English of Saadalla (2008); Shakely (1992), as well as Yildirim's Turkish rendition (2011). I am grateful to them all.
7 Xanî (2019: 237).
8 Bruinessen (2003: 3).
9 Leezenberg (2019b); O'Shea (2004).
10 O'Shea (2004: 174).
11 Maxwell and Smith (2015).
12 The problem of disunity among the Kurds (whether one construes it in terms of tribes, emirates, or a class of warriors) was around well before Xanî (in the *Sharafnama*) and continued long after him (in Haji Qadir Koyî or Bediuzzaman Said Nursi). About his people, Sharaf Khan, for example, says, "[T]hey do not follow and obey each other and do not have concord" (Hassanpour 2003: 113).
13 Hobbes (1996).
14 Khani (2008).
15 Khani (2008: 11).
16 Yildirim (2011: 239); Zaza (1996: 55-6).
17 Tek (2018: 417).
18 Bruinessen (2003: 10); Shakely (1992: 103).
19 Mem (2005).
20 Bulut (2011).
21 Hassanpour (2003); Shakely (1992).
22 Leezenberg (2019a); Tek (2018: 418).
23 Dale (2010).
24 Özoğlu (2004).
25 Eppel (2016: 28).
26 Ciwan (2015).
27 Ateş (2019: 397).
28 Ateş (2013: 4).
29 Özoğlu (2004: 31).
30 O'Shea (2004, 162).
31 Ateş (2013).
32 Alsancakli (2017a: 246).
33 Hassanpour (2003: 40).
34 El-Rouayheb (2015: 14–59).
35 Ibid., 57.
36 El-Rouayheb (2008: 213).
37 Alsancakli (2018: 192).
38 Eppel (2016: 27–44); Özoğlu 2004: 47).
39 Hassanpour (2003: 128).

40   Tek (2018: 419).
41   Leezenberg (2019b: 211).
42   Ibid., 212.
43   Tek, 421.
44   Machiavelli (2003: 107).
45   Mansfield (1996).
46   A prime example of this tendency is posed by Said Nursi in his dialogues with
     Kurdish tribes on liberty and constitutionalism (in 1911). Nursi employs a certain
     rhetorical technique to highlight the future-oriented nature of the ideas he is
     presenting to his otherwise peasant audiences. When they fail to see what he depicts
     as the benefits of liberty and constitutional government, he says, "If so, I am not
     talking to you. I am turning this way, speaking to the people of the future: O Saids,
     Hamzas, Omers ... and others who are hidden behind the high century ... [i.e.,
     people of the twenty-first century] quietly listening to my words and watching me
     with an invisible gaze! I am addressing you. Raise your heads and affirm by saying
     'correct'! Let those contemporaries of mine not listen to me, if they wish. I am
     speaking to you over the wireless telegraph stretching from the river valleys of the
     past called history to your elevated future. What can I do? I hurried and came in the
     winter, but you will come in a paradisal spring." See Nursi (2006: 119–20).
47   Ozkirimli (2010: 68–70).
48   Hobbes (1996: 104).
49   Lie (2004: 1).
50   Yildirim (2011: 50).
51   Tezcur (2019b).
52   Hobbes (1996: 106).
53   Tek (2018: 418).
54   Smith (1974: 120).
55   Nasstrom (2007: 634).
56   Giddens (1990).

HISTORICAL AND POLITICAL DIMENSIONS OF YEZIDI IDENTITY BEFORE AND AFTER THE *FIRMAN* (GENOCIDE) OF AUGUST 3, 2014

Majid Hassan Ali

Introduction

The Yezidis constitute the largest non-Muslim religious minority in Iraq. Yezidi communities also exist in Turkey, Syria, and the former Soviet Union. Additionally, there is a large Yezidi diaspora, especially in Germany. In terms of geographical spread of the community, northern Iraq is widely acknowledged as the historic homeland of the Yezidis. A majority of Yezidis in Iraq reside in the so-called disputed areas.[1] Sheikhan,[2] which is a religious and political center for the Yezidi community, and Sinjar are the most important Yezidi centers in Iraq.[3] The Yezidis have been subject to various ethnic, national, and religious projects and to many military campaigns and pogroms during their history. In Yezidi oral tradition, these massacres, most of which occurred during Ottoman times, are called *firmans*.[4]

After the American occupation of Iraq, the Yezidis were subject to many attacks and kidnappings. Hundreds of Yezidis lost their lives in such religiously motivated attacks.[5] The August 2007 suicide bombings, considered to be the largest and most deadly attack to have taken place in the post-2003 Iraq, killed hundreds of Yezidi and caused the (almost complete) demolition of two Yezidi towns located in the south of Mt. Sinjar, Siba Sheikh Xidir and Til Ezer.[6] On August 3, 2014, IS occupied Sinjar and the other Yezidi villages in Nineveh plains,[7] killing and enslaving thousands of women, men, and children.

After the 2014 attack, a significant change in political identity took place among Yezidis of both Iraq and diaspora. Increasingly vocal calls emerged among Yezidis to recognize the attacks as genocide based on religion in reaction to the IS

I acknowledge the helpful and constructive comments of Janelle Carlson and Gert Lou (Yan) who edited and proofread an earlier draft of this paper.

atrocities and the sudden and panicked withdrawal of the Kurdish armed forces from the Sinjar region, leaving the Yezidis in the hands of IS. Tens of thousands of Yezidis fled to Mt. Sinjar. Those who were unable to reach the mountain were killed or captured, while those who reached the mountain remained there with little food or water for several days until the Kurdish Protection Units (YPG) fighters from Syria and the People's Protection Forces (HPG) from the Qandil Mountains—a stronghold of the Kurdistan Workers' Party (PKK)—opened a safe passage for them toward Syria. As a result of the IS attacks, a majority of the Yezidis were placed in IDP camps and the cities of the KRI. About 10,000 Yezidis remain in camps in the YPG-controlled areas northeast of Syria. According to official statistics,[8] 350,000 Yezidis out of a population 550,000 became displaced by the IS invasion. More than 100,000 Yezidis have emigrated from Iraq to Western countries.

The number of victims in the first days of the attack was approximately 1,293 and the number of children who became orphans was 2,745. The number of Yezidis abducted by IS was 6,417, including 3,548 females and 2,869 males. More than 50 percent of these abductees were eventually liberated. The number of survivors totaled 3,509 people, including 1,192 women, 337 men, 1,033 girls, and 947 boys. The fate of 2,908 individuals, including 1,323 females and 1,585 males, was unknown.[9] The number of mass graves discovered in Sinjar as of October

Figure 3.1 An overview of containers in the Rwanga camp populated by Yezidis (Zakho-Duhok road, May 2018)

Figure 3.2 A street in the Rwanga camp populated by displaced Yezidis (Zakho-Duhok road, May 2018)

2019 is eighty. This is in addition to dozens of smaller sites and individual graves. The number of religious shrines and holy places destroyed by IS was sixty-eight.[10]

The attack and its aftermath have redefined the dimensions of Yezidi relations with their Muslim neighbors. It has led to the collapse of the relationship between the Yezidis and the Sunni Arabs and Sunni Kurds.[11] A primary reason for the Yezidi mistrust toward the KRI was due to its failure to protect the Yezidis from the IS attack. The absence of an independent investigation and convincing justification for the withdrawal of the Kurdish Peshmerga was a major disappointment for the entire Yezidi community, from the Mir (Prince),[12] the Yezidi Spiritual Council,[13] and to the ordinary people. A pressing question remained unanswered: "Why did the Kurdish Peshmerga abandon us and leave us unarmed?" Other salient questions remain unanswered as well. Why did the Yezidis become a primary target of the IS? The IS invasion reminds the past *firmans* (genocides) committed against the Yezidis due to their non-Islamic religious identity. Many Yezidis believe that their distinctive religious faith is one of the most important reasons for the withdrawal of the Peshmerga, even if there could be also political reasons.[14]

These events and developments have a significant impact on the entire Yezidi community within and beyond the borders of Iraq. It has led to a reassessment of the religious, ethnic, and national aspects of their identity. There are also many regional differences among Yezidis from Rojava (Syria),[15] Bashiqa and Bahzani (where Arab-speaking Yezidis live), Sinjar and Sheikhan (Iraq), or Russia, Armenia, and Georgia. Given this diversity, there has never been a political unity among the Yezidis. At the same time, it is puzzling to note the absence of the Yezidi from international media coverage and from political and academic discussions until very recently, despite their shared suffering alongside other minority and sectarian groups in Iraq and other countries. This chapter reflects on the reasons for this absence and offers an examination of the formation of an ethnoreligious identity among the Yezidis, intra-Yezidi conflicts, and between Yezidis and other nationalist political movements and groups.

The Yezidis as an Ethnoreligious Group

Scholars consider many of the doctrinal elements of the Yezidi faith as linked to other religions, such as Islam, Christianity, and Zoroastrianism.[16] Notwithstanding the deep-rooted ethnogenesis of the Yezidis, they were formed as an ethnoreligious group, approximately in the twelfth and thirteenth centuries, based on an ancient Mesopotamian cult and on the teachings of Sheikh Adi ibn Musafir, who died in 1162 CE.[17] He drew from a mixture of ancient traditions and rites and blended them with the mysticism, which he believed offered a means of attaining "direct fusion" or oneness with God. He is considered the great reformer of the Yezidi religion. After its reestablishment during the era of Sheikh Adi, the Yezidi belief system became more open and allowed outsiders to embrace the religion. Members of different clans in the regions gathered around Sheikh Adi and converted to the Yezidi religion, many of whom spoke the Kurmanji-Kurdish language,[18] along with other tribes that spoke Persian, Turkish, and Arabic.[19] In time, the Yezidi community became an ethnoreligious unit established on the basis of Yezidi religious teachings.

There are new academic studies on the issue of Yezidi identity, including some of my studies that deal with historical and sociopolitical aspects, including the evolution and transformation of Yezidi identity from a scientific perspective. These studies suggest that Yezidi identity is based on ethnoreligious concepts. Based on the hypothesis adopted by some scholars, the Yezidi religion was revised and reestablished between the twelfth and thirteenth centuries.[20] It was the religion of different nations and peoples of Mesopotamia, such as Kurds, Arabs, the Persian and Turkish speakers, and other followers of Sheikh Adi. According to a new study,[21] the ethnogenesis of Yezidis originated centuries before the coming of Sheikh Adi to Lalish in the twelfth century. Religious communities can be said to exhibit diverse identities. The Yezidi community presents many layers of identity. This is geographical, as is reflected in the Yezidi sub-identity demarcation Sinjarian (Shingali) and Walati. Yet there remains an identifiable core Yezidi identity. However, prior to the emergence of Arab and Kurdish nationalism that led to the need to assert Yezidiness in the face of Kurdishness or Arabness, perhaps people constructed their identities primarily in relationship to other Yezidi social groups, primarily based on tribe or caste. Because their whole world was constructed within the Yezidi community and not vis-à-vis Kurdish Muslims, for example, their identity categories were all Yezidi. Many probably lived their entire lives without any contact with non-Yezidis, so naming a Yezidi identity per se was not urgently important in their daily lives in the absence of an external challenge to that identity. There is a coherent Yezidi identity, but there is also tremendous diversity within the Yezidi community, which can also change over time. Yezidi identity is very complex and rich, as there exists a range of identities within it.

As aforementioned the majority of Yezidis speak standard Kurmanji, which is considered the principal Kurdish dialect. Linguistically, Yezidis are not homogenous. Some Yezidis speak other languages as a mother tongue, such as the Bahzanian language (dialect), which is close to some Levantine Arabic dialects. There are several Yezidi religious texts in languages other than Yezidi Kurmanji. Of the total remaining 175 texts, about 160 are read and recited in Yezidi Kurmanji, while 15 are in other languages such as Persian, Turkish, and Arabic. For example, the *Qawwl* (hymn) of Shams-e Tabrizi is read and recited in Farsi, the *Qawwl* of Pir-Sini Bahri is in Turkish, and the *Qawwl* of *Gayyib-Kuni* and several other prayers are in Arabic.[22] It should be noted that the number of texts mentioned here was counted by clerics and could be compared with the findings of some scholars.[23]

In time, the Yezidi community became an ethnoreligious unit established on the basis of Yezidi religious teachings. The distinction between the Yezidi religion and other belief systems has been confirmed by some orientalists[24] who claim that Yezidi ideology and beliefs differed significantly from those of the Islamic Kurds, Arabs, and Turks adjacent to Yezidi territories. They subjected Yezidis to oppression. In light of the religious reforms established by Sheikh Adi and the societal outcomes of these reforms, this hypothesis appears to be convincing to some extent. However, the religious reforms of the twelfth and thirteenth centuries were the conglomeration of ancient traditions the Yezidis had been practicing before the coming of Sheikh Adi and his mysticism, along with the reforms that he brought about.

In terms of Yezidi ethnoreligious identity, it is worth mentioning some Yezidi characteristics, such as isolation or self-concealment, the non-missionary nature of the Yezidi religion, and the practice of endogamous marriage. Endogamous marriage and the complex and strict caste system, known as the system of *Hadd-u-Sad* (measures and laws), are social and religious conventions within the Yezidi religious tradition. This socioreligious system was established after the coming of Sheikh Adi. Its application within the Yezidi community is based on a sacred Yezidi religious text preventing marriage across the three main endogamous castes—the Pir, Sheikh, and Murid—[25]and to those who are not adherents of the Yezidi religion. This system was probably introduced with the intention of protecting the continuity of the Yezidi from the encroachment of proselytizing religions. Endogamous marriage would serve to foster the self-isolation of the Yezidis. Assuming that endogamous marriage and its consequences originated with Sheikh Adi in the twelfth century, it has been ongoing for nine centuries.

This long period of isolation and endogamous marriage has, over time, caused the Yezidi to have a very distinctive identity. Moreover, emphasis was placed on preserving the purity of Yezidi blood (kinship). Members of other religions were not allowed to convert to the Yezidi religion and public preaching was prohibited. The blood bond constitutes a strong peculiarity that may be said to lend the Yezidis a strong collective identity.

The State of Iraq and the Yezidis

On the issue of nationalism and the ethnic affiliation of the Yezidis, it is of vital importance to note that the British mandate in Iraq considered the Yezidis to be a small nation: "[T]his people [the Yezidis] is also indigenous to the country that it now inhabits, and was also treated as a small Nation by the Turkish [Ottoman] Empire."[26] The identity issues confronting Iraqi Yezidis are somewhat different from those facing Yezidis in Armenia or Russia, or those in Europe, due to the different contexts and circumstances in which they find themselves. It is possible that the British colonial officers conflated the term *nation* with the term *millet* that originated before the modern European doctrine of nationalism. Were the British correct to classify the Yezidis in this way? If so, the British assumed that the Ottomans viewed the Yezidis as a *millet*.[27] This recognition by the Ottoman authorities could have applied for only a short period because the Ottomans did not tolerate Yezidis and did not consider them to be adherents of a *legitimate* non-Muslim religion. The Ottomans tried to exterminate the Yezidis several times. There is no historical evidence that the Ottomans classified the Yezidis as a distinct *millet*.[28]

The Iraqi history, from the foundation of the modern state under British tutelage in 1921 to the US occupation in 2003, was characterized by periods of instability and insecurity for non-Muslim religious minorities. After the First World War, Iraq became a separate entity and most Yezidis became part of the emerging Iraqi state, with the resolution of the so-called Mosul problem and its annexation to Iraq in 1925. This region holds the Yezidi areas of Sinjar and Sheikhan, the historical and religious center of the Yezidi faith and home to the sacred valley and main temple of Lalish.

From 1921 to 2003, the Iraqi government subjected the Yezidis to numerous military campaigns for various reasons. These campaigns included the settlement of Arab and Muslim tribes in their areas, which led to several rebellions, especially in the Sinjar region. The most important of these armed uprisings occurred between 1925 and 1935 and was led by Dawud al-Dawud and Hamu Shiru, who demanded the return of Yezidi land and the expulsion of the Arab tribes that had been brought to the region.

The 1960s saw renewed Yezidi uprisings, especially the 1966 rebellion led by Saydo Hamu Shiru, the chieftain of the Faqira clan, and Murad Atto, the chieftain of the clan of Habbabat. These Yezidi leaders declared an insurrection on Mount

Sinjar in March 1966. The main reason for this insurrection is their refusal to settle the Arab tribes in their areas.[29] Mt. Sinjar offering a natural fortress, the first rebels were joined by members of many Yezidi clans from Sinjar and its adjacent villages. After this rebellion, the government initiated a long-term program to prevent any future revolt. Government plans included demolishing Yezidi villages on the top of Mt. Sinjar, grouping them into residential compounds and settling Arab tribes around their old villages. However, there was no mass Yezidi immigration out of Iraq until the 1990s. In the aftermath of the 1991 Gulf War, the Yezidis and other minorities were divided between the CGI and the KRI, which was formed in 1991. A migration of the Yezidi began as a result of the war and its aftermath, the economic blockade, as well as the formation of a no-fly zone in northern Iraq, which led to the separation of three Kurdish governorates (Duhok, Erbil, and Sulaymaniyah) from the control of the CGI, which at the same time divided the Yezidis between the CGI and the KRI.

Political Dimensions of Yezidi Identity in Iraq

In light of the controversy surrounding the Yezidi identity, political movements with opposing agendas have developed competing theories about the identity of Yezidis.

The Iraqi Arab Nationalists and Political Parties

The 1960s was a period of great regional change in general and in Iraq in particular. During this time that Arab nationalism peaked and a number of the Arab nationalist and pan-Arabism parties came to power. It was also the time when the armed conflict between the central government and the Kurdish movement intensified.[30] The rise of Arab nationalist currents in Iraq, especially the Ba'th Arab Socialist Party, had major implications for the evolution of the Yezidi identity. The Arab call for the Yezidi Umayyad movement[31] was announced by a wing of the opposition Yezidi princely family in 1964. When the Ba'th Party firmly established its power in 1968, they officially recognized the "Arab Call of Yezidi Umayyad" in its "Umayyad Office," which was located in Bab al-Sharqi quarter in Baghdad. That recognition was explained in 1972 by the Umayyad Office as follows: "The Yezidi *Ta'ifa* [community] inland and abroad responds to the call of nationalism and wishes to preserve itself [as a distinct community] on the basis of two main principles: 'Umayyad nationality and Yezidi faith.'"[32] Subsequently, the government recognized Yezidi religious holidays.[33] Similarly, other religions were granted religious holidays under the new legislation. The Umayyad office continued to exist officially in Iraq until 1981. In the same year, all religious communities that were officially recognized in Iraq were listed by law. In this new law, the official name of the Yezidi community name was changed to the "Yezidi Umayyad Cult."[34]

Despite these politics of recognition, mutual distrust between the Yezidis and the government remained. Mir Tahseen Beg (1933–2019) was accused of participating in a conspiracy against Saddam Hussein, for example (probably because of his joining the Kurdish Movement in 1969), which caused him to flee to Britain in the 1970s. Nevertheless, the office of *al-Daawa al-Umawiya* (the Umayyad Call) became a link between the government and the Yezidis. The government-appointed Bayazid (a member of Yezidi princely family) as government representative of the Yezidis passed a special decree in April 1980 that made him president and prince of the Yezidis. Bayazid remained in office until his death on June 13, 1981. Shortly after his death, Prince Mir Tahseen Beg returned to Iraq, having been pardoned by the Iraqi president, Saddam Hussein.[35] After the death of Bayazid, this current was led by the children of Bayazid and Moawiyya al-Umawi (Umayyad). Among them is Anwar Muawiyya al-Umawi and a number of other members of the princely family of Ismail Chol Beg (uncle of Prince Tahseen), especially after the Second Gulf War.[36] This current rejected the imposition of the Kurdish ethnonational identity over the Yezidi; however, the power and influence of this current diminished after 2003 as a result of the emergence of other Yezidi currents.

The Kurdish Nationalists and Political Parties

In the monarchical era (1921–1958), Yezidis were not considered ethnically Kurdish.[37] Despite the Yezidis' refusal to submit completely to the laws and policies of the country, which their revolts, movements, and mutinies of monarchy exemplify, the Yezidis had never publicly gravitated toward any nationalist movement, be it Arab or Kurdish. For instance, in the 1930s, although Khoybun, the Kurdish nationalist association based in Lebanon and Syria, idealized the Yezidi religious minority as the one true Kurdish religion, it did not have prominent Yezidi members. Some sources claim[38] that Hajo Agha Heverki, the chieftain of the Heverkan Kurdish tribe and a Khoybun member, was a Yezidi, but it is generally accepted that he was not openly so.

After the establishment of the Republic of Iraq in 1958, the Yezidi prince, Mir Tahseen Beg, was called to join the Kurdish movement and this was the first official contact between a Kurdish political movement and the Yezidis.[39] The Kurdish movement and the Kurdistan Democratic Party (KDP) engendered hitherto unprecedented support among the Yezidis in the 1960s. For the first time, Yezidis became politically and militarily active in the struggle between the Iraqi government and Kurdish nationalist movement. The political influence of the KDP on the Yezidis remained significant in the subsequent decades.

The unprecedented involvement of the Yezidis in the Kurdish armed revolt and in the KDP raises an interesting question as to why the Yezidi attitudes in Iraq changed in the 1960s, particularly attitudes toward the Kurds. The phenomena of Kurdish and Arab nationalism had already existed for decades. Nevertheless, 1963 was a pivotal moment in that it marked a new form of political pressure on minorities to conform to identity expectations of the larger groups. Therefore,

Yezidi ethnicity became an increasingly contested issue with the escalation of Arab nationalism in Iraq.[40]

After the outcome of the Second Gulf War in 1991, which included the imposition of a safe zone (by the United Nations Security Council Resolution 688, which was adopted on April 5, 1991),[41] the Kurdish political parties and currents took over regions that included three major governorates of Iraq. One of these governorates, Duhok, included the four Yezidi towns of Sharya, Khanke, Dayrabun, and Baadre. Due to the administrative and security vacancy created after the withdrawal of the CGI institutions from those governorates, the Kurdish political parties decided to hold the first provincial election in KRI in 1992. The idea of a Yezidi religion being the original Kurdish religion became part of the official ideology and state propaganda of some Kurdish political parties, especially the KDP. In the words of Massud Barzani, the KDP leader, "if there are such a people as Kurds, then Yezidis are the original Kurds."[42] These developments divided the Yezidi community between the CGI and the KRI. Yezidi within the CGI was unable to organize themselves politically due to the repressive political system and the dominance of the Ba'th Party. This situation continued until the overthrow of the Ba'th regime in 2003. The Yezidi Umayyad movement was abandoned. In the KRI, there were some cultural, social, and political developments that affected the Yezidis, the most important of which was an agreement reached by the first generation of Yezidi intellectuals to establish a center for Yezidi culture, history, and heritage. This agreement saw the establishment of the Lalish Cultural and Social Center in 1993, which became pro-KDP after the 1994 Kurdish civil war. However, the Yezidis refrained from establishing a political party at that time. Although the option of establishing a Yezidi party was discussed within the Yezidi elite, this was strongly discouraged by the dominant Kurdish political parties, the KDP and the Patriotic Union of Kurdistan (YNK), which included a significant number of the Yezidi political elite.

In their political and ideological programs, those Kurdish parties considered the Yezidis to be ethnic Kurds. Accordingly, from their point of view, there was no need to establish a political party peculiar to the Yezidi people based on religious differences as they share the same ethnic origins as the Muslim Kurds. It was also in the interests of the Kurdish political agenda to assimilate the Yezidi population, rather than to support and encourage their self-determination. This is why the Yezidi continued to be represented by the Kurdish parties after 2003. At the same time, this situation displeased many Yezidis in that there were many Kurdish Islamic parties established on the basis of religious ideology. They felt that they were deprived of a political right permitted to others.

Yezidi Political Movements in Iraq

Following the Third Gulf War in 2003, the KDP security forces expanded their control over the disputed areas, which include Yezidi towns and villages in Sinjar. Following the political developments and the ongoing conflict between the CGI and the KRI, the Yezidis established political movements and parties for the first time in their history.

The first movement was the ethnonationalist "Yezidi Movement for Reform and Progress" that had its headquarters in Sinjar. It gained the Yezidi quota seat in the Iraqi parliament three times from 2005 to 2014.[43] The Yezidi Movement for Reform and Progress was headed by Ameen Farhan Jejo and Hamad Matto,[44] who subsequently broke away from it and established the Yezidi Progression Party on April 6, 2008, which was also located in Sinjar.

It is noteworthy that Ameen Farhan Jejo, the president of the movement, tried to follow in the footsteps of past Middle Eastern nationalists by writing books that contain political and ideological theorization. One of them is entitled *The Yezidi Nationalism: Its Roots, Constituents and Sufferings*. The second is entitled *Yezidi-Arabic Dictionary*, while another is entitled *The Origins of the Yezidi Language*.[45] Through these books, he argued for an autonomous Yezidi nationality in a way similar to that of Kurdish, Arab, and Turkish nationalisms. He attempted to prove that Yezidism is an independent ethnonationality whose roots reach back to Mesopotamia. Despite the scarcity of historical and methodological scientific documentation, it remains an attempt on the part of the writer and his political movement to bring attention to a belief that had not been covered by other writers and researchers. His second book, a dictionary, depended upon an alphabet that had been published in some studies and research, as the sacred alphabet of the Yezidi religious texts. In the third book, he claimed to link the Yezidi language with ancient Iraqi languages by returning to semiotic languages. These claims were not based on scientific evidence but represented an attempt to imagine the Yezidis as a national ethnic group.

In addition, the Yezidi Movement for Reform and Progress demands that the Iraqi parliament officially list the Yezidi as a people in the official documents of Iraq. This demand is refuted by those Yezidi political elite adhering to the belief that the Yezidi are of Kurdish origin.[46] The idea that the Yezidis are an independent ethnonationality and religion, separate from the Kurds and Arabs, challenges the positions of the Kurdish ethnonationalist parties, especially the KDP who consider the Yezidi to be ethnically Kurdish.[47] This ideological difference has caused a power struggle in the Yezidi regions. It is noteworthy that the power of the Yezidi Movement for Reform and Progress expanded in Sinjar but not in the Sheikhan district,[48] which is directly subject to the dominant KDP security.

In 2004, the Yezidi Free Democratic Movement (TEVDA) was established. It was founded in Mosul on January 2, 2004, and held its first conference on March 18–20, 2004. In addition, it declared that it aims to represent all members of the Yezidi community, saying it "opposes intolerance and the limited clannish traditions." It also stressed the freedom of women and the creation of a fully aware community.[49] This organization remained active in Sinjar and its role grew after IS occupied Sinjar in 2014 in which it formed the basis for the establishment of the Protection Units of Shingal—*Yekîneyên Berxwedana Şingal* (YPŞ). They are a military force, based out of Khanasor town in Sinjar. The KDP and Turkey have accused them of being affiliated with the PKK. It is worth mentioning that most of the YPŞ fighters are Yezidis from Sinjar.[50]

Yezidi resistance fighters in Sinjar established special forces named *Hêza Parastina Êzîdxan* (the Ezidkhan Protection Forces), headed by Haider Shesho, a member of the central committee in the YNK. Although these forces raised their own flag, they, at the same time, asked to be part of the Kurdish Peshmerga system, which enjoys the support of the Kurdish parties. The Ezidkhan Protection Force officially established a political party in 2017, called the Ezidi Democratic Party, and it inaugurated a center in Sulaymaniyah.

In addition to these forces, the central government and the Popular Mobilization (*al-Hashd al-Sha'abi*),[51] as well as the Peshmerga of the Kurdish parties, competed with each other for control of the area due to strategic importance near the Syrian and Turkish border, and because it is likely to contain untapped minerals and oil resources.

The Transformations of the Yezidi Identity in the Caucasus

In the Soviet Union, the Yezidis and the Muslim Kurds were considered ethnonationally distinguishable. The Yezidi were thus registered in official documents as an independent ethnonationality, and on their civil identity documents their nationality was registered as Yezidi. Similarly, in 1919, the Yezidis were granted permission by the Georgian government to register an organization in Tbilisi, called the Yezidi Ethno-Nationality Consultative Council,[52] which indicated that the Yezidis saw themselves as a distinct nationality. Moreover, educated Yezidis in the Soviet Union considered themselves representatives of the Yezidi nation in their publications. They also considered their dialect of Kurmanji to be a Yezidi language: Yezidiki. Accordingly, many Armenian Yezidi refused to acknowledge that they speak Kurmanji, insisting instead that they spoke Yezidiki, a separate language. However, the majority of Yezidi clearly speak Kurmanji. Any differences between Kurmanji and the language spoken by the Yezidi in Armenia, Georgia, Russia, and Syria are regional variants.[53]

However, during the era of Joseph Stalin, the measures adopted during the Stalin era about linguistic and nationalistic groups led to the changes in Yezidi perceptions.[54] In the census of 1939, there were 46,000 Kurds in the Soviet Union, and there were 59,000 in the 1959 census. According to Bennigsen,[55] about 20 percent of them were Yezidis, with the written language for Yezidis appearing in Cyrillic script. Some Yezidi writers and educated Yezidis were influenced by the development of the Stalin era about linguistic and nationalistic groups, and in their writings and publications, they declared themselves Kurdish, despite having claimed in the past that they were Yezidi.[56] In addition to the influence of Stalin's policies, the Yezidi may have begun calling themselves Kurds because identities based on religion were considered undesirable in the Soviet Union. These Yezidi writers and academics, therefore, went about publishing their writings under the rubric of Kurdish literature and heritage.

Since the fall of the Soviet Union in 1991, many Yezidis in the Caucasus have not made a sharp distinction between Yezidi and Kurdish nationalist identity. In the meantime, moreover, many Yezidi leaders in Armenia disavow Kurdish roots. For instance, in an official US communication,[57] one such leader "characterized his own pro-Armenian position as a question of loyalty to the government" in gratitude that it "finally recognized the Yezidi as a distinct ethnicity." It could be that Armenia wants to emphasize that Yezidis are not Kurds given the problematic history between Armenians and Kurdish Muslims. This position represents a significant change after years of Soviet insistence that the Yezidi were Kurds, and marked a shift toward Yezidis trans-ethnonationalism.

Manifestations of the Transformation of Yezidi Identity after 2014

The Yezidi armed groups that formed on Mount Sinjar after the IS onslaught raised a peculiar flag with three colors: red and white with a yellow sun in the middle.[58] They also introduced a national anthem[59] that symbolized an independent Yezidi identity. In most demonstrations that have been organized by Yezidi societies abroad, the same flag that was raised on Mt. Sinjar has been waved. Supporters of this current believe the flag to be a symbol of an independent Yezidi identity, not just a military or political group. It has been raised by many social, intellectual, and religious Yezidi institutions in European countries and Armenia, Russia, and Georgia to denote the independence of the Yezidi identity.

Dozens of institutions have been established by Yezidis in Western countries since the nineties, but most of them are connected to the Kurdish parties and assume the Yezidi Kurdish nationalist identity. After 2014, however, various new international civil organizations and institutions outside Iraq were established. They embraced the Yezidis' idiosyncratic identity.[60] The Yezidis organized a number of demonstrations independently for the first time. The first purely Yezidi demonstration occurred in 2007, when the house of the prince and the Yezidi centers were burned by Kurdish Muslims. This was because the Kurdish Muslims believed that the Yezidis in Sheikhan had kidnapped a Muslim woman. That was a false claim and this episode reflected religious hatred toward the Yezidi community in that district.

After this, a series of other demonstrations and protests were organized, especially when kidnapping and Islamization of Yezidi girls took place in the KRI. In addition, individual attacks and the burning of Christian and Yezidi stores occurred in the cities of Zakho and Duhok in 2011. These events were followed by a series of incidents, explosions, and killings.[61] The last is the genocide in 2014, all of which pushed Yezidi societies abroad to stage further demonstrations in protest. The majority of these demonstrations were purely Yezidi, without the participation of Muslim Kurds or others.

Conclusion

Yezidis, because of their religion, spend their lives confronted by challenges, which in turn affect their distinct identities as they continuously encounter various modes of inclusive and exclusive practices. Discrimination and marginalization serve to heighten Yezidi claims to a separate ethnoreligious or peculiar identity. At the same time, those suffering under religious and ethnic discrimination themselves can become discriminatory and reproduce the discourse of religious hatred.

Political developments and societal changes affected the reformation of the Yezidi ethnoreligious identity. The transnational nature of the Yezidis as an ethnoreligious unit has raised the issue of the Yezidi identity in the former Soviet Union during the 1920s. In Iraq in the 1960s, both Kurdish and Arab nationalists aimed to co-opt Yezidis into their agendas and formulated contested claims associating Yezidis with Kurdish or Arab ethnicity, respectively. Such claims were the products of internal and external aspects of the conflicts and originated in the political discourse of the nationalist movements. But there was no independent Yezidi ethnonationalist position before 2003.

After the US invasion of Iraq in 2003, it is notable that the Yezidi political movements allied with preexisting political movements, which resulted in the growth of intellectual and organizational relations with these parties and other political movements. Many of those who believe in the Yezidi Kurdish identity are activists and members in the Kurdish parties, especially in the KDP and in the YNK, where they present a multifaceted image of the allies of the Yezidi parties and institutions with the other political parties and currents. All of them have failed to gather the Yezidis under one political umbrella.

The occupation of Sinjar and the Nineveh Plain in August 2014 by IS, as a consequence of the failure of the Iraqi army and the Peshmerga forces in protecting Yezidis, had a great impact on Yezidi public opinion. As a result, these security and military systems lost credibility among the Yezidis. Consequently, the question of identity has become a prominent issue for the Yezidis after the August 3, 2014 event and subsequent developments. The outcome of this study shows that the nationalist and political parties must accept Yezidis the way they are, with no attempts to change them and their identity by imposing unfamiliar ideologies upon them. Yezidis, on the other hand, must understand that the confrontation with the other groups will not lead to peace.

Notes

1   These areas are part of the dispute between the Central Government of Iraq (CGI) and the Kurdistan Region of Iraq (KRI), as defined in the article 140 of the Iraqi constitution of 2005. For more details, see Ali (2017: 46, 293–5).

2   Sheikhan is a geographical area northeast of Mosul. The majority of its inhabitants were Yezidis, but it was subjected to gradual demographic Islamization until the Yezidis eventually became a minority.

3 Sinjar is located 125 km west of Mosul, at the foot of the southern face of Mt. Sinjar.
4 The Arab and Islamic campaigns and invasions against Yezidis, known in the literature and heritage of the Yezidis by the term *firmans*, which literally means genocidal campaigns according to modern terminology. For more information, see Ali (2019b).
5 Danish Immigration Service (2009: 38–9).
6 Suicide truck bombings targeting Yezidis near the northern town of Sinjar in August 2007 killed as many as 500 people, the worst single attack since 2003; HRW (2008: 479).
7 "PAX for peace," 2015: 52–3.
8 This statistic is taken from the statistics of BRHA (2016).
9 The "Office for Yezidi Abductees" revealed these figures to the author. Interview with Hussein Kuro Ibrahim, director of the office for Yezidi abductee, August 12, 2019.
10 See RSHID (2019).
11 Barber (2017).
12 The Mir (Prince) is considered both the religious and political leader of all Yezidis.
13 The Spiritual Council is a religious institution that regulates the Yezidi communal affairs. Its aims are to preserve the beliefs of the community, to educate clerics, and to find ways of resolving religious issues.
14 Ali (2019c).
15 I mean Yezidis who joined the Kurdish nationalist movement in Syria.
16 Fuccaro (1999b: 9).
17 Yezidis pronounce his name as Shaykhadi, while in Arabic, it is pronounced Sheikh Uday.
18 It is called Êzdîkî (Yezidi)-Kurmanji by many groups of Yezidis in Caucasus; for more details, see the section "The Transformations of the Yezidi Identity in the Caucasus" in this chapter and Yilmaz (2018).
19 Ali (2019a).
20 Ibid.
21 The basis for their statements on the origins of Yezidis is their fieldwork among Yezidis and their study of the Yezidi oral tradition; see Ali (2019a); Ali, Pirbari, and Rzgoyan (2014: 175).
22 Ali (2019a).
23 Kreyenbroek and Rashow (2005).
24 al-Damaloji (1949: 170–6); Arakelova (2010: 12).
25 In Yezidi, Kurmanji, and Persian literature, the term *Pir* denotes a venerable old man. It is also a mystic term that corresponds to the Arabic term *Sheikh*, which means "spiritual chief and nobleman." In Yezidi, *Murid* (Mirîd) means "layman" or "disciple" and indicates a person who does not belong to the sacerdotal caste but is of the caste of ordinary people. There is no historical evidence that Sheikh Adi created the caste system or that it did not already exist before his time, but Yezidis say that the second cast (Sheikh) was created after Sheikh Adi and also has a spiritual connotation.
26 "The Kingdom of Iraq and its minorities," 2001: 580.
27 The word *millet* means a religious nation; it is an Islamic term. It comes from the Arabic word *millah* and literally means nation or people. However, millet is also a term that was used to refer to ethnoreligious communities in the Ottoman Empire. It refers to the separate legal courts in which religious minorities ruled on the civil cases of minority citizens. For more details, see Ali (2017: 58–9, 96).
28 For the Ottoman campaigns targeting Yezidis, see the chapters by Bahadin Kerborani and Güneş Murat Tezcür, Zeynep Kaya, and Bayar Mustafa Sevdeen.
29 Ali (2017: 117–33, 220–70).

30 Aziz (2011: 66–70).
31 Yezidi Umayyad movement was established in Baghdad in 1964 by some members of the Yezidi princely family who were closed to the Arab nationalist movement in Iraq, and they considered Yezidis as Umayyad Arab ethnically. This movement collapsed with the fall of the Ba'th authority in 2003.
32 Al-Maktab al-Umawi (The Umayyad Office), a special report, the Members of the Umayyad Call in Baghdad, in 1972, cited in Ali (2017: 288).
33 "Al-Waqa'I" al-Iraqiyya', 1972.
34 "Law No.1," 1982.
35 Ali (2017: 288–9).
36 Ali (2019c).
37 Excerpt by the Khoybun Kurdish political organization, which considered Yezidism as an ancient Kurdish religion.
38 Bruinessen (1994: 23–4); Fuccaro (1994a: 22–240).
39 Although there were Yezidi members of the KDP, founded 1946, this can be considered as an individual activity rather than an indicator of collective commitment.
40 Ali (2019a).
41 UN Security Council (1991).
42 Spät (2018).
43 Salloum, Salah, and Hassan (2015).
44 Hamad Matto disappeared after the IS occupation of Sinjar. His fate is unknown since August 3, 2014.
45 Jejo (2010, 2013, 2014).
46 Ali (2019c).
47 Related to the argument is that the Yezidi were the original Kurds, some Yezidi intellectuals claim that the Kurds came later, due to social evolution, and that they are ethnically Yezidi and not the other way around.
48 "Lone Yezidi Parliamentarian Criticizes Kurdish Treatment of Minorities," 2006.
49 TEVDA 2004a, 2004b.
50 It is notable that the Yezidi parties did not take up arms until after the 2014 invasion by IS and the withdrawal of Kurdish Peshmerga forces from Sinjar.
51 *Al-Hashd al-Sha'abi* (Iraq's Popular Mobilization Force) is an organization composed of some ten militias that are mostly Shia Muslim, but also includes Sunni Muslim, Shabak, Christian, and Yezidi individuals as well. It was established to fight IS in 2014.
52 Ali, Pirbari, and Rzgoyan (2014: 182).
53 "Assessing Kurdish Militancy in Armenia—So Far, Not Too Much," 2006.
54 Сталин ИВ [Stalin I.V.] (1953).
55 Bennigsen (1971: 171).
56 Ali, Pirbari, and Rzgoyan (2014: 183).
57 "Assessing Kurdish Militancy in Armenia—So Far, Not Too Much," 2006.
58 "Statement on the occasion of the Day of Ezidkhan National Flag," 2015.
59 "Êzîdxan - Ezidi Anthem," 2017.
60 Among these organizations are *Eziden Weltweit* EWW [Initiative for Yezidis around the world], established in Germany on February 7, 2015. Yazda is a global Yezidi organization of great activity and influence on a global scale. Its main center is in the United States and it has various branches in Europe, Australia, and Iraq; see Ali (2019c) for more details.
61 "Yezidi Protest at Embassy," 2007.

4

POLITICAL IDENTITY AND KURDISH REFUGEES IN THE KURDISTAN REGION OF IRAQ

Arzu Yılmaz

Introduction

Throughout the twentieth century, refugee flights among four parts of Kurdistan have been a recurrent pattern of the Kurdish experience. Kurdish people faced forced migration and oppression especially after revolts in Turkey, Iran, Iraq, and Syria where they make significant minorities. In some cases, they fled from one part to another. The Kurds, for instance, fled from Turkey to Syria after the Sheikh Said Revolt in 1925; from Iraq to Iran after the failure of the Gulan Revolution in 1975; and from Iraq to Turkey and Iran after the failed Kurdish uprising in 1991.[1] In these episodes, the Kurds fled across the frontiers primarily to reach safety and the geographical proximity has been the determinant factor in terms of the choice of destination.

In this search for safety, however, the availability of resources for shelter provided by the Kurds living across the borders has also been an important factor. During and after revolts, Kurdish refugees regrouped among close kin or joined other Kurds in exile.[2] Yet solidarity based on shared ethnic kinship didn't necessarily turn into a transformative political force in the host country. This was primarily because of the central authorities' strong military and political control over Kurdish-populated regions that undermined sustained transborder political activism. Kurdish refugees' access to a relative safety in exile was conditional on their contribution to the efforts to dampen the Kurdish movement in the host country.[3] As a consequence, the vast majority of the Kurdish refugees fled across the frontiers eventually returned back to their home countries, took refuge in third countries, or melted in the host country (e.g., stateless Kurds in Syria).[4]

This chapter is based on fieldwork for my dissertation, which has been published as a book in Turkish: Yılmaz 2016.

This state of affairs, however, changed by the emergence of a de facto autonomous Kurdistan in Iraq. As the state violence against the Kurds escalated in Iran in the 1980s and Turkey in the early 1990s, the flux of Kurds from these two countries took refuge in the Kurdistan Region of Iraq (KRI). First, the Iranian Kurds fled to the KRI in 1992. Around 9,000 Kurdish refugees fled Iran were already settled in Iraq during the Iraq-Iran War in 1980s. However, the number of Kurdish refugees fled from Iran to the KRI reached 23,000 in 1992 once the Iraqi Kurds established their autonomous rule.[5] Then, in 1994, the forced migration from Turkey resulted in approximately 15,000 Kurdish citizens of Turkey taking refuge in the KRI.[6] Finally, after the Qamishli Uprising in 2004, and after the Syrian civil war in 2011, hundreds of thousands of Kurds from Syria fled to the KRI. As of 2017, there were 238,347 Syrian, 20,833 Turkish, and 13,616 Iranian Kurdish refugees, mostly in the refugee camps, in the KRI.[7]

By the 1990s, the rise of the KRI as the choice of destination for Kurdish refugees was basically related to the replacement of central state authority with Kurdish rule in northern Iraq. Moreover, the Operation Provide Comfort led by the United States and other Western countries in the aftermath of the Gulf War in 1991 provided a "safe haven" not only for the Iraqi Kurds fleeing Saddam's vengeance, but also for the Kurds in neighboring countries who sought a sanctuary from the state violence.[8]

It should be emphasized that the Kurdish refugees who fled to the KRI during and after the 1990s do not lack political agency. To the contrary, they have formed highly organized refugee communities with a political leadership structure and armed sections engaged. For instance, most of the Kurdish refugees from Iran in the KRI have been affiliated with the Iranian Kurdish political parties, namely Kurdish Democrat Party of Iran and/or Komala Party of Iranian Kurdistan. The Kurdish refugees who fled Turkey have strongly been engaged with the Kurdistan Workers' Party (PKK). The Atrush Camp and then the Maxmur Camp, where most of them have been settled, were perceived by Turkey as the "PKK bases" despite their refugee camp status determined by the UN Refugee Agency (UNHCR).[9] Similarly, the Kurdish refugees who fled from Syria to the KRI constitute the backbone of both the Syrian Kurdish National Council (ENKS, e. 2012) and Roj Peshmerga, the armed unit of ENKS.[10]

In this regard, the Kurdish refugees in the KRI represent a different category called "refugee warriors," which differs them from other refugees who are conventionally defined as a matter of humanitarian issue in a depoliticized manner. Peter Nyers argues that refugee warriors complicate the civilian and nonpolitical character of being a refugee by disrupting and unsettling the prevailing binaries, which define the refugees merely as victim, passive, and voiceless.[11] Given this definition, what identities are constructed by disrupting and unsettling the prevailing binaries of refugeeness? What political implications does this identity construction have for refugees and their political representation?

I will address these questions by focusing on the political mobilization of the Kurdish refugees fled from Turkey to the KRI, in particular, and discuss the transformation of their political identity, which is torn between humanitarian and political spaces. By problematizing the distinctions between refugee-warrior, victim-agent, passive-active, voiceless-vocal classifications, I will argue that the political identity of the Kurdish refugee warriors in the KRI is not given but constructed in a way to transcend those classifications. In addition, these constructions reflect the limits and opportunities of the changing political contexts and power relations that they face throughout the long-lasting refugee experience while a pan-Kurdish political identity is being formed beyond their country of origin and/or the Kurdish political party engagements. Given this, finally, I will argue that in contrast to the conventional definition of migration, for the Kurdish refugees in the KRI, migration has been a practice of reengagement with the ancestral home country namely Kurdistan.

The Emergence of Kurdish Refugee Warriors Community

The phenomenon of refugee warriors associated with the national liberation movements of the decolonization process. While the wars of national liberation produced large flows of refugees, the refugee camps mostly built in the borderlines of a neighboring country provided supporting services for the military operations and became a resource for recruitment for the armed wing of the national movements.[12]

The flow of Turkish Kurdish refugees to the KRI in 1994 was in fact a consequence of the forced migration that Turkey pursued during its irregular war against the PKK that erupted in 1984. As a result of Turkey's counterinsurgency campaign intended to deprive the PKK of its logistical support, around 2,685 villages and hamlets in Turkey's southeastern provinces were completely or partially depopulated. Most of this forced migration occurred by 1992 and an estimated range from 275,000 to two million people were displaced.[13] The Turkish Kurdish refugees who fled to the KRI were mostly the inhabitants of those forcibly evacuated villages close to the Iraq-Turkey border.[14] According to UN categories based on the causes of the refugees' departure, then, they were a mere victim, and thus, soon after their flight, the UNHCR recognized the refugee status of the Turkish Kurdish refugees in the KRI.[15]

It has always been arguable whether their choice of destination was voluntary or involuntary. On the one hand, the narratives of the flight of the Turkish Kurdish refugees indicate clearly that the Turkish soldiers pushed the villagers in the borderlands deliberately to the KRI. Even some villagers who attempted to migrate to the western provinces of Turkey were stopped by soldiers who established roadblocks.[16] On the other hand, as the prominent PKK commanders confirmed, the PKK also tried to move these refugees into the KRI.[17] The goal of the PKK was captured by a maxim, "If you run into a problem and you can't solve, then, make it bigger."[18] In other words, by driving the Turkish Kurdish refugees into the KRI, the PKK aimed to internationalize the Kurdish Question as a matter of humanitarian crisis. The goal was, ideally, to pave the way for international protection similar to the one the Iraqi Kurds achieved with the Operation Provide Comfort.

The outcome of such efforts, however, was a disappointment both for the PKK that failed to realize its goals and for the Turkish Kurdish refugees who expected to return back to their homes soon. Upon Turkey's military and political pressure, the Turkish Kurdish refugees settled disorderly throughout the border zone were forced to resettle in the Atrush Camp built far from the Turkish border by UNHCR in 1995.[19] By that time, the significance of the distinction between voluntary and involuntary displacement disappeared as most refugees refused to move to the Atrush Camp. The PKK, for instance, had difficulty convincing all refugees to leave the border zone and resettle in the Atrush Camp. Paradoxically, the UNHCR's persistence on moving the refugees to Atrush to secure their protection contributed to the PKK's efforts. Particularly after UNHCR's restrictions on the delivery of humanitarian aid to the refugees who remained on the border zone, all refugees gradually joined to several thousands who initially relocated to the Atrush Camp.[20]

The total number of the refugees in the Atrush Camp was recorded as 15,000.[21] This number was fewer than the total estimated number (approximately 30,000) of the Turkish Kurdish refugees who fled to the KRI in 1994.[22] Yet some of the refugees, especially the ones with kinship networks, moved in villages, towns, and cities in the KRI. A few others reached the western provinces of Turkey through illegal ways. Meanwhile, the PKK, soon after, established full control over the Atrush Camp despite the presence of the refugees who distanced themselves from its activities to some extent. In the words of a refugee interviewed for this research, "As the victims of Turkey's brutal violence against us, we were eventually siding by the PKK. But some of us were resisting to hand our will over the PKK despite its persistent requests."[23]

After its failure to reframe and internationalize the Kurdish Question as a matter of humanitarian crisis, the PKK revised its goals about the flight of the Turkish Kurdish refugees. The new goal was aimed to create a "Kurdish state" within the KRI.[24] In this regard, the Atrush Camp turned into the "Republic of Atrush" as the PKK designed and proposed the model of "United, Independent, and Free Kurdistan."[25] Regardless of the PKK's success in realizing this revised goal, the reorganization of the management of the camp with a promise of self-rule helped the PKK mobilize all the refugees. At the same time, the Kurdish Turkish refugees were not merely victims but also political agents engaging the PKK. They were positioned in a sense that they were the "chosen people" of the Kurdish nation to regain the essence and purity of Kurdishness on the way to United, Independent, and Free Kurdistan.[26] For instance, they showed great interest in participation in the elections held in the Atrush Camp in 1996 to form a government mainly responsible for the management of the camp affairs.

These developments put the Atrush Camp at the frontline of the ongoing armed conflict between the PKK and the Kurdistan Democrat Party (KDP) in the KRI. The KDP, then, in alliance with Turkey, claimed that the Atrush Camp provided shelter to the PKK.[27] It was almost impossible to distinguish the PKK members and the refugees in the Camp. The refugees joined the PKK members in defense of the camp against the KDP attacks. Consequently, the UNHCR decided to stop supplying humanitarian aid and food to the camp even though the UN flag kept flying over the camp.[28] The embargo became a harbinger of the closure of the Atrush Camp in 1997, but the Kurdish refugee warriors community was already formed by then.

The Closure of Atrush Camp

The closure of the Atrush Camp weakened the belief that a United, Independent, and Free Kurdistan would ever be founded. The failure of the Republic of Atrush experience was not the only reason for pessimism. The PKK's armed resistance had also been defeated to a great extent in Turkey and Iraqi Kurdistan by the end of 1990s. Consequently, not only did the Kurdish refugee warriors community lose the opportunity of becoming agents of a Kurdish state at the scale of the Atrush Camp, but they also lost the chance of becoming citizens of an United, Independent, and Free Kurdistan. Hence, being a refugee was no longer a temporary status that would disappear with the realization of a political objective. Instead, it became a long-lasting exile while the transitivity between the victim and agent positions has gradually ended by the closure of Atrush Camp. The refugees were not merely the victims of Turkey's brutal policies or the agents of the PKK's political objectives, but the agents of their own political act.

As Nyers argues regarding the opportunities that the refugees enjoyed in the absence of a centralized political power in the post–Cold War era,[29] the Kurdish refugee warriors community also found the opportunity to put their political choices into practice in Iraqi Kurdistan under conditions of fragmented and contested sovereignties. Accordingly, the political choices of the Kurdish refugee warriors community following the closure of the Atrush Camp overlapped with neither the PKK's nor the KDP's political objectives.

In this context, the KDP offered the refugees: "To return to Turkey under UN protection, to stay here [KRI] as refugees on the condition of abidance to the UN and ourselves [KDP], or to settle here [KRI] permanently, with [refugees] residence permits in the city of their choice."[30] The PKK, on the other hand, gave up the establishment of an administrative model that was originally proposed during the founding of the Atrush Camp. For Osman Öcalan, a high-ranking leader until his defection in 2004, this was because of the PKK's inability to carry the burden of the refugees without the UNHCR support. In addition, the objective of internationalizing the Kurdish issue by instrumentalizing the course of refugees also failed in the absence of UNHCR protection.

Therefore, the refugees would initially be free in choosing one of those options raised by the KDP. However, the facts on the ground were in fact different:

When Osman Öcalan came to speak to us at the Atrush Camp, he did not allow us to leave. He told us about how they were forced to close the camp due to the deal they struck with the KDP and the pressure from Turkey. According to the plan, some of us would go to Sulaymaniyah, while others would be relocated to the PKK controlled Gare Mountain. Some others would be dispatched to Semel town [in Duhok Province]. Another group would go to Saddam controlled Mosul and Kirkuk. This was the plan and would weaken Turkey's pressure on the KDP, which had devised this plan according to a deal with the YNK.[31]

In this context, similar to the circumstances under which Kurds from Turkey took refuges in the KRI, the choices available to the refugees were shaped by the political objectives of political actors. This time, there was no coherence between refugee choices and political objectives. Some refugees voiced objection over being sent to mountainous territories under the military control of the PKK, such as Gare Mountain, the Zap area, and the Çiya Spi region. Other refugees protested against being sent to military camps with their families. As the disputes ensued, about 1,500 men among the refugees went to Gare Mountain, only to return about one month later.[32]

Under such circumstances, then, a small group of refugees mostly from villages located in the Gever (Yüksekova in Turkish) and Şemzinan (Şemdinli in Turkish) districts of Turkey settled in Erbil's Harir town in February 1997. This resettlement was the only instance of one of the options offered by the KDP: "[To] join us [KDP held provinces in the KRI] instead of remaining as refugees." For refugees choosing Harir, the presence of relatives was the determining factor. Like Gever and Şemdinli, the residents of Harir were members of the Herki tribe. However, the vast majority of the remaining refugees considered this development as an indicator of support for the KDP.[33] While tribal relations played an important role in the choices of other refugees, they tried to keep a relative distance from the KDP. Accordingly, keeping a safe distance from areas subject to Turkish incursions was another factor shaping the choices of the refugees. Gele Qasrok region, for example, was not preferred due to concerns about being "too close to the border and subject to infiltration by the MIT [Turkish National Intelligence Service]."[34]

Consequently, the total number of refugees going back to Turkey was just 1,217 after the closure of the Atrush Camp. About 13,000 refugees resettled in Iraqi Kurdistan.[35] At this stage, it was apparent that the PKK lost the image of being "a project of survival and building a future" while the KDP was not regarded as an alternative that could meet the needs of the Kurdish Turkish refugees. Instead, the refugee status became the only political position that prevailed following the closure of Atrush Camp. For the first time, refugees defined their identities based on personal migration and exile independent from any sort of political objective. The prevailing refugee identity became the expression of a new political position against local and international actors. In this regard, refugeeness was transformed into a sense of political agency without being a subject of any political authority. Likewise, refugeeness has also been the expression of a permanent position that goes beyond the reach of political boundaries and abilities. Such a position, however, did not lead to deterritorialization as happened in many diaspora communities. On the contrary, refugeeness has turned into an experience of reconstructing everything territorial in the case of Kurdish refugees experience in the KRI. Migration which conventionally refers to an actual disengagement from country of origin, has functioned as a pattern of reengagement with the origins of Kurdishness and Kurdistan, the ancestral home country of the Kurds. In this regard, the significance of the country of origin and/or political party affiliations, which have deepened the fragmentation of the Kurds as a nation itself, vanished, and the Kurdish refugees repositioned themselves as the agents of Kurdish unification within a given territory.

The Rise of Refugee Agents

Following the closure of the Atrush Camp, the Kurdish refugee warriors community dissolved. While a group headed to the settlements designated by the KDP within the KRI, another group resettled in the Maxmur Camp located around 60 kilometers southwest of the KRI capital Erbil but in the territory controlled by the Iraqi central authority. The majority of refugees headed to the settlements in the KRI justified their choice on the grounds that it was unsafe to live in territories controlled by Saddam Hussein. With memories of the Halabja Massacre of 1988 still vivid in people's minds, the idea of going to a region of Iraq outside the KRI was rejected.[36] Overall, the number of refugees preferred to settle in the KRI was 7,754, whereas 6,800 moved to the Maxmur Camp built by the UNHCR soon after the closure of the Atrush Camp.[37]

The majority of the refugees moved to the Maxmur Camp were families who had daughters, sons, or siblings fighting for the PKK. Although this finding is not based on hard data, the refugees interviewed for this research frequently expressed that "people who surrendered their freedom to PKK" moved to the Maxmur Camp. Meanwhile, the PKK also tried to influence the decision of the refugees once the UNHCR decided to build a new refugee camp after the closure of the Atrush Camp. A refugee who played an active role in the process of resettlement in the Maxmur Camp explained this process as follows:

> The administration told us, "Anyone is free to go but do not release the people of Hilal and Mijîn as refugees from these two large villages constituted the spine of the camp. Those from Hilal and Mijîn were about 100 households. We identified more than 2,000 additional households and we chose them from among those we thought would convince others if they were on our side. We would go to Iraq together."[38]

Despite such efforts, however, neither in the Maxmur Camp nor in the settlements in the KRI, it was possible to reconstruct the Kurdish refugee warriors community as a group subordinate to the political agendas of Kurdish parties.

Settlements in the KRI

The Kurdish refugee warriors community mainly consisted of villagers living along the Turkey-Iraq border. Based on their tribal relations and cross-border trading, they had vibrant contact with the Iraqi Kurds. However, these transborder contacts did not entail shared political solidarities. In fact, political distinctions became sharper during the PKK-KDP armed conflict in 1995. So much so that refugees regarded Iraqi Kurds as "KDP but not Kurds" whereas Iraqi Kurds considered refugees to be solely the "PKK."[39] The borders of both political identities and Kurdistan itself were redrawn based on loyalty to a party. Accordingly, for every party member, the defense of Kurdistan was invariably limited to the area under the military control of that party.

However, the political options that became available during the closure process of the Atrush Camp reduced these stark differences. Above all, as the process presented the alternative of a return to Turkey, the majority of the Kurdish refugee warriors community chose to remain in the KRI. This could be regarded as the first instance of the refugees acting as autonomous political actors whose interests coincided with neither the PKK's nor the KDP's political objectives.

Life for refugees was subject to intense political pressure at Mısirik, Gregewre, Darato, Hassaniye, and Mala Berwan, the settlements, which formed during the resettlement process in Iraqi Kurdistan following the closure of Atrush Camp. In fact, stuck in the civil war between the PKK and the KDP, which re-erupted soon after the resettlement, refugees were regarded as a threat by both the KDP and the local population. The presence of refugees was considered a source of tension facilitating infiltration by the PKK's armed forces. This is why entries and exits from the settlements were heavily controlled by KDP *Asayish* (domestic intelligence forces). Refugees were only allowed to leave their settlements for reasons limited to work, health, marriages, and condolences. There were also significant efforts to prevent refugees contacting the local population. The settlements were positioned on the periphery of the villages, which further marginalized the refugees. The KDP authorities aimed to avert the potential risk of refugees preaching the PKK propaganda to the local population. As a matter of fact, attempts were made by the village headman (*Agha*) to establish a civilian security network in every village with a settlement. Süleyman Hasso Kelki, the *Agha* of the region, which includes Mısirik and Gregewre, gave an account of the meeting he attended on this matter: "The District Governor of Semel arrived. First, he asked me permission. He said, 'We will be bringing refugees from Turkey and settling them here'. Then added, 'But keep an eye on them, do not let them among you. No one talks to them. They are PKK. Be wary.'"[40]

The situation was no better in the realms of education and commerce where refugee interaction with the locals was relatively unregulated. Children under the age of twelve started education at village schools after a three-month Arabic language course. As all the children had learned to read and write in Kurdish with Latin alphabet at Atrush Camp, this language course was mandatory. Despite such efforts, however, refugee children labeled as "Zarokên Kempê PKK [Children of the PKK Camp]"[41] by locals experienced discrimination by their peers and suffered from adaptation problems. Besides, the UNHCR aid was never adequate, which forced almost all refugees to work in the fields. Actually, most refugees wished to continue their practice of livestock trade, but with a ban on free movement, getting a job in the agricultural fields became the only option. Even this was only possible if a local broker took unconditional responsibility for the refugees. In each settlement, *Asayish* officers would check the list of names as the workers left in the morning and returned in the evening.

Meanwhile, the KDP party membership cards were the only available official document for the refugees to travel across a wider area within Duhok province. Early on, refugees resisted pressure from *Asayish* to become members of the KDP. However, over time, membership gained appeal based on the conveniences granted to cardholders. Having a KDP membership gave advantages in going through checkpoints or finding jobs. However, membership did not mean that refugees took part in KDP activities or assumed positions within the KDP organization.

Finally, life in the settlements between 1997 and 2003 was more about a fight for survival. In a sense, refugees under economic, social, and political pressures paid the price for their perceived affiliation with the PKK but refrained from any political activity during this period. They had no chance of communicating with the PKK under tight security measures in place. As for the KDP membership, it was not a form of political activity, rather a condition of meeting basic living standards at best.

A refugee describes the situation, "Actually, what we experienced here [in Iraqi Kurdistan] was no different than what happened to us in Turkey."[42] Above all, choosing to be a refugee was a demonstration of defiance against the political authority in both Turkey and Iraqi Kurdistan. Accordingly, they distanced themselves from the PKK authority as well by choosing to live in settlements instead of the Maxmur Camp. Their refugee status was the expression of a political position beyond party affiliations. In this political setting, each refugee privileged the requirements of basic living standards over the requirements of political choices while trying to maintain a sense of political agency. Nevertheless, the refugees developed a new way of organization in the settlements, which was independent from all types of political authority. In fact, there were *Muhtars* (headmen) appointed by the *Asayish* in each settlement. *Muhtars* were responsible of representing the refugees in their relations with the UNHCR, local authorities, and the public. The title of *Muhtar* was an official and paid position.[43] However, *Muhtars* did not have much say on the running of settlements. For example, disputes within the settlements were resolved by a committee consisting solely of refugees but not by *Muhtars*. These committees were composed of representatives directly endorsed by the refugees. Although the experienced elders known as *rîspî*[44] had an important place in the committee, their vote in the decision-taking process was equal to other members. The remaining committee members could be representatives from the village or family. Age, education, or feudal titles did not give any privileges in committees. The number of members was relative to the number of refugees living in each settlement. Committee members did not change with periodical elections. They were replaced in the event of a death or the decision of the group they represented. The joint decisions of these committees were implemented in these settlements on a broad spectrum of issues including the punishment of criminals, compensation of victims, determination of alimonies, and inheritance distribution. In the meantime, a registry of births, deaths, and marriages was kept by the *Melle* (imam) who was also a refugee.[45] In this regard, the law that regulated public life in the settlements was practiced completely independent from the local authority. There has not been a single judicial case brought from the settlements to the local courts until 2012.

The refugees embraced this order in the settlements as an un-hierarchical alternative to the existing political authority in practice:

> We never have any fights here. If there is a problem, we convene to discuss solutions. It was like this 100 years ago and it still is. But there is one thing. If we were in Mijîn [hometown]there would have been disagreements among us, but not here. We are laci (refugees) here. For example, the [non-refugee] Kurds here are part of a tribe, the *Agha* takes the decisions. But this is not the case for us. Everyone is equal and like members of a big family. If we fall out, we will be assimilated among them. If we do not stand united they will swoop down on us, we will break up.[46]

The refugee identity shaped by the experience in the settlements became the source of this newly established collectivism. Ethnic, political, and sociocultural ties played no role whatsoever. Refugeeness expressed a position, which does not exclude these ties but also stands above them. Ultimately, this position eased the tension not only in the settlements but also in the Maxmur Camp after 2003.

Maxmur Camp

The Maxmur Camp was established in 1998 next to the Green Line in the Nineveh province separating the KRI from the Saddam regime. As the camp fell under the control of the Saddam regime with extremely strict security policies, any chance of a relation with the Kurdish refugees remaining in the KRI was absent. Refugees leaving the Maxmur Camp were only allowed to visit Maxmur town or, in some exceptional conditions, the city of Mosul. In spite of the Saddam regime's security measures, however, the PKK enjoyed full control over the camp. The daily course of life for refugees in the camp was shaped due to the PKK rules and regulations. Despite periodical visits, even the UNHCR officials failed to help overcome this grip of authority. Refugees who witnessed the establishment of the camp reported that the UNHCR officials were in fact mostly Iraqi citizens who would avoid direct contact with the refugees, but instead, dealt with Iraqi troops responsible for exterior camp security and PKK's armed forces responsible for domestic camp order.

However, it was not that the refugees at Maxmur Camp quietly obeyed the PKK's authority. First of all, the refugees arriving at Maxmur on May 25, 1998, objected to being settled at the selected campsite. No preparations had been made on this site, which was situated on a stretch of desert. In fact, according to refugee accounts, an expedition was organized with the UNHCR officials on May 6, 1998, and a new location was identified in the Iraqi regime-controlled Sinjar (Shingal) region to the east of Mosul. Asked to board buses at Nehtara, the refugees thought they were being transferred to Shingal, but instead, they were dropped off at Mosul's Maxmur town. So, in a way, refugees were forced to comply with this imposition. A refugee gives an account of the chaos he witnessed on arrival to Maxmur:

> There was dispute because Maxmur was simply no place to stay. It was in the middle of a desert and without water. Maxmur town had been evacuated of almost all its residents. No one wanted to get off the buses but we had no choice. There was no means of going back and we were all too exhausted to go anywhere in that heat.[47]

In the end, the refugees were dropped off at a site some 5 kilometers to Maxmur town despite their objections. Early on, however, the lack of access to clean water and/deaths of refugees because of scorpion bites made the PKK control over the Maxmur Camp almost impossible. At this stage, a speech from PKK leader Abdullah Öcalan addressing the refugees via satellite phone connection became a turning point in the establishment of the Maxmur Camp. According to witnesses, Öcalan appealed to the refugees in these words: "I know you are in dire straits however your mission is vital. You shall become a bridge between Kandil and Lebanon. More hardship awaits you. You will be creating miracles by prevailing."[48]

In fact, the "vital mission" emphasized by Öcalan signaled a military necessity for the PKK that had recently been forced to retreat significantly from the KRI border regions with Syria and Turkey. Under such circumstances, it was imperative for the PKK to establish a corridor between its military headquarters in Qandil and its military bases in Syria and Lebanon. Geographically speaking, Maxmur Camp was key to building this corridor. As the speech implied, living conditions might be grueling for the refugees but setting up camp at Maxmur was an absolute necessity for PKK's military and strategic interests.[49] It can be argued that PKK leader Abdullah Öcalan's speech appeared to be the most important motivation for refugees to settle at Maxmur Camp. According to the accounts of several first-hand witnesses, Öcalan's speech was considered to mark the beginning of Maxmur Camp. A refugee explains how everyone was persuaded: "Once the leadership spoke, you were either going to stay or escape. There was no third option."[50]

The growth of the Maxmur Camp took place with the efforts of the refugees. Four refugee neighborhoods were identified in the first phase. Each family chose a site in each of these neighborhoods and started to build a house with bricks, timber, and cement provided by the UNHCR. Health clinics were opened in the neighborhoods and a larger medical center was completed at the center of the camp. The construction of schools started in the second phase. A school was built in each neighborhood with the communal help of refugees; however, they lacked furniture and educational material. The students started school sitting on benches made from wooden beams raised on stones.

The implementation of order inside the camp was similar to the Atrush Camp. Refugees took responsibility for security, as militia forces, but it was PKK's armed forces who were really in charge. Neighborhood committees were formed and organized as administrative units to provide solutions to refugee problems inside the camp. There was also a foreign affairs unit, which oversaw relations with the Iraqi regime and the UNHCR. As one of the first administrative units in Maxmur Camp, the municipality was founded to provide utility services such as water and electricity and waste collection.

The PKK, the key player in organization and operation across the camp, demanded loyalty from camp residents. The PKK leader Abdullah Öcalan himself had absolute authority over the camp while the refugees living at Maxmur Camp were called "People of the Leadership." The Abdullah Öcalan factor in the reconstruction of the Kurdish refugee warriors community at the scale of Maxmur Camp was significant. Such that, refugees' commitment to the Maxmur Camp ceased to be an issue after Abdullah Öcalan was captured in Kenya by Turkish security forces on February 15, 1999. A refugee recalls the events that unfolded that day:

> The day after the leader was arrested, men who had been ready to flee the camp with their family at any given chance handed their children over to the guerrilla. Two hundred fifty people from Maxmur Camp joined the guerrilla on February 16. Besides that, 250 or so went for training at [PKK camps] at Gara, Qandil, Metina, Zap, Zagros and Haftanin. This level of involvement was not even seen at Atrush.[51]

The most prominent effect of Öcalan's arrest on the Maxmur Camp was that refugees embraced the PKK at an unprecedented level. This was not limited to refugees joining the PKK's armed forces; everyday life at Maxmur Camp also became identical to the discipline implemented at PKK's military bases. Life at the Maxmur Camp according to a refugee was "like an ant who grew wings just before dying."[52]

The construction of a new life at Maxmur Camp, then, quickly turned into a display of existence under existential threats. Under such circumstances, both the past and the future became envisioned differently. The experiences of immigration and being a refugee were reinterpreted. It was no longer an exodus but a voluntary choice.[53] Therefore, instead of being a temporary station in exile providing shelter from oppression, the Maxmur Camp became the final stop in the journey of resisting oppression. The refugees now defined themselves as "Gelê Maxmur [People of Maxmur]" at the expense of refugee identity. Refugeeness was now regarded as a past experience despite maintaining its significance as the main reason of how the "Gelê Maxmur" came into existence.

The reimagination of the future was also shaped according to contemporary developments. Knowledge distilled from the previous refugeeness experience and the everyday camp order became the future. The new way of life was constructed on a communal understanding in which the boundaries of private property disappeared. Likewise being a member of the people of Maxmur gained more importance than the nuclear family.

One of the most important events with mass turnout was the "Wednesday Meetings," which started after the conviction of Abdullah Öcalan in a Turkish court. Imprisoned at İmralı Island, Öcalan's letters were brought back by his lawyers and read out to the refugees at the meetings held each Wednesday. The meetings took place at the Martyrdom building, one of the first units to be completed at the Maxmur Camp. If a letter did not come that week, passages from Öcalan's books were read and information about weekly political developments were shared. Refugees were also dressed in black and fast each year on February 15 in protest of Öcalan's arrest.

This course of developments in the Maxmur Camp, however, came to an end when a "social reform" process took place within the PKK by 2002.[54] Upon significant changes in its ideological and military framework, a group of the PKK commanders attempted to reorganize the PKK in accordance with the changing political context on the eve of the upcoming US occupation of Iraq. The foundation of the KADEK (Kurdistan Freedom and Democracy Congress) was the first concrete step taken in this regard. The statements made at the meeting establishing the KADEK provided important clues about the state of the PKK in 2002. For example, KADEK's European spokespersons gave media statements claiming that "PKK had fulfilled its historic mission of laying claim on the destiny of the Kurdish people" and that KADEK was founded to act as an all-inclusive congress based on the conviction that violence was unable to offer solutions.[55] Meanwhile, although Abdullah Öcalan's ideological leadership continued, announcements were made about a Presidential Council replacing him as concerns over his prison conditions became widespread. Ultimately, the aim was to establish a new organization model, which would remove PKK's armed and central powers and instead allow organizations in each part of Kurdistan to reshape itself based on local conditions and focus potential on problem solving.[56] However, objections to the new organization model, particularly from within PKK, hindered the so-called social reform process.

The attitudes of the refugees toward social reform have indicated a turning point in terms of the fate of both social reform and the Maxmur Camp. The Maxmur Camp was a pilot site for the implementation of the reform itself. The camp was chosen as a "rehabilitation" center that especially focused on integrating armed forces into civilian life while hundreds of the PKK fighters headed to the Maxmur Camp from the mountains.[57] The construction of new buildings became the first notable change at Maxmur Camp following the new arrivals. Confined to rudimentary village dwellings at best, refugees started to feel resentment about the source of the money needed for construction and how it was being spent. Considering that refugees suffered great difficulties in acquiring their most basic needs for many years, there was a lot of uneasiness about these new activities. Rumors on the activities being financed by the United States triggered anti-imperialist reflexes,[58] which had been aggravated with the capture of PKK leader Abdullah Öcalan. The unrest among the refugees grew further as they witnessed an increasing number of active armed force members getting married.[59] The number of couples putting their names down on the matrimony lists opened at the Maxmur Camp continued to rise during the social reform. Keeping in mind that there were many PKK-supporting civilians who had postponed the idea of marriage until after the revolution, it was easy to understand the objections towards the marriage of active guerrillas. This practice led to security concerns and considerable disappointment among refugees who accepted hardship of the camp life as a necessary sacrifice in the collective struggle to revolution. This development led to disputes, which undermined the PKK's absolute authority over the civilians in the camp. In the words of a refugee, "Celal [a prominent PKK commander] told me, 'It does not matter if you agree or not. The party does.' I urged him to gather the people and apologise ... confess that they were exhausted and were stepping down. I told him, 'All the families suffered so much ... was it all just for this?'"[60]

The combination of discontent among the refugees at the Maxmur Camp and their objection to social reform within the PKK marked the beginning of a new phase at the camp. Preparations to discuss the objections within the PKK at a congress reflected on the Maxmur Camp with a letter sent directly to the refugees by the PKK Executive Committee Member Cemil Bayık. Bayık urged the refugees not to believe the social reformers before discussions at the PKK's Qandil headquarters were concluded.[61] The final ruling, announced on October 15, 2003, led to a new restructuring under the name Kongra-Gel.[62] The previous model foreseen by the social reform was shelved while the PKK members who advocated the model were dismissed from the ranks.

The impact of these developments was not felt immediately at the Maxmur Camp as the social reformers tried to maintain control of the camp. However, the refugees took a decision among themselves and forced this group out of the camp.[63] The major fracture inside the PKK, which emerged with the Kongra-Gel process, lasted until June 2004. Ultimately, the decision to terminate the ceasefire that was announced on June 1, 2004, marked the beginning of a new period for the PKK and Maxmur Camp. A guerrilla group advocating social reform left the Maxmur Camp.

The refugees who played a key role in this outcome initially appeared to favor prolonged armed resistance against the Turkish state. In this context, an important turning point took place on July 14, 2004, when seventy refugees representing Maxmur visited Qandil. The refugee delegation demanded the easing of controls at entries and exits from Maxmur Camp as the KRI had taken control of the region including Maxmur Camp from the Iraqi regime. The refugees demanded freedom of movement and permission to work in the KRI-controlled territory. Another request concerned granting students educated at Atrush and Maxmur the right to be admitted to universities across Iraqi Kurdistan. Asking for financial support from the KRI for the infrastructure and schools at the Maxmur Camp was also voiced as an urgent need during the visit.

Murat Karayılan who was the spokesperson for the PKK leadership during this meeting with the refugees admitted that the requests initially caused concern within the organization. This was mainly because granting their requests would mean that the KDP would inevitably establish control over the refugees. However, Karayılan also confirmed the final verdict in favor of the refugees on the grounds that PKK had to consider the fact that the refugees should decide on the future of the camp.[64]

Pursuant to the decision, the armed group remaining at Maxmur Camp could only act in the capacity of "observer." Although the refugees were promised to have the only and absolute say in the management of the camp, it is hard to say that this was fully materialized. Armed groups continued to have presence, especially in the units like Asayish and *Foreign Affairs* (responsible for operating the communication/relation of the Maxmur Camp with the local and central authorities and the international institutions like UNHCR, etc.). That said, with KDP taking significant responsibility in municipal services and education, it became harder for the Maxmur Camp to be labeled as a PKK bastion. As things stood, Maxmur Camp was not under the sole control of neither the PKK nor the KDP. In other words, Maxmur Camp recognized the authority of both the PKK and the KDP. Ultimately, it was the refugees who determined the form and nature of power these two authorities could practice inside the camp, and the pressing necessities of a civilian lifestyle gained gradually more importance. The refugee identity became important again and, similar to the settlements, became a form of political agency, which gave the opportunity to the refugees to distance themselves from hierarchical political forces.

Conclusion

The formation and dissolution of a Kurdish refugee warriors community in the KRI indicate that the relations between refugees and armed groups are shaped by the refugee experience rather than the initial shared political objectives. Moreover, the opportunities derived from the current political context determine the distance and alliance between the refugees and armed groups. Political identity of the refugees transcends conventional binary distinctions of the refugee-warrior, victim-agent, passive-active, and voiceless-vocal. The PKK's already weakened authority over the Turkish Kurdish refugees is further loosened by the emergence of the Kurdistan Regional Government (KRG) after 2005 as a Kurdish semi-state making transborder appeals to all Kurds. The refugees both in the settlements and the Maxmur Camp have joined the reconstruction of the KRG, while they constituted a balanced political position between the PKK and the KDP. A refugee from Maxmur, for instance, stated that in the past, she would fight against the KDP if a clash occurred between the PKK and the KDP. After a long-lasting experience of exile in the KRI, however, she shifted her positions and said that she would be neutral in the midst of such a clash.[65] Accordingly, in the eyes of Kurdish refugee warriors community, the refugee status is just a symbol of Turkish occupation of their villages and towns, but not identifying their actual presence in the KRI. Nevertheless, they refuse to be named as refugees; in their own words, they are simply the "Kurds in Kurdistan." Then the repatriation that is seemingly conditional with the realization of the political objectives of the PKK (i.e., the formation of some sort of a Kurdish self-rule in Kurdish areas of Turkey) would not necessarily entail a decision to leave the KRI on their part. In conclusion, there is no doubt that the Turkish Kurdish refugees in the KRI who formed a refugee warriors community given their affiliation with the PKK are autonomous political agents rather than just instruments in Kurdish power politics.

Notes

1　Altuğ (2010); Chatty (2018); Olson (1996); Randall (1997); Sasson (2009).
2　Chatty (2018: 132).
3　Romano (2006).
4　Jwaideh (2009); Kardam (2013).
5　IDPs and Refugees in Duhok Governorate Profile and General Information 2016.
6　"BM Göçe El Attı," 1994.
7　IDPs and Refugees in Duhok Governorate Profile and General Information 2017.
8　"BM'den Kürt Göçmenlere Güvenli Bölge," 1994.
9　"Mülteci Cumhuriyeti," 1996.
10　"US Wants Kurdish Groups to Reconcile in Eastern Syria," 2019.
11　Nyers (2006: xviii).
12　Zolberg, Shurke, and Aguayo (1989: 234).
13　HRW (1996).
14　"Kuzey Irak'a Göç," 1994.
15　"BM Göçe El Attı," 1994.
16　"Kürtleri Sınırdışı Etmek Cinayettir," 1994.
17　Interview with Murat Karayılan, May 25, 2013.
18　Interview with Osman Öcalan, July 11, 2011.
19　"Humanitarian Situation of the Kurdish Refugees and Displaced Persons in South-East Turkey and North Iraq," 1998.
20　"Kürt Göçmenler Eylemde," 1994.
21　Humanitarian Situation of the Kurdish Refugees and Displaced Persons in South-East Turkey and North Iraq, 1998.
22　"Göçenler Güney'de de Hedef," 1994.
23　Interview with M. A. (In this study the names of the refugees interviewed are marked with the first letters of their names and surnames to keep their identity anonymous), March 16, 2011.
24　Interview with Osman Öcalan, July 11, 2011.
25　"Mülteci Cumhuriyeti," 1996.
26　Interview with M. Z., May 13, 2012.
27　"Atrosh Camp: Facts of the Cause and Practices of PKK," 1999: 88.

28 "Türkiye Göçmenler için Güney'e Heyet Gönderdi," 1997.

29 Nyers (2006: 110).

30 Interview with Abdulaziz Tayyib, former Governor of Duhok, 2011.

31 Interview with M. Ş., 2012. The YNK is the Patriotic Union of Kurdistan, the other major party in Iraqi Kurdistan.

32 "Dağ'a Çıkarız," 1997.

33 Interview with Osman Öcalan, 2012.

34 Interview with B. A., 2012.

35 Yılmaz (2016), Appendix 2: 354.

36 Interview with M. C., 2012.

37 "Atrosh Camp: Facts of the Cause and Practices of PKK": 174–5.

38 Interview with R. K., 2012.

39 Interview with M. F., 2012.

40 Interview with Süleyman Hasso, 2012.

41 Interview with M. F., 2012.

42 Interview with S. A., 2012.

43 By 2012, Muhtars were paid 50 thousand ID per month.

44 An informal committee generally consisting of senior members of the community who are respected for their knowledge and experience, which assembles to develop solutions for the community and take decisions on issues that regulate communal life.

45 Interview with M. A., 2012.

46 Interview with L. Y., 2012.

47 Interview with H. A., 2012.

48 Öcalan's speech to refugees in Maxmur Camp took place in July 1998. The refugees couldn't agree on the exact date of this speech but according to their accounts it was in the first week of July 1998.

49 Interview with R. K., 2012.

50 Interview with S. H., 2012.

51 Interview with H. R., 2012.

52 Interview with R. O., 2012.

53 Interview with M. H., 2012.

54 For further reading on social reform, see Yılmaz (2016: 306–14).

55 "PKK'nın yeni adı KADEK," 2002.

56 Interview with Osman Öcalan, 2012.

57 Osman Öcalan stated that 700 guerrillas moved to Maxmur Camp in 2002. However, refugees claimed that 700 was the only number of guerrillas sidelined by the social reformers, and the total number of guerrillas headed from Qandil to Maxmur Camp was approximately 1,300.

58 Interview with Abdurrahman Belaf, former governor of Maxmur district, 2012.

59 Romantic relations were forbidden in the PKK. Nizamattion Taş, a prominent leader of the social reform in the PKK, claimed that the idea of guerillas marriages in fact belonged to Abdullah Öcalan. Interview with Nizamettin Taş, 2014.

60 Interview with M. Z., 2012.

61 Interview with S. T., 2012.

62 Anonymous (2003).

63 Interview with S. T., 2012.

64 Interview with Murat Karayılan, 2013.

65 Interview with L. I., 2013.

5

SURVIVAL, COEXISTENCE, AND AUTONOMY: YEZIDI POLITICAL IDENTITY AFTER GENOCIDE

Güneş Murat Tezcür
Zeynep N. Kaya
and Bayar Mustafa Sevdeen

Introduction

In contemporary Yezidi discourse, violence has a cyclical character, in contrast to interpretations of history that posit the progressively declining role of violence in human affairs.[1] A sense of historical victimhood is central to the formation of Yezidis communal identity whose very survival was at stake in different time periods. Accordingly, the IS attacks in 2014 were perceived as the latest in a series of atrocities Yezidis experienced since the medieval times. The attacks are called "the 74rd *firman*" implying continuity with previous episodes of mass-scale violence targeting the community. While the IS attacks involving mass executions and enslavement shocked the conscience of the international community, for Yezidis, the tragedy of August 2014 was not unprecedented in terms of its harm. In the words of a Yezidi leader, "[In 1832], [t]hey took away a thousand of our girls. A thousand was plenty. Our population was much smaller by then ... You now see lots of [Sunni] Kurds around. Their fourth or fifth generation ancestors were Yezidis."[2] In his eyes, Yezidis have historically been targeted because of their religious beliefs and subject to sexual violence and forced conversions. The main difference between the past massacres and the current one was the widespread publicity characterizing the IS violence that triggered an international humanitarian intervention, which was in fact unprecedented.

This prevailing discourse of victimhood implies that Yezidis were subject to violent campaigns primarily due to their religious identity. In fact, Orthodox

The fieldwork informing this chapter has received an approval from IRB at UCF (#SBE-18-13819).

Islamic perspectives define Yezidis as polytheists or unbelievers and do not treat them as "People of the Book," unlike Christians and Jews who are entitled to certain rights and a limited degree of autonomy in their internal affairs. This liminal status, similar to the experience of other religious groups that emerged after the rise of Islam such as Alevis, Kakais, and Bahais, put Yezidis in a precarious position and more vulnerable to violence justified on religious grounds over centuries from the fatwas of the leading Ottoman jurist Ebussuud Efendi in the sixteenth century to the IS in the twenty-first century. From this perspective, the very existence of Yezidis as a non-Islamic group has been a source of major security concern and religious challenge to the political order in Muslim societies. While the rise of political secularism with the formation of the Iraqi national state provided a semblance of stability for Yezidis, the post-2003 period was characterized by the collapse of the state authority and violent sectarianism signified the return of religious violence targeting Yezidis *qua* Yezidis.

This chapter suggests that the IS attacks of 2014, which exhibit certain similarities with the past violence, has had unique implications for Yezidis. The contemporary forms of Yezidi identity exhibit two distinctive characteristics in the post-genocidal era. First, Yezidis have gained unprecedented recognition and interest in the international arena. While Yezidis had a long history of contacts with Western diplomats, scholars, and travelers going back to the first half of the nineteenth century, the community as the victims of religious intolerance and persecution brought the community under global limelight in the post-2014 period. In particular, captive Yezidi women subject to extreme forms of sexual violence have come to embody the experience of the community. This gendered experience facilitated a context for Yezidi women to express their perspectives and become vocal voices, such as Nadia Murad, to communicate the experiences of the Yezidis to the international community and make political demands. Given the long history of entrenched patriarchal practices in the community, the increased visibility of Yezidi women and their increased engagement with issues that affect their community represents a paradoxical outcome of the IS violence.

Next, the massive displacement suffered by the community contributed to the fragmented nature of Yezidi politics. This process of fragmentation has taken place at two parallel levels. On the one hand, Yezidis are subject to the authority of an increasing number of political actors with opposing agendas. The failure and inability of the Kurdish military forces to protect the Sinjar area against the IS onslaught in early August 2014 generated sentiments of disillusionment and resentment among large sections of the Yezidi community. This development drew a wedge between the Yezidis and Sunni Kurds despite their common linguistic characteristics. Even if the Kurdistan Regional Government (KRG) pursues a policy of co-optation and symbolic empowerment toward the Yezidis, the debacle of August 2014 has had a strong negative impact over the popular appeal of a hyphenated identity of "Yezidi-Kurds." Meanwhile, the rise of the PKK as a significant military force in the Sinjar area and the capture of most parts of the Sinjar by the Iraqi government and Shiite militias led to the proliferation of political forces. On the other hand, there has been a notable increase in the number of Yezidis who claim to speak on behalf of the community and pursue different goals both in Iraq and Western countries. Ironically, the relative demographic and political weakness of the Yezidi community has contributed to its political fragmentation, as different Yezidis seek the support of a variety of local and international entities.

The chapter first offers a historical overview of the Yezidis' interactions with local and imperial rulers since the rise of the community with its distinctive religious belief system by the thirteenth century. Yezidis always remained outsiders to the Ottoman *millet* system offering limited tolerance and autonomy to certain non-Islamic groups such as Christians and Jews. At the same time, large-scale military campaigns targeting Yezidis were not exclusively or primarily religiously motivated. The Ottoman pashas led many expeditions against Mt. Sinjar inhabited by several Yezidi tribes primarily in order to protect the caravan routes linking northern Syria and southeastern Anatolia with Mesopotamia. With the advent of the nineteenth century, Yezidis became targets of Ottoman centralization efforts aiming at tax collection and conscription that continued after the establishment of the Iraqi state in the 1920s. Next is a narrative of the violence experienced by the Yezidis in the post-2003 era. The general atmosphere of sectarian insecurity and rise of radical Islamist groups have made Yezidis more dependent on the KRG that perceived the Yezidi community as an important

Figure 5.1 The entrance of the Khanke camp populated by displaced Yezidis (Duhok, May 2018)

Figure 5.2 The courtyard of the Lalish Temple, the most sacred place for the Yezidis (Nineveh, May 2018)

leverage in its claims over disputed territories in the province of Nineveh. However, the IS blitzkrieg in 2014 undermined this dependency and exposed the vulnerability of Yezidis lacking a defense force of their own. The remaining sections of the chapter focus on the rise of an ethnoreligious national identity in intersection with gender identity among Yezidis amid political fragmentation in the post-genocidal period. The chapter concludes with a brief reflection on the future evolution of Yezidi politics.

A Liminal Existence: Yezidis under the Ottomans

Yezidism, primarily a set of beliefs and practices transmitted orally across generations, has an inherent tendency to defy orthodoxy associated with religions with a history of extensive records. As eloquently articulated by Philip Kreyenbroek, no dogmatic and official form of the faith exists. The pursuit of defining Yezidism according to an authoritative and canonical textual source overlooks oral traditions central to its lived experience.[3] Unlike Mandeans who claimed to have sacred books of their own, probably to escape persecution in the hands of powerful Muslim rulers, Yezidi went to lengths to hide their purported books from outsiders.[4] Nonetheless, the attempt to identify the textual origins of Yezidism has been a major occupation of both Western and Muslim travelers, scholars, and intellectuals who often perceived the community as an exotic group with strange and arcane customs for an extended period of time.[5] In particular, the widespread usage of the epithet of "devil-worshippers," which mischaracterizes the sacred status of Peacock Angel for Yezidis as an affront to the Muslim God, suggests that the community remained *illegible* for outside observers for centuries.[6]

The Yezidis remained an illegible community in the eyes of Ottoman rulers who established their dominance over territories inhabited by Yezidis in the early sixteenth century. At the same time far from being defenseless and helpless subjects, Yezidis were autonomous political actors with significant capacity for coalition-building, negotiation, and resistance, as discussed by Bahadin Kerborani in his chapter. There are numerous records of Yezidi tribal chiefs being appointed as local Ottoman rulers and engaging in alliances with or against Sunni tribal chiefs.[7] The community presented two overlapping but distinct challenges to the Ottoman order. First, Ottoman rulers perceived Mt. Sinjar, an arid and narrow mountain range with commanding views of the trade routes between Baghdad and Mosul, in the southeast, and Aleppo, Diyarbakir, Mardin in the northwest, as a bastion of insecurity and banditry.[8] They organized a series of punitive expeditions against Yezidi tribes who engaged in raids targeting caravans. For instance, Evliya Çelebi, the renowned Ottoman traveler, was an observer in such an expedition in 1655. He described Yezidis of Sinjar as "wild savages, rebellious, ghoul faced, hairy infidels" who worshiped a black dog.[9] He also narrates a previous expedition by the ruler of Diyarbakir in 1640 resulted in massacres and enslavement of thousands of Yezidis.[10]

Evliya Çelebi's dehumanization of Yezidis was not untypical and pointed out to a second dynamic characterizing the Ottoman-Yezidi relations. Yezidis with their "illegitimate" belief system remained outside of the Ottoman moral order. Even if the campaigns against Mt. Sinjar were often motivated by security concerns (i.e., securing the caravan routes and recovering stolen goods), large-scale and indiscriminate violence against Yezidis were justified on religious grounds.[11] In this regard, it is possible to draw parallels between the Ottoman state's perception of Sinjar and the Ottoman and later Turkish state's perceptions of Dersim in eastern Anatolia.[12] Using the concept developed by James Scott, these two mountain ranges with their natural defenses against invading forces can be described as stateless zones with a long history of indigenous people resisting or fleeing state authorities, Yezidis in Sinjar and Zazaki-speaking Alevis in Dersim.[13] In both cases, the state authorities perceived these regions as a *stateless zone* inhabited by a group whose "deviant" religious beliefs foster disloyalty and make them potentially rebellious.[14]

The history of Ottoman-Yezidi interactions during the last century of the empire demonstrates several tendencies shaping the imperial policies and priorities. The advent Ottoman modernization of the nineteenth century involved the imposition of conscription, improvements in tax collection, and projection of central state authority into remote corners of the empire. Meanwhile, the Russo-Turkish wars, especially the conflict in 1877, resulted in thousands of Yezidi being subjects of the Russian

Empire.[15] The 1830s and 1840s saw a series of campaigns against Sinjar that remained a geopolitically important area controlling the line of communication between Diyarbakir and Mosul.[16] A permanent Turkish garrison in the more accessible southern Sinjar was established only after 1849.[17] At the same time, the Ottomans were less successful in conscripting Yezidis.[18] After the powerful British ambassador in the Ottoman capital intervened on their behalf, Yezidis of Sheikhan and Sinjar were able to obtain an exemption in 1850.[19] In a petition submitted to the Ottoman authorities and representatives of European powers, Yezidi leaders demanded exemption from obligatory military service on religious grounds. This was the first time Yezidis presented a stylized version of their belief systems to the outside world in a written document. Even if the Ottoman state continued to treat Yezidis as a liminal minority not qualified to be included in the *millet* system, it also showed flexibility and accepted that Yezidis made a payment in lieu of serving in the Ottoman army.

Religious considerations became more central to how the Ottoman state dealt with the Yezidis during the reign of Abdülhamid II. The project of making loyal subjects out of Yezidis involved systematic attempts at their conversion at a time when increasing presence of foreign representations and missionaries in the eastern provinces aggravated the threat perception of the Ottoman state. The conscription of Yezidis would facilitate their Islamization, and make them immune to the appeal of foreign influences, and ensure their loyalty to the Ottoman order. An Ottoman pasha entrusted with the task of dealing with the

Figure 5.3 An overview of the Khanke camp populated by displaced Yezidis (Duhok, May 2018)

"Yezidi question" who arrived in Mosul in 1892 engaged in a campaign of terror and destruction that ultimately backfired. Hundreds of Yezidis were killed; the Lalish, the spiritual center of Yezidis, was converted to a madrasa; sacred religious objects were confiscated; mosques were built in Yezidi villages; leading figures of the community were forced to convert.[20] When the word of these coercive practices reached the Ottoman capital, the pasha was dismissed. Apparently, the Ottoman state did not approve pasha's brutal methods that sow disorder and insecurity in the region and recognized the limits of violence in achieving mass conversion.[21] The remaining decades of the Ottoman era did not see any large anti-Yezidi violence except for brief expeditions against Sinjar during the First World War. Overall, this historical overview offers a nuanced picture of Yezidi victimhood under the Ottomans. While religious violence against Yezidis, a heterodox group excluded from the legitimate Ottoman intercommunal system, became salient in certain time periods, the community developed a strong sense of political autonomy and often achieved significant concessions via resistance or negotiations.

In the Crossfire: The Formation of Yezidi Political Identity in Post-2003 Iraq

During the Mosul dispute between the nascent Turkish Republic and the British-controlled Iraq, most Yezidi leaders preferred Iraq under a European mandate over a Turkish or Arab government.[22] Nonetheless, Yezidis remained on the margins of the newly established Iraqi state. Conscription continued to be a major concern for the community and triggered small-scale acts of rebellion in Sinjar, which gained a new geopolitical importance as a border zone between Syria and Iraq.[23] Ironically, the marginal political influence of Yezidis could be a major reason for the absence of large-scale violence targeting the community in Iraq during the twentieth century.[24] Nonetheless, the rising appeal of Kurdish nationalism among Yezidis starting with the early 1960s led to repressive policies by the Baghdad governments.[25] The ruling Ba'th regime initiated a systematic campaign of resettlement and Arabization targeting the Sinjar region.[26] Yezidis of the mountain villages were forced to relocate to eleven collective settlements surrounded by Arab villages receiving preferential treatment.[27] In the 1980s, a significant number of Yezidis served in the Iraqi army and lost their lives in the war with Iran. In the early 1990s, the establishment of an internationally enforced no-fly zone and the formation of de facto Kurdish autonomy saw the partition of Yezidi lands between Baghdad and Erbil. While the Sinjar area and southern Sheikhan remained under the Iraqi rule, Yezidi communities in Duhok, other parts of Sheikhan district, and the Lalish temple fall under the Kurdish control.

In the post-2003 order, Yezidis became a crucial demographic bloc to KRG's claims over disputed territories and its power politics in the Nineveh province, one of the most contested areas in the entire country. In the 2005 referendum on the new Iraqi constitution, around 55 percent of the voters said no in the

Nineveh province that also includes Sinjar. This was still short of the two-thirds of the vote that would result in the defeat of the new constitution.[28] Since the Kurds were the main beneficiaries of the new constitutional order, obtaining the Yezidi support in Nineveh was essential to their political goals. Article 2 of the constitution drafted in 2006 and passed in the KRG parliament in 2009 included Sinjar as part of Iraqi Kurdistan. Yezidis, who were subject to Arabization policies during the Saddam era, also benefited from the Kurdish patronage. For the first time, Sinjar district had a Yezidi governor. Some Yezidis joined the Iraqi army or Peshmerga and worked as translators for the US army. Other Yezidis found employment opportunities in Duhok and Erbil and benefited from the Kurdish economic boom that lasted until 2014.[29] These developments generated some resentment among the Sunni Arabs and Turkomans in the area who lost their privileged positions and increasingly perceived the Yezidis as being part of the Kurdish power structure.[30] At the same time, a significant number of Yezidis were uncomfortable with the rising ethnic tensions and Kurdish exclusion and repression of Yezidis political activism espousing an independent communal identity. They were fearful that their community was becoming pawns in the Kurdish-Arab territorial struggle and characterized the KRG policies as "Kurdification" of Sinjar.[31]

Like other religious minorities in Iraq, the fall of the Saddam regime in 2003 generated an atmosphere that was highly dangerous for Yezidis. As early as 2004, targeted killings of Yezidis because of their religious identity started to proliferate.[32] It became increasingly dangerous for Yezidis to get services, work, or study at Mosul, which emerged as a hotbed of Sunni militant groups.[33] The self-proclaimed Islamic State of Iraq (ISI) imposed a siege on the delivery of food, fuel, and construction materials to Sinjar as it considered Yezidis unbelievers.[34] After a Yezidi girl was stoned to death by her relatives and community for allegedly having an affair with a Sunni man in April 2007, the ISI urged its followers to kill Yezidis wherever they found them. Two weeks later, armed men stopped a bus, checked passengers' identification documents, and ordered non-Yezidis off the bus. Then they drove the hijacked bus to Mosul and executed twenty-three Yezidis there.[35] The most lethal terrorist attack in post-2003 Iraq, suicide bombings in Al-Qahtaniya (Til Ezer) and Al-Jazeera (Siba Sheikh Xidir) collective towns inhabited by Yezidis, killed several hundreds of people on August 14, 2007.[36]

These developments made Yezidis of Sinjar more dependent on the Kurdish authorities for their security who increased their control of the area especially after the 2007 bombings. Between 2005 and 2009, Kurdish parties increased their vote share at the expense of autonomous Yezidi parties in Sinjar. While the Kurdish Alliance received 44,224 votes (approximately 60 percent of the valid votes), the Yezidi Movement for Reform and Progress received 17,055 votes (app. 22 percent) in the Sinjar district and Qahtaniya subdistrict in the December 2005 parliamentary elections.[37] In comparison, the Kurdish alliance received 101,606 votes (app. 78 percent) while two autonomous Yezidi parties received only 7,787 votes (app. 6 percent) in the January 2009 provincial elections.[38] By that time, the Yezidi support for the Kurdish political goals in Nineveh became even more important as the Sunni Arabs now started to actively participate in the electoral politics.

At the same time, the KRG authorities do not recognize Yezidis as a distinct ethnoreligious group but as ethnic Kurds with distinct religious beliefs. In the eyes of KRG leaders, Yezidism is the "original Kurdish religion" that set Kurds historically apart from Arabs, Persians, and Turks, their Muslim neighbors Muslim populations. In this regard, Yezidism was incorporated into the Kurdish nationalist discourse.[39] Article 6 of the draft KRG constitution explicitly mentions only Turkomans, Chaldeans, Assyrians, Armenians, and Arabs as distinct national groups. Article 7 states that the Islamic law is one of the sources of legislation while indicating the rights and freedoms of Christians and Yezidis and other religions are to be protected.[40] The KRG parliament has 111 seats with 11 of these seats reserved for Chaldeans, Assyrians, Armenians, and Turkomans and none for Yezidis.[41]

In summary, the fall of the Saddam regime had a mixed blessing for the Yezidis. On the one hand, there was an improvement in the material well-being of the Yezidis in the post-2003 era. Some Yezidis, especially the ones serving in the Iraqi army or working for the US army, improved their economic situation, built themselves houses, and purchased cars.[42] Moreover, Yezidis affiliated with the KDP, the dominant party in the KRG, gained access to greater political patronage and resources. On the other hand, the rise of sectarian extremism made the situation of Yezidis, a historically marginalized community, even more precarious. They were disproportionately targeted by extremist groups and became increasingly dependent on the Kurdish Peshmerga for their very survival. Besides, the KRG's attempts to reconstruct Yezidi identity by emphasizing its common linkages with Kurdishness generated some backlash among Yezidis of Sinjar who were fearful that increasing ethnic conflict over disputed territories in Nineveh would result in their scapegoating.

An Ethnoreligious National Identity?

In the early hours of August 3, 2014, the so-called Islamic State (IS), which already captured Mosul and the surrounding areas in less than two months ago, staged a coordinated attack against the Sinjar region. As the Kurdish forces withdrew in panic, the IS quickly overrun any feeble defense shown in Yezidi collective towns. During this campaign, at least 1,500 Yezidis were executed while almost 1,500 died on Mt. Sinjar from dehydration or starvation.[43] Around 6,400 Yezidis, mostly women and children, were kidnapped. Many of them were subsequently sold as "slaves" by IS.[44] Women were raped repeatedly; children were forced to convert and brainwashed to serve as soldiers for the IS. Although other religious minority groups in northern Iraq were also targeted by IS, the scale of anti-Yezidi violence was unparalleled. Testimonies by survivors suggest that many local Muslims, including former friends, "blood brothers," and godfathers of Yezidi children, took an active part in the killings and kidnappings. Accordingly, most killings and kidnappings took place in towns such as Siba Sheik Xidir, Til Ezer, and Kocho that were close to Arab settlements.[45] Yezidis in the northern part of the mountain had more time to take refuge in Mt. Sinjar.[46] The IS control of the Sinjar city center ended in November 2015; the entire Sinjar district was liberated by spring 2017. Yet the scope of destruction, poisoned intercommunal relations, and prevailing political instability have prevented reconstruction efforts. Five years after the attacks, most Yezidis of Sinjar either stayed in IDP camps in Iraqi Kurdistan or sought refuge in Western countries.[47]

This catastrophic development had a monumental impact on Yezidi political identity and had three specific consequences. First, for the first time in their history, Yezidis emerged as a political community attracting significant international interest and concern. The Obama administration's decision to authorize airstrikes against the IS was triggered by the human tragedy experienced by the Yezidis stranded on Mt. Sinjar.[48] International organizations including the United Nations described the anti-Yezidi attacks as genocide.[49] A Yezidi survivor woman, Nadia Murad, became the co-recipient of the Nobel Peace Prize in 2018 for her global activism against sexual violence in war. The German federal state of Baden-Württemberg initiated a humanitarian admission program specifically for Yezidi women survivors and their children (but not necessarily adult male members of their family).[50] While it would take some years to fully assess its effects, this global spread of the community led to the diversification and internationalization of Yezidi activism with the formation of various associations by Yezidis based in Western countries.[51] With support from various international actors, these associations have made two core demands influenced by political liberalism and transitional justice discourses: (a) the recognition of the IS attacks against Yezidis as genocide and (b) the formation of international tribune to try and convict individuals who participated in these attacks. The fact that the International Criminal Court (ICC) does not have automatic jurisdiction over Iraq and Syria, which are not part of the Rome treaty of 2002 that created the ICC, complicated these efforts.[52] The captured IS militants were tried in Iraqi courts where many of whom were found guilty and sentenced to death. Thousands of IS fighters from many different countries were detained by PYD forces in northern Syria after the liberation of the last piece of land held by the IS in March 2019. Yet not a single IS member was put on trial for crimes specifically committed against Yezidi people.[53]

Another important consequence of the IS attacks on Yezidi political identity is the strained links between Yezidis and the KRG. As indicated before, the KRG established political and military control over Yezidi-inhabited territories and extensive patronage networks incorporating a large number of Yezidis between 2003 and 2014. However, the panicked withdrawal of the Kurdish forces from Sinjar in August 2014 was a major disappointment. While some Yezidis argued that the Kurdish forces lacked the capacity to resist against the IS onslaught, many others portrayed the withdrawal as an act of betrayal demonstrating the dispensability of Yezidis for the Kurdish leadership.[54] In response, the KRG authorities undertook several initiatives including the establishment of an office responsible for rescuing Yezidis kidnapped by the IS and diplomatic efforts aiming to have the anti-Yezidi attacks recognized as genocide.[55] The term *genocide* evokes a strong emotional and political meaning for Iraqi Kurds given the legacy of Saddam Hussein's Anfal campaign involving chemical weapons attacks, massacres, sexual violence, and mass deportation against Kurdish people in the late 1980s. The description of Anfal as genocide has been central to the legitimacy of Kurdish pursuit of statehood and independence from Iraq.[56] By labeling the IS violence against the Yezidis as another genocide victimizing ethnic Kurds, the Kurdish authorities sought international support for the formation of an independent Kurdistan where religious minorities would be safe from extremist violence. The KRG authorities organized polling stations in IDP camps and strongly urged Yezidis displaced from Sinjar to vote in the 2017 independence referendum.[57] In this regard, the recognition of Yezidi victimhood has been made central to Kurdish victimhood and pursuit of independence. At the same time, the failure of Kurdish forces to protect Yezidis fostered demands for the formation of an autonomous region for religious minorities in Nineveh under international supervision. For instance, Yazda, one of the most well-known Yezidi humanitarian and lobbying organizations, explicitly calls for such autonomy.[58] Similar demands were also put forward by various Christian groups.[59]

A final transformation following the IS attacks concerns the end of the KRG control over Sinjar. While the KRG forces gained back parts of Sinjar from the IS, they withdrew completely from the area in the face of the Iraqi and Shiite militia advances in October 2017. As a result, for the first time, a Shiite political force asserted military supremacy over Yezidis lands and aimed to cultivate its own patronage networks among Yezidis by taking advantage of intra-Yezidi divisions.[60] Besides, the PKK, a Kurdish nationalist force with a history of rivalry with the KDP, made significant inroads among Yezidis in the post-2014 period.[61] During the attacks, the PKK militants played a highly visible role in opening up a humanitarian corridor between Mt. Sinjar and the Syrian border controlled by the PYD, a PKK affiliate. This corridor enabled desperate Yezidis who took refuge in Mt. Sinjar to reach safety. The PKK established a permanent presence in the area and successfully recruited a significant number of Yezidi men and women, who were disenchanted with the KDP, to its militia.[62] Like the KDP, the PKK also emphasizes Kurdishness of Yezidis but offers a distinct ideological alternative. In particular, the PKK with its secular, equalitarian, and gender progressive platforms presented itself as a vehicle of empowerment for Yezidi women subject to extreme levels of sexual violence and patriarchal practices.[63] Moreover, the PYD forces rescued many kidnapped Yezidi women and children from the IS captivity in northeastern Syria. Building on a blueprint that was implemented successfully in northern Syria (and unsuccessfully in Kurdish areas of Turkey), the PKK declared "democratic autonomy" for Sinjar and sought international support. The rise of the PKK as a viable force vying for support among Yezidis contributes to further fragmentation of Yezidi political identity and complicates the formation of a unified stance among Yezidis who are more spread out than ever before.

Gender and Politics among the Yezidis

IS's attacks against the Yezidis revealed once again the centrality of gender in political violence. Indeed, sexual violence has been used as a deliberate and systematic tool to commit genocide and ethnic cleansing against religious and ethnic communities in many other contexts in recent decades as well, such as in Bosnia, Kosovo, Rwanda, Sudan, Uganda, and the DRC.[64] Groups such as IS use specific, typically patriarchal, gender norms in intersection with identity perceptions toward religious or ethnic groups to justify violence.[65] The precarious position of the Yezidi minority in Iraq, as explained earlier in the chapter, played an important role in IS's targeting of this community. The lawlessness and insecurity created by sectarian violence in Iraq further exacerbated existing discriminatory attitudes toward the Yezidis, as well as other minority communities.[66]

IS explicitly justified its gendered violence against the Yezidis through its interpretation of certain Islamic rules and practices. It defined the Yezidis as a "pagan" minority and nonbelievers and treated them differently from members of other religions such as Christians. According to IS ideology, Christians and Jews are considered as the "People of the Book" who can be treated as immune from certain practices during war, such as abducting and raping female members of these communities.[67] IS believed that it was allowed to kill male members of the Yezidi community if they do not convert to Islam, and to abduct, rape, and sell the Yezidi women and girls and force them to do house labor.[68] After their capture, the Yezidi women and children were shared among IS fighters that participated in the occupation of Sinjar, and after that one-fifth of the captives, in IS terminology "slaves," were transferred to the IS authorities to be divided as "profit."[69] Captured Yezidi women and girls lived under circumstances in which they had no control, and they were entirely stripped off their ability to control their life, body, and dignity.

The Yezidi community's own gender norms, especially the embodiment of men's and families' "honor" in women's bodies, made these attacks particularly unsettling for the community. Yezidis' gender norms were used as a tool by IS to discourage abducted Yezidi women not to escape. Yezidi survivors were reported to say that their captives told them that if they returned to their communities, they would be killed, referring to the practice of "honor" killing, or would not be accepted back home.[70] The Yezidis, including Yezidi leaders, consider the sexual violence perpetrated by IS against Yezidi women and girls as an attack against the whole of the community. As Mir Tahseen Beg, the hereditary leader of the Yezidis, stated the Yezidis could have maybe reconciled and gone back to living with their Arab neighbors even after killings, but IS's treatment of thousands of Yezidi women and girls would make it very hard to reconcile.[71] The experiences of the Yezidis left lasting scars for the community and led to extreme levels of postwar trauma and PTSD.[72]

Sexual and other forms of violence experienced by the Yezidis cannot be treated as simply an outcome of IS's extreme methods or the result of conflict. There is a wider context of inequality and structures in place that made such violence thinkable and feasible. Interviews with members of the Yezidi community suggest that the community is aware of these wider circumstances. They associate their experiences of violence and sexual violence to the long-term disadvantages of being a minority group in the disputed territories in Iraq and the historical prejudices against their community. Like many other minority communities in Iraq, a large section of the Yezidi community is located in disputed territories (between the Kurdish regional government and the Iraqi government). Being in this location puts them in a precarious position because these areas are typically neglected in terms of infrastructure, economic investment, and provision of security and protection. Moreover, the history of religious prejudice against the community and the distrust among Yezidis, Iraqis, and Kurds has exacerbated the precariousness of their position. Gender norms also played a key role in these outcomes. The idea that women can be bought and sought for sexual purposes like a commodity and that they can be entirely stripped off their agency is a clear example of this. This extreme form of discrimination and violence practiced against Yezidi women can be seen as part of a continuum of wider discriminative practices and violences perpetrated against women in Iraq in general.[73]

Yet, alongside this, the community's experience of gendered violence by IS has had a transformative impact on the political and social life among the Yezidi community. These impacts can be analyzed in three interrelated aspects. First, IS's attacks and its violence against Yezidi women had significant effect on Yezidi attitudes about survivors of sexual violence. Female survivors who were held captive by IS and exposed to sexual and other forms of violence were initially hesitant about returning to their families and communities. They feared they would be rejected or killed for "tainting" the "honor" of the family.[74] With the February 2015 Declaration by the Yezidi religious authorities, survivor women as well as women and men who were forced to convert to Islam were reaccepted to the community. After this declaration, the number of women and girls returning to their community increased. However, this does not mean stigma around being sexually assaulted has disappeared and life after return has been easy for returnees. Moreover, many of these women and girls continue to live with untreated trauma and in difficult conditions of displacement away from their homes. Some of these women have migrated to European countries and were experiencing other difficulties such as being away from home and family and adjusting to life in a different culture.[75] Finally, the situation of children born to Yezidi women raped by their IS captors is a particularly challenging issue.[76]

Another significant impact of sexual violence against Yezidi women and girls is that taboos around talking about sexual violence in the Yezidi community have weakened after this experience. Generally, sexual violence is considered as a difficult issue to make public and acknowledge in most societies, as previous cases of sexual violence in armed conflicts across the world showed.[77] There has been a public silence about the experiences of Kurdish women sexually assaulted during the Anfal campaign.[78] In sharp contrast, sexual violence has become part of the public discourse and Yezidis integrated it into their communication with outsiders and Iraqi and Kurdish authorities to explain their situation, request support, and express their needs and demands. Male community leaders, and brothers, fathers, and husbands of survivors of sexual violence have openly discussed the issue. This is an interesting development because rather than shying away from it, Yezidis are openly talking about sexual violence in national and international platforms. Nadia Murad, a Yezidi sexual violence survivor herself, is seen as a spokesperson for communicating Yezidis' experiences and needs and demanding justice and protection for her community. These novel developments are unprecedented in the history of the Yezidi community.

Finally, there are indicators of changing perceptions about women's role and position in society among the Yezidi community. This is for two reasons. First, the experience of genocide and sexual violence made the community once again realize that their position as a community in Iraq is precarious. They do not have the necessary political and economic support structures and protection mechanisms. Therefore, some of the community members believe that empowering girls through enabling them to access education and jobs can provide them some form of protection. A number of interviewees said that if their people in Sinjar were more educated and more aware of their life outside their communities, the genocide against their community would not have happened.[79] The second factor that contributed to changing perceptions about women's position is displacement. Displaced Sinjari Yezidis in Sheikhan and Duhok were able to meet with Yezidis living in these areas and interact with members of the Yezidi diaspora. Yezidis in Sinjar have generally more conservative norms about women's position in society compared to Yezidis in the Duhok region that have been under Kurdish rule. After the attacks, several educated and experienced local Yezidi women in Duhok and Sheikhan began to work with women's rights organizations and humanitarian organizations to provide support for surviving and displaced Sinjari Yezidis and met and worked with them. One of the interviewed humanitarian NGO workers, who is a Yezidi herself, said, "[T]he Shingali[80] women were initially reluctant but then started to participate in training and even started working." She attributed this partly to the exposition of the more conservative Sinjari (Shingali) Yezidi communities to the more open life of the Yezidis in Duhok: "[T]he Shingali community became more open towards women because they saw other Yezidi women, like those from Sharya. They saw that their women are open, they go to work, they go to school, so they thought to be a little bit more open with their women as well."[81]

Conclusion

The general feeling of insecurity characterizing post-Saddam Iraq, the rise of Sunni extremism, the conflict between the KRG and Iraqi central government involving Yezidi lands, and the further fragmentation of the community via migrations and forced displacements have made it increasingly difficult, if not impossible, for Yezidis to seek political accommodation and security as a compliant minority group. The genocidal attacks in 2014 have strongly reinforced this trend and contributed to a proliferation of voices and platforms about distinctive Yezidi identity at local, national, and international levels. In this regard, Yezidis are latecomers to the global politics of recognition, challenging allegedly difference-blind policies and demanding dignity for particular group identities.[82]

The Yezidi politics of recognition represents a major change in the community's self-identification and representation given the long history of Yezidis as a liminal community lacking official recognition during the Ottoman times and widespread prejudices about their belief systems persisting until now. It entails a strong emphasis on the distinctive nature of Yezidi identity and history and a request for accountability of the crimes committed against Yezidis informed by discourses of transitional justice and feminism. This request for recognition also entails a strong gender dimension. The traumatic experience of systematic sexual violence pushed the community to question gender-related taboos and norms and women's position in private and public life and to initiate some changes. In their demands for protection and recognition, Yezidi advocacy groups and activists have explicitly incorporated Yezidi women, gender dimension, and sexual violence. All these have led to significant symbolic gains that elevated Yezidis from an obscure minority into an internationally recognized religious minority suffering from crimes against humanity and deserving respect and protection.

Ironically, this rise of autonomous Yezidi politics is accompanied with an increasing communal fragmentation and dispersion and an involvement of an even greater number of external actors in Yezidi affairs. The postwar conditions in Sinjar remain prohibitive for the revitalization of the Yezidi life there; geopolitical rivalries involving multiple local and regional forces make the formation of an autonomous zone for Yezidis highly implausible. Under these circumstances, one can expect that the Yezidi diaspora would increasingly play a more important role in sustaining Yezidi collective identity, shaping its global image, and transforming relations within the community.

Notes

1   Pinker (2011).
2   He is referring to the atrocities committed by a local Kurdish ruler, Mir Mohammad Kor of Soran. Interview with a Yezidi religious authority, September 27, 2017.
3   Kreyenbroek (1995).
4   Khenchelaoui (1999: 23–5).
5   Allison (2008).
6   As late as 1935, *The New York Times* described Yezidis as "devil-worshippers" in an article about a punitive Iraqi expedition to Mt. Sinjar. "Rebellious Yezidis Are Subdued in Iraq," 1935.

7   Mir Mohammad of Soran, whose violent campaign left a strong legacy in Yezidi oral traditions, attacked Yezidis because they were allied with his rival, the Behdinan Emirate. Layard (1850: 276–7); Longrigg (1925: 28); Guest (1993: 67–9).

8   In Yezidi historiography, these campaigns make a plurality of *firmans* targeting the community. Cindî Reşo (2014).

9   Evliya Çelebi (2013: 50). Kreyenbroek (1995: 36) observes that the violent events between the fourteenth century and the campaign of Mir Mohammad Kor of Soran in 1832 left little trace in the collective memory of the Yezidis.

10 Evliya Çelebi (2013: 51–4). He writes that this campaign took the revenge of Karbala (54). In fact, there is a widespread association between Yezidis and Caliph Yazid whose soldiers massacred the grandson of Prophet Mohammad and his followers in Karbala in 680. This monumental event gradually led to the schism between Sunni and Shiite Muslims. For a detailed and nuanced discussion of the reverence shown to Yazid in Yezidi tradition, see Kreyenbroek (1995: 37).

11 Gölbaşı (2013: 3–4).

12 Dersim was the scene of state-led massacres in 1937 and 1938. For the Ottoman/ Turkish perception of Dersim and its people, see Goner (2017: 31–64).

13 Scott (2009: 13) calls the great mountainous zone in Southeast Asia, Zomia, as "one of the largest remaining non state spaces in the world, if not *the* largest."

14 This interpretation disagrees with Gülsoy (2002) who argues that religious differences never had primary influence on the Ottoman treatment of Yezidis. He argues that Ottomans targeted Yezidis only when they threatened the public order (134–5).

15 For Yezidis in contemporary Transcaucasia, especially Armenia, see Nicolaus and Yuce (2019).

16 A British officer visited Sinjar during this period (Forbes 1839).

17 Fuccaro (1999a: 4).

18 Gölbaşı (2009) provides a highly informative narrative of the Ottoman-Yezidi relations regarding conscription.

19 Guest (1993: 104); Gölbaşı (2009: 95).

20 Erdem (1996: 46, 59–60) writes that the post-1856 era brought an end to the Ottoman practice of enslavement of disobedient populations. At the same time, Parry (1895) observes that this fin de siècle campaign entailed the kidnappings of Yezidi women and girls and their forced marriage to the Ottoman soldiers.

21 Deringil (1999: 71–5). The Ottoman state eventually returned the possession of the Lalish temple and sacred objects to the Yezidi religious leadership.

22 League of Nations (1925).

23 Fuccaro (1997).

24 There was little modern political participation among Yezidis. For instance, the Communist Party of Iraq that attracted marginalized ethnic and religious groups such as Christians, Kurds, and Shiite Arabs had very little Yezidi representation. Batatu (1978: 1190).

25 Ali (2019a).

26 It also aimed to generate a historiography linking Yezidis to the Umayyad caliphate and arguing for their Arabic roots. See Majid Ali Hassan's chapter in this volume.

27 Savelsberg, Hajo, and Dulz (2010).

28 Heavy majorities (more than two-thirds) in Anbar and Salahuddin voted no. Had the no vote in Nineveh also reached the two-thirds, the constitution would be rejected. "Iraq Voters Back New Constitution," 2005.

29 A Yezidi politician affiliated with a Kurdish party resembled Dinjar to the Darfur region of Sudan given its underdevelopment. Interview conducted in Duhok, May 27, 2018.

30 Interview with Khidir Domle, Duhok, May 28, 2019.

31 UNAMI 2009 (we thank Peter Bartu for sharing this document with us); HRW (2009). A US diplomatic cable from 2008 published by WikiLeaks notes that Mir Tahseen Beg, the foremost Yezidi leader, was worried with forceful transfer of Yezidi property to Kurdish ownership in Sheikhan with the goal of increasing the number of Kurds in the disputed territories of Nineveh. "Yezidi Protest at Embassy," 2007.

32 UNHCR (2005).

33 UNAMI (2009).

34 UNAMI (2009). According to UNHABITAT (2015), the Sinjar region had a population of 339,000 before the August 2014 attacks. Yezidis made around 74 percent of this population.

35 HRW (2009).

36 Some Yezidis label these attacks as "the 73rd firman."

37 This Yezidi party won the parliamentary seat allocated for Yezidis in the 2005 Iraqi elections.

38 UNAMI (2009); USIP (2011). There was a significant increase in the number of voters in Sinjar between 2005 and 2009 leading to the allegations of voting fraud.

39 Spät (2018: 426) observes this idea of fusion between Kurdish and Yezidi identities found a less receptive audience among the Yezidis of Sinjar than the Yezidis living east of the Tigris, who have a longer and more intense history of contact with the Kurds.

40 This draft constitution also talks about religious freedom of Yezidis in Articles 65 and 124. For an analysis of and text of the draft, see Kelly (2010).

41 There was a single Yezidi politician affiliated with the KDP, Sheikh Shamo, in the KRG parliament elected in 2013. Two Yezidis, one each from KDP and YNK, gained seats in the September 2018 parliamentary elections. The inability of Yezidis from Sinjar, many of whom lived in camps in the Duhok province, to vote significantly undermines electoral powers of the Yezidis in the KRG elections. Ironically, these displaced Yezidis were allowed to vote in the Kurdish independence referendum in September 2017.

42 Dinç (2017).

43 Cetorelli et al. (2017).

44 As of August 2019, 3,509 of these captives were liberated, mostly through ransom payments, according to the statistics announced by the KRG.

45 Kocho, where the worst atrocities took place, remained under siege until August 15 when the IS militants raided the town, executed adult males in groups, and enslaved women and children. According to survivor testimonies, IS militants included Arabs from neighboring villages.

46 The exception to this pattern is the town of Hardan, located in the northwestern part of Mt. Sinjar, which was attacked by the neighboring Sunni Turkomans.

47 As of February 2017, there were around 36,000 families in IDP camps in the Duhok province of the KRG. Around 77 percent of these families were Yezidis (BRHA 2017: 18).

48 "Obama Allows Limited Airstrikes on ISIS," 2014.

49 OHCHR (2016).

50 McGee (2018).

51 The most well-known of these associations are Yazda and Free Yezidi Foundation.

52 The ICC has jurisdiction over crimes committed by IS militants who are citizens of
    the countries that are members of the court. It is also possible for the UN Security
    Council to refer a case to the ICC, as it happened with atrocities in Darfur in 2005.
    Because of this referral, the ICC prosecutor issued an indictment of then Sudanese
    President Omar al-Bashir and accused him of committing the crime of genocide. Yet
    the Trump administration, which is openly hostile to the ICC, was not willing to refer
    the case of IS atrocities to the international court.
53 HRW (2017).
54 Interviews in Duhok, May 2018.
55 In a statement delivered on the fourth anniversary of the IS attacks, then KRG Prime
    Minister Nechirwan Barzani described the events "as one of the most barbaric
    genocides of the 21st century." "PM Barzani pledges continued support for Yezidis on
    genocide anniversary," 2018.
56 Baser and Toivanen (2017).
57 While many Yezidis were agnostic about the Kurdish referendum in 2017,
    Mir Tahseen Beg, who died in January 2019, asked Yezidis to support Kurdish
    independence. "Ji Mîre Êzidiyên Cîhanê banga referandûmê," 2017.
58 'Press Release' 2016.
59 Demands for autonomy have a long history among the Assyrians going back to the
    formative years of Iraq. Joseph 1961: chapter 8.
60 ICG (2018). Shiite views of Yezidis are complicated by the widespread perception
    that Yezidis are followers of Caliph Yazid, the most hated figure in the Shiite
    historiography. At the same time, there is no history of Yezidi-Shiite intercommunal
    conflict in recent history given their limited geographical contact. In fact, Yezidis
    and Shiites of Sinjar were participating in similar rituals and venerating the same
    shrine in the post-2003 period. Lajnat al-Buhuth wa al-dirasat (2016: 95). Moreover,
    Shiite authorities strongly condemned the IS cruelty against Yezidis and Ayatollah Ali
    Sistani met with a Yezidi delegation. Ibid., 404–5.
61 For an overview of KDP-PKK tensions over Sinjar, see Yılmaz (2018).
62 The PKK presence in Sinjar aggravated threat perception of the Turkish state that
    conducted airstrikes in the area numerous times.
63 For the motives of women joining the PKK and its gender politics, see Tezcür (2019a).
64 Jefferson (2004).
65 Davies and True (2015: 505).
66 Maisel (2008); Oehring (2017). Shi'iite Turkmen women and girls, albeit at a
    significantly lower scale, were also among minorities in Iraq that were exposed to
    sexual violence by IS. Bor (2019).
67 In practice, this distinction was not always kept. IS members also kidnapped, raped,
    and enslaved Christian women. "Christian women kidnapped by IS reunited with
    father after four years," 2018.
68 "The Failed Crusade," 2014: 14–15.
69 Ibid., 15.
70 Interviews with members of Yezidi community, May 2018.
71 Interview with Prince Hassan, May 2018.
72 Erdener (2017); Kizilhan (2018).
73 Geneva International Center for Justice (2015: 18–22).
74 Interview with two Yezidi sexual violence survivors, May 31, 2018.
75 McGee (2018).

76 According to three different NGO sources, the number of mothers with children
    from IS was around 200 as of May 2018. Some women gave their children to the
    PKK and some of them returned and took shelter with their child under the PKK.
    Yezidi survivors with children sometimes find different strategies to navigate in this
    situation. Some claim to their families that they met a husband (usually dead or
    missing) at some point and the child was his. Even though this is not true, and the
    family knows this, they accept it. Some mothers want to keep the child; some do not.
    Interviews in Duhok and Sheikhan, May 2018. The topic remains highly controversial
    among Yezidis. On April 24, 2019, Yezidi Supreme Spiritual Council issued a
    declaration accepting these children to the community before reversing it three days
    later.
77 Jefferson (2004); Turshen (2001: 66).
78 Moradi (2016).
79 Interviews with Yezidi community members, December 2017 and May 2018.
80 Shingal is the local name for Sinjar.
81 Interview with a Yezidi female humanitarian NGO staff, May 29, 2018.
82 From this perspective, the lack of recognition or misrecognition can be a form of
    oppression; Taylor (1994).

Section II

PERCEPTIONS: KURDS AND YEZIDIS IN THE EYES OF OTHERS

PAYING THE PRICE OF DASHT-I KARBALA: HISTORICAL PERCEPTIONS OF YEZIDIS IN THE OTTOMAN ERA

Bahadin Hawar Kerborani

Introduction

This chapter investigates how Yezidis, a Kurdish-speaking religious group, were represented in Ottoman and Kurdish sources in the sixteenth and eighteenth centuries. I focus on how the history of Yezidis and their relationships with other actors can be examined from alternative perspectives in Ottoman Kurdistan. We have studies that mainly emphasize the history of Yezidi groups in the Ottoman Empire and under the rule of local Sunni Kurdish leaders as a history of violent victimization, persecution, and *firmans*.[1] My goal is not to deny or minimize the violent actions of the Ottoman and Kurdish rulers against Yezidis. However, analyzing and understanding the history of Yezidis in terms of their culture, economic, and social life and as active participants in the life of the region depict a broader picture of local dynamics.

One of the issues that scholars have faced is the lack of sources about Yezidis from this period. Additionally, there are not many written materials produced by Yezidis about their own community. Scholars such as Christine Allison, Khanna Omerkhali, and Philip G. Kreyenbroek and many others have documented the richness of Yezidi oral tradition.[2] One of the main sources I utilize is Evliya Çelebi's *Seyahatname*, or *Book of Travels*, which consists of ten volumes. I draw especially from volume 4, which can be called *Kurdistan-name (The Book of Kurdistan)* as it provides great details about Ottoman Kurdistan, its people, and also covers some part of Iranian Kurdistan. Another significant account was written by a local *imam/hatip*[3] of the city of Van, Ibn-i Nuh's *Van Tarihi* (1716). Ibn-i Nuh supplies substantial information about local dynamics between the Yezidis of Hoshab,

I would like to thank Güneş Murat Tezcür and Lydia Shanklin Roll for their assistance and suggestions during the writing of this chapter.

a fortified settlement southeast of Van, and the Ottomans during the period when these two forces fought in 1715–1716. Additionally, I utilize Sharaf Khan's *Sharafnama (1596/7)* and a few fatwas from the time period.

Evliya Çelebi's *Seyahatname* is a distinctive account that provides substantial information and details related to almost the entire territory of the Ottoman Empire, including people, architecture, literature and languages, religion, history, customs and traditions, geography, food, and foreign affairs of the empire. Çelebi wrote *Seyahatname* in the later years of his life, in seventeenth-century Cairo. Çelebi was raised and received his education at the Ottoman Palace in Istanbul. He had close connections with the palace through his kinsman, Melek Ahmed Pasha, who led an expedition against Yezidis on Sinjar Mountain in 1640s. Çelebi was an Istanbuli gentleman who spent a good deal of time in the Ottoman capital, one of the great centers of the world. He served many pashas and traveled to almost all parts of the empire as a secretary, *imam* and *müezzin* (prayer leader and caller to prayer), courier, and messenger.[4]

As Nelida Fuccaro[5] and Gerald MacLean[6] present in their works, Western travelers also wrote about Yezidis during the same period. Çelebi's account and experiences, however, provide a unique angle about the Ottoman-Yezidi relations given his position as an Ottoman source. Overall, *Seyahatname* has been an important source for Kurdish studies and scholars who analyze the relationship between Sunni Shafi'i Kurds and the Ottoman Empire and the status of Kurdistan in the sixteenth and seventeenth centuries. For example, two prolific scholars of Ottoman and Kurdish studies, Robert Dankoff and Martin van Bruinessen, have consulted *Seyahatname* frequently in their works on and the interactions and reactions of Sunni Kurds (and partially Yezidi Kurds) with the empire and surrounding communities. Dankoff's three books, *Evliya Çelebi in Bitlis*[7] (1990), *Intimate Life of an Ottoman Statesman: Melek Ahmed Pasha*[8] (1991), and *An Ottoman Mentality: The World of Evliya Çelebi*[9] (2006), describe in great detail how Çelebi perceived the indigenous people and the role of the state in the region. They also provide important insights into Çelebi's way of thinking and how to use *Seyahatname* as a source. In comparison, van Bruinessen, who regarded Evliya Çelebi as the first Kurdologist,[10] authored *Evliya Çelebi in Diyarbekir*[11] with Hendrik Boeschoten, focusing on the relevant section of the *Seyahatname*. Additionally, he wrote about statuses of Kurdish local rulers in Kurdistan, as well as the Kurdish language and literature, also based on *Seyahatname*.[12]

The historically rooted perception that Yezidis are followers of the second Umayyad Caliph who ordered the killing of Hussain, the grandson of Prophet Muhammad, in Karbala in 680 shaped how Ottomans treated Yezidis. This perception played an important role in Çelebi's understanding and representation of the Yezidi community in his writing. Çelebi provides significant details about the wealth in the hands of the Yezidi community. I argue that his hostility and unpleasant attitudes toward the Yezidi community were not only based on the "unusual" religion and practices of Yezidis or their unruly actions against other neighboring communities and people. The wealth and other commodities in the hands of the Yezidi community are another excuse used by Çelebi to justify his hostile attitudes toward the community. The issue of wealth also plays a role in fatwas against Yezidis, as well as with the authors of *Seyahatname* and *Van Tarihi*. These individuals used the Yezidi community as a foil to highlight their *pak* (pure) Sunnism and their role as protectors and servants of the Muslim world.

Çelebi attempts to show the Yezidi community as one of the main players at the Battle of Karbala through providing different episodes and stories about the role of the Yezidi community at the battle. Çelebi formulates his narration in such a way as to make sure that Yezidis were cast as the main perpetrators of the violence who had to be penalized in his *Seyahatname*. In this chapter, I will explore how Evliya Çelebi perceived the Yezidi community and reconstructed the role of Yezidis at the Battle of Karbala a millennium after the battle. I will also address how the Yezidi community was represented and understood by different figures, from the points of view of the capital and localities.

Yezidis in Evliya Çelebi's Seyahatname

Dankoff's *An Ottoman Mentality: The World of Evliya Çelebi* explores the world of Çelebi as an individual and how the environment around him played a significant role in his writing and positionality. As Dankoff points out, researchers should be careful with the text because of concerns about Çelebi's reliability and narration, especially in terms of numbers and factual information. He uses many stories and information he witnessed and collected personally. At the same time, he is not always an eyewitness, or sometimes he retells the same story at another point in his account. Dankoff calls this aspect of Çelebi's writings "anecdotal inventiveness,"[13] by which he means that while Çelebi was not an eyewitness to a particular incident, he narrates as though he were actually there. Dankoff says:

> Evliya's narrative style, it seems to me, oscillates between anecdotal inventiveness and epic formulaicness. The latter is especially prominent in the descriptions of war and battle, feasts and gift exchanges, and the like. The Sincar episode (Chapter 5) is a good example. Here there is only the slightest pretense to eyewitness. Evliya, responding to Firari Mustafa's insistent queries, elaborates with obvious rhetorical flourishes on one of Melek's martial deeds, which occurred fifteen years before. After the victory, "some of the Yezidis, seeing that their wives and children were taken captive, gouged out their own eyes."[14]

Çelebi uses many terms to describe Yezidis including *Saçlı Kürdü* (hairy Kurds), *Yezidi Ekrad* (Yezidi Kurds), *Saçlı Yezidi Kürdleri*[15] (hairy Yezidi Kurds) *kavm-i na-pak* (impure group), *bed-mezheb*[16] (bad sect), *bî-dîn*[17] (faithless), *savm u salât ve hacc u zekât vermezler*[18] (they do not know anything about these pillars of Islam), *kelb-perest*[19] (dog worshippers), and *fırka-ı dal*[20] (heretic sect). Additionally, Çelebi includes many details related to the appearance of Yezidis and how much they love onions and dogs.[21]

The Battle of Karbala was an important moment in the Islamic history and numerous accounts were written related to the battle, such as two well-known books: Kasnifi's *Rawdat al-Shuhada* (The Garden of the Martyrs), written in 1504 in Persian, and Fuzûli's *Hadiqat al-Su'ada* (The Garden of the Blessed), written in the sixteenth century in Turkish. Fuzûli explains the reason behind writing his book in the preface: "Whilst the Arabs and Persians could read the history of the martyrs in their own languages, the Turks possessed no such record, and Fuzûli feld called upon to supply that deficiency."[22] Fuzûli had a close relationship with the Ottomans and he states that Kanuni Sultan Suleyman was the sovereign sultan. He also dedicated his book to the governor of Baghdad, Mehmed Pasha. Syed Akbar Hyder stated that "in 1596, this work [*The Garden of the Blessed*] was illustrated under the patronage of the Ottoman Sultan Murad III."[23] As we can see, the Sunni Ottoman Empire and the sultan were closely interested in this historical event.

The language of Çelebi is very hostile to the Yezidi community when he articulates his experiences and thoughts about them. This leads to a speculative question: Did Evliya Çelebi see the Yezidi community as both perpetrators of the Battle of Karbala and the followers or descendants of Yezid ibn Muawiya? Is this one of the reasons for his severe hostility against Yezidis?

One of the most interesting justifications Çelebi offers for the Ottoman army's attacks was to describe them as acts of revenge for the martyrs in Karbala and the blood of Hussein.[24] I will provide some passages from *Seyahatname* to show how Çelebi identified and blamed Yezidis as one of the main perpetrators at the Battle of Karbala (680). Melek Ahmed Pasha fought against the Yezidis after he heard that they raided and plundered the villages of Mardin in 1640–1641. The following passage might provide some information about Çelebi's hostility toward Yezidis: "All of them Abkhazian and Circassian and Georgian braves who shamed one another in battle, and never held back their reins, and who knew what Muhammedan honor meant. They invested Mt. Saçlı with one heart and mind, intent on avenging upon these Yezidi devils the blood of imam Hüseyin and the martyrs of Karbela."[25] He told the same story in book VI: "The revenge of the martyrs on the plain of Karbala taken through killing thirteen thousand Yezidi Kurds on Mountain Sinjar."[26] When he goes on to describe the abundance of the Yezidi areas, he addresses how these prosperous areas were in the Yezidis' hands.[27] The spoils of Ottoman army attacks targeting Yezidi were described in the following manner:

> These Yezidis were as wealthy as Croesus. All the multitudes of troops from the provinces of Van and Diyarbekir and Mardin who came to the aid of Melek Ahmed Pasha, all the Kurdistan soldiery who participated in plundering the money and food and drink and copper vessels and household furnishings and the like which emerged over ten days from the Saçlı Dağı caves, could not carry away more than a drop in the sea and a mote in the sun. For ever since the event of Kerbela these people have been rich, and no king ever conquered them before.[28]

Evliya Çelebi portrays Melek Ahmed Pasha as a hero of Islam and an avenger of the blood of the martyrs of Karbala.[29] He also provides rich details of the bounty the pasha gained with the conquest of Mount Sinjar:

> To conclude: Melek Ahmed Pasha got as his royal tithe of the booty 1.060 purses of silver, 11 purses of gold, 13.000 muskets, 300 bales of silk, several hundred bales of gunpowder, 300 mules, 1.800 captives young and old, and countless precious cloth items. Only god the Generous knows the amount that fell to the other emirs and nobles and officers and *gazis*. Certainly, each tent got five or ten lovely lads and lasses and other captives. There were no sheep, horses, or water buffalo; but there were many mules and goats.[30]

As we can see, the empire's military expedition on the Sinjar was not only based on religious concerns. The military campaigns did not only aim to punish this Yezidi group because of their actions against other neighboring communities. According to Çelebi's *Seyahatname*, the Ottoman campaign was motivated by greed and material gain as well.

Another example from volume 4 is how Çelebi associates Yezidis and one of their most important sites, Sinjar, with the Battle of Karbala. Evliya Çelebi placed Sinjar and Yezidi tribes at the heart of the Battle of Karbala by saying that Yezid ibn Muawiya collected soldiers from Sham, Sham-1 Tarablus, Kurdistan, and Sinjar and put them under the control of Ubeydullah ibn Ziyad ibn Ömer.[31] We do not have any other information about the role of soldiers from Sinjar or Kurdistan at the Battle of Karbala in the late seventh century. However, Çelebi claims that Yezid ibn Muawiya collected soldiers from the Yezidi area.

There are still unanswered questions regarding how Çelebi formed his ideas about Yezidis. Most likely Çelebi read or heard stories about the Battle of Karbala and attributed some anecdotal features of the incident to Yezidis. For example, he provides intricate details about the role of dogs in Yezidi life and how Yezidis treated dogs. He says that dogs were very important for Yezidis and that they washed dogs with onion juice when they died.[32] The first time Çelebi recounts this story it sounds strange. How could Yezidis find enough onion juice to wash dogs when the Yezidis' favorite vegetable was supposedly onion? Çelebi wants to construct a story to show the importance of dogs in the life of Yezidis, because he also believed that dogs were important figures at the Battle of Karbala. This may have stemmed from the same volume; there is a section about the dogs of Kerbela Der-beyan-1 kelb-1 Kerbela. Çelebi says the dogs of the Caliph (Yezid ibn Muawiya) drank the blood of martyrs on the battlefield.[33] It seems that one of Çelebi's goals is to use the figure of the dog, and the connection between Yezidis and dogs at the Battle of Karbala, to highlight what he considered to be the unusual and vulgar habits of Yezidis.

Çelebi tells another interesting story about Yezidi Daseni (Dasni) leader. He says, "Most of these devils keep war tools at their houses from the Martyrs on the Plain of Karbala and they proudly tell each other, 'Our ancestors killed that many Hussain supporters.'"[34] Çelebi uses the term *Şehidan-ı Deşt-i Kerbela* ("The Martyrs on the Plain of Karbala") throughout *Seyahatname*, but he only focuses on Yezidis as being responsible for the murder and deserving revenge. I have not encountered any other groups who paid a price for the Battle of Karbala in *Seyahatname*. As mentioned, it is unclear how Evliya Çelebi collected information about Yezidis. He probably witnessed some vicious actions against Yezidis on Mountain Sinjar when he was with Melek Ahmed Pasha. Çelebi also spent considerable time with Kurdish local rulers. He mentions Yezidis in his conversations with these rulers. Çelebi states that he traveled for eleven years in Kurdistan[35] and he shares a story of when he encountered a group of Yezidis from the village of Karabaş. He recounts how Yezidis attacked his group near Çöldepe, on their way to Van from Diyarbekir. During the fight, Çelebi's group killed a few Yezidis and chased the others to their village.[36] Overall, these various anecdotes suggest that Çelebi witnessed a few incidents firsthand even if he mostly relied on stories he heard or read about Yezidis.

Çelebi's favorite Kurdish group was the Shafi'i Sunni Kurds because they fought with the Ottomans against the Safavids and they built their own symbols of Islam, mosques and madrasas. However, Yezidi villages did not have any of these religious structures.[37] Çelebi does not say anything about the architectural structure of Yezidi temples in the Sinjar region. Çelebi only describes Yezidis as living in the mountains and far from civilization without buildings or any other symbols of "civilization." According to him, Yezidis traveling to cities would not be welcomed by others and could be killed. For example, the people of Cizir did not give corn to Yezidis and they refused to allow them into the city.[38] Çelebi provides another example: "Imadiyye [Amedi] people killed Yezidis when they see them in the city because Yezidis worshiping dogs and Imadiyye people are pure followers of the Shafi'i madhab."[39] In another similar example about Sunni Kurds of Vestan, he says there were not any Yezidis among the Vestanis and if they were to see them, they would kill them as soon as possible.[40]

Çelebi's hostility against Yezidis is also reflected in his views of their language. He provides examples of language and literary works of different groups from different parts of the empire including commentaries on different Kurdish dialects and literary samples in Kurdish. For example, he includes a poem by Monla-yı âlim Ramazân-ı Abbasiyân or Ramazân Kürdikî.[41] By doing so, Çelebi comes up with a new barrier tool, language, to separate Yezidis from other Kurdish groups and civic life. Çelebi says none of the Kurds can understand the language of the Bapirisi [Yezidis] on Mountain Sinjar[42] or the language of the Haliti Yezidi. Moreover, he claims twenty-four groups of Kurds cannot understand the language of the Haliti Yezidi.[43] Even if Yezidis come down from their mountains to the city area, they will not be understood even by their own people and neighbors. They cannot interact with other communities and be integrated into civic life.

As mentioned above, onions and dogs are common elements of Çelebi's story. He uses these two elements all the time to show the strange way of life of Yezidis. It seems that Çelebi deliberately uses stories of dogs and onions to construct his view of Yezidis as devil worshipers, impure, "uncivilized," not able to be understood, and engaging in an odd way of life while constructing a peculiar historical narrative. According to this narrative, Yezidis were assembled by Yezid ibn Muawiya from

Kurdistan, Sinjar, and other places; they killed Hussain and his followers at the Battle of Karbala; the dogs of Yezidi ibn Muawiya drank the blood of Hussein and his companions at Karbala; in Çelebi's day Yezidis treated dogs as holy creatures and wash them with onion juice; they feed their baby with the milk of black dogs,[44] and they still have some items in their homes from the Battle of Karbala of which they are very proud.

He offers different reasons why the Ottomans, the protectors of the realm of Islam, should get rid of Yezidis. From his state-centric, orthodox, and imperial position, Yezidis were disrupting the polity of the empire and weakening the legitimization of the state through attacking and plundering people. Yezidis, who were able to rule their own territory, should be conquered by the army of Islam. From his Sunni Muslim perspective, these "unbelievers" did not have any mosques and did not know anything about the pillars of Islam. Moreover, Yezidis kept great wealth in their region, and a group who worshiped dogs, the devil, and Yezid ibn Muawiya should not possess that much wealth. As coming from one of the global centers, Istanbul, which was one of the hubs of civilization and knowledge, his enmity against Yezidi Kurds reflects his position as a loyal representative of the imperial order.

Seyahatname as an Alternative Source in Yezidi Studies

Seyahatname can be looked at from different perspectives and it can open new avenues for understanding more about Yezidis. First of all, Yezidis can be found in different cities. Based on Evliya Çelebi's account, Yezidis did not only live in the Sinjar area. Rather, Yezidis can be seen in numerous places in the seventeenth century, such as in Bingöl, Bitlis, Van, Hazo, Amedi, Diyarbekir, Hasankeyf, Cizir, and Dühük. They were not a small and insulated marginalized group; they were visible and active in numerous central locations.

Der-beyan-ı futuhat-ı cebel-i Saçlı, ya'nî Sincar, be-dest Melek Ahmed Paşa yı serdar, or "The Story of the Conquest of Mt. Saçlı, That Is Mt. Sinjar, at the Hands of Melek Ahmed Pasha, the Serdar,"[45] in book IV is one of the most popular sections when historians and scholars describe the violence of the Ottoman Empire against Yezidis. It is probable that some of these violent actions were taken against Yezidis, but we should keep in mind who draws the picture. Dankoff warns us about the use of numbers by Çelebi in *Seyahatname*.[46] Çelebi says 3,060 Yezidis were killed on the mountain, which sounds highly inflated. One can imagine that getting the exact number of casualties in this kind of situation would be impossible.

Çelebi's account provides a larger picture for understanding the role and activities of Yezidis in Ottoman Kurdistan. As Nelida Fuccaro describes the situation of Yezidis in the fourteenth and fifteenth centuries, Fuccaro says, "The expansion occurred relatively rapidly: in the 14th century Yazidism became the official religion of the principality of Jazira, a semi-independent political unit ... and in the same period seven of the most powerful tribes of Kurdistan were also Yazidi."[47] Tutku Ayhan also discusses in her chapter, Yezidis were not passive actors in the region. Yezidi leaders occupied important positions in the Ottoman provincial system. "Yezidi Hussein Beg of the Daseni tribe to be governor of Erbil ... Kara Ahmed Pasha appointed the Daseni Mirza Beg governor of Mosul with the rank of pasha."[48] Moreover, the Ottoman rulers gave control of the city of Tikrit, northwest of Baghdad, to the son of Yezidi Hüseyin, Davud Beg, and the city of Kerek to the son of Yezidi Hüseyin Beg, Said Beg, in 1556.[49]

Yezidis were not only active in ruling and fighting; they were active participants in the commerce and river transportation of their region through interactions with other religious and ethnic groups as well.[50] Çelebi says, "The quality of Yezidis' grapes and honey is priceless, and their raisins are high priced in Baghdad, Basra, and Lahsa markets. They have many berry trees. Sinjar has important mineral as well."[51] Yezidis played an important role in commerce in many places. Çelebi highlights that Yezidis collected fees when they took people from Hasankeyf to the other side with their *keleks* (ferries).[52] John Guest also provides information on Yezidi transportation business. He says, "After this time few Yezidis are reported south of the Great Zab, though for over a century they operated the principal ferry across the river at a point appropriately called Kelek."[53]

Yezidis had a sizable population in different cities of the empire, especially in the cities of Kurdistan, and they mostly ruled their own communities. For example, Daseni Beg was one of the Yezidi leaders that Çelebi writes about. The Yezidis were not a marginalized group who lived on a mountain without any sign of civilization. Çelebi claims that when Yezidis go to cities they will be killed by other Muslim groups. However, historical records suggest that Yezidis were active participants in the commerce of their region through interactions with other religious groups.

Figure 6.1 Yezidi shrines on hilltops northeast of the city of Mosul (Nineveh, September 2017)

Yezidis in Local Accounts

A local imam of the city of Van, Ibn-i Nuh's account, *Van Tarihi* (1715/6),[54] is another important text deserving attention to better understand the religious attitudes of Ottomans toward Yezidis, from a local perspective. Ibn-i Nuh devotes a section to why he wanted to write this narrative. He decided to write the history of the city because there have been not many books about the city of Van. His account provides the point of view of a local religious figure regarding Yezidis, when the Ottomans attacked the Yezidi population of Van in 1715. It addresses the Yezidi defeat of the Ottoman army in the first wave of attacks and Yezidis capturing the pasha of the city of Van during the battle.[55] Under the section titled *Harb-i Yezidiyan Der Sahra-yi Canik Ba-Vaniyan* (The Battle of Yezidis with Vanis at the Desert of Canik), Ibn-i Nuh recounts the names of important people who lost their lives in the battle and describes a dreadful situation for Muslims and Islam at the hands of *Cünd-i Şeytan* (the Army of Devil).[56] Ibn-i Nuh refers to the same historical incident as Çelebi, the Battle of Karbala, when describing the victory of Yezidis over the Ottoman army. He articulates the situation of the city in this following way: "This sorrow and calamity in the land of Cânik– this land seems like it became the desert of Karbala."[57]

One of the local *mullas* of the city, Ibn-i Nuh, witnessed the event and narrated how the state reacted to Yezidis under the section *Maktel-i Yezidiyan ve Intikam-ı Şüheda-i Van* (The Killing of Yezidis and the Revenge of the Martyrs of Van).[58] The pasha of the city assembled around 7,000 soldiers from Ahlat, Adilcevaz, and Erçiş to take on the Yezidis. Ibn-i Nuh recounts the incident as a great victory for the empire and Muslims against infidels, troublemakers, and Yezidis. He says, "[T]his place did not pay *cizye* or poll tax so considered to be the Abode of War and some Christians lost their lives and many women and children held as captives."[59]

Unfortunately, Ibn-i Nuh does not provide as many details as Çelebi did, but the similarities and the use of the same language and historical events by different persons can give us some clues related to how Ottoman scholars and elites perceived Yezidis from the capital, as well as at the local level. Having alternative sources from the ground can give us a broader scope of local dynamics. As we can see, Yezidis were spread out in different parts of Ottoman Kurdistan. They had a sizable population in different parts of the empire and Yezidis were powerful enough to make the Ottoman Empire call for help from other cities in order to defeat their insubordination.

Yezidis in the Holy Book of Kurdish History: Sharafnama

Kurdish local rulers played an important role during the ideological and geopolitical rivalry between the Ottoman and Iranian Empires due to dwelling on the borderlands and being able to maneuver between these two entities, as also discussed by Bilici in his chapter. A large part of historical Kurdistan was de facto ruled by local Kurdish rulers until the second half of the nineteenth century. Kurdish intellectuals and leaders contributed to history writing and the circulation of knowledge in the region and produced numerous historical accounts under the patronage of the Ottoman and Safavid rulers.

An important historical chronicle, *Sharafnama*, was written in Persian by Sharaf Khan, the local Kurdish ruler of Bedlis (Bitlis in contemporary Turkey), in 1596–1599. *Sharafnama* provides an important account from a local point of view and demonstrates how a Kurdish leader and intellectual made sense of political dynamics concerning local principalities and empires. Sharaf Khan's depiction of other Kurdish tribes, dynasties, and non-Sunni Kurds (i.e., Yezidis), assists historians in analyzing and understanding the internal dynamics between different Kurdish groups. Sharaf Khan divides Kurds into four branches, Kurmānj کرمانج, Lur لر, Kelhur کلهر, and Gurān گوران. Moreover, one of the earliest specifications of the borders of Kurdistan was made by Sharaf Khan. He identifies the sphere of Kurdistan as the following:

> The realm of Kurdistan on the coast of the Strait of Hormuz which borders on the shores of the Indian Ocean. From thence, it extends forth on the straight line, terminating with the provinces of Malatya and Mara'sh. To the north of this line are the provinces of Fars, Persian Iraq, Azerbaijan, Armenia Minor and Armenia Major. To its southern side lies the Arabian Iraq, Mosul and Diyarbakir.[60]

This work is mainly devoted to highlighting important dynasties, emirates, and families of Kurdistan. Sharaf Khan presented his book to the Ottoman sultan, Mehmed III (r. 1595–1603).[61] Sharaf Khan attempts to reveal details about some important Sunni Muslim Kurdish figures who played an important role in the earlier centuries of the Ottoman Empire, including the teacher of Orhan Gazi (1326–1359), Mawlana Taceddin Kurdî, and the teacher of Sultan Murad (1421–1444), Mewlana Saddeddin.[62] He emphasizes his Sunniness and mentions that he follows the path of the Shafi'i school of law. "They [Kurds] pay homage to the Prophet's grand companions and caliphs, and obey the great *ulema* in their dispensation of the requirements of prayers, alms, pilgrimage to Mecca and fasting with utmost diligence."[63] After these details about Sunni Shafi'i Kurds he reveals substantial information about Yezidis. He describes Yezidis as follows:

> This is excepting a few districts and dependencies of Mosul and Syria, such as the Tasini, Khalidi, and Psiyan, and some of Bokhti Mahmudi and Dunbeli who maintain the doctrine of Yezidism. They are followers of the Shaykh Adi b. Musafir, who was a client of the Marwanid [Umayyad] caliphs and ascribe themselves to him. Their wrongful belief is that Shaykh Adi whose shrine is found the hills of Lalish in Mosul district, has done "for us in his own days the requisite daily prayers and the fasting. Thus, on the Day of Judgment, we

will be taken into paradise without being reproached or questioned." They bear unlimited animosity towards the exoteric ulema.[64]

Sharafnama is an important source to locate Yezidi tribes and population groups in the sixteenth century. Yezidis could be found in many regions. For example, Yezidis were present around the city of Kilis (a city bordering Syria in contemporary Turkey) and around Aleppo.[65] Moreover, Sharaf Khan provides some anecdotes and details about various tribes such as Mahmudi, Dunbuli, and Khalidi. Emphasizing his loyalty to the Ottoman sultan, Sharaf Khan claimed that Yezidi Kurds did not like Muslim *molla*s and scholars.[66] At the same time, he highlights the conversion of Yezidis to Islam in certain passages. For instance, he writes,

> This great ruler [Hasan Beg] and merciful destroyed the temple of Yezidism among the Mahmudi tribe. He obligated the pillars of Islam such as fasting, prayer, pilgrimage, and alms on followers of Sunnah and community. He ordered them to study the Qur'an and other traditions and requirements of Islam. Not only these, he built a mosque and *medrese* in every village.[67]

Similarly, he writes in another passage, "Cezire Emirate was following the sinister and inauspicious religion of Yezidisim but later they met with glory of Islam and Sunnah and they built many mosques and *medreses*."[68] In another anecdote related to Yezidis, he observes, "The members of Dinbili tribes were Yezidi but one of their leaders named Isa Beg with some other families converted to Islam. However, there are some Yezidis who still follow their old religion, Yezidisim."[69]

An important reason for Sharaf Khan's emphasis on conversions of Yezidism could be sought in his own political position. During the time of Sharaf Khan, the Ottoman and Safavid Empires each attempted to obtain the loyalty of Kurds in the frontier zone.[70] The Bedlis Emirate changed sides many times between these two imperial rivals. Sharaf Khan was educated along with the Shah's children.[71] Therefore, when Sharaf Khan decided to change sides, to ally with the Ottoman Empire, he needed to display his loyalty to the sultan. He attempted to show his loyalty through stressing his Sunni identity and his position as a member of an ideal group of Kurds.

Yezidis in Fatwa Writing

Sharafnama refers to an anti-Yezidi fatwa written by a cleric of Kurdistan, Mawlana Muhammad Barqal'i who permits for the looting of Yezidis' properties and taking of married Yezidi women who renounce their community by Sunni Kurds.[72] In fact, a number of other Muslim clerics wrote fatwas targeting Yezidis. The purpose of a fatwa issued by a Muslim cleric could be any of a wide range of ways to clarify an issue when it was requested by ordinary people or even by the sultan when he needed to provide a reason for campaigns or for other purposes. Muhammad Khalid Masud describes fatwa in the following way:

[A]cross time and space two distinct categories of legal interpreters have stood at the meeting points of law and fact. The domain of legal procedure, including adversarial cases, rules of evidence, binding judgements, and state enforcements, belongs to the judge (*qadi*); the issuance of nonbinding advisory opinions (*fatawa*, or *fatwas*) to an individual questioner (*mustafti*), whether in connection with litigation or not, is the separate domain of the jurisconsult (*mufti*).[73]

The text of a fatwa can be just a word, such as yes, no, permissible, or impermissible. Or a fatwa can be a very long answer to a certain question and provide details via examples and information from a variety of Islamic sources.[74]

Some of the salient questions addressed by scholars are the origins of the Yezidi faith and how their belief system was reformulated after the death of the founder and the most important figure of the faith, Sheikh Adi. During the sixteenth century when the Yezidi faith took on some new elements, such as the role of Sheikh Adi, a number of Sunni scholars wrote down their perspectives on the Yezidi faith.

Mustafa Dehqan who discovered different versions of these fatwas[75] brings out a pivotal dynamic about Kurdish religious figures and their perception of Yezidis. Provincial judges played an important role in producing legal and religious texts in the Ottoman Empire and Kurdistan. Mala Salih al-Kurdi al-Hakkari, or the "Mufti of Kurdistan," wrote a fatwa on Yezidis and their religion in the sixteenth century.[76] Al-Hakkari provides details about Yezidis and their faith and explains why their manners and belief system are unlawful and illegitimate. Al-Hakkari states, "[T]hey are pure unbelievers; as it has been stated in religious books in connection with the essence of religion,"[77] and that, as a result, plundering their property is lawful. The following made Yezidis pure unbelievers:

> They deny Koran, and Religious Law, calling them lies, … they express enmity to the *ulema* and harbor rancor against them in the heart. Indeed, if they are victorious over them, they will kill them in a terrible manner, as has happened frequently. If they find Islamic books, they throw them into filth, and even tear them up, and urinate, and defecate on them. And this is a well-known matter which cannot be concealed.[78]

Al-Hakkari reveals some religious principles that were being practiced by Yezidis and explains that they were against Islam because

> they attribute to God such qualities as eating, drinking, sitting, and the like, which are related to the body and they tell stories about God, His Prophet, and Sheikh Adi including the objects which place God and His Prophet lower than Sheikh Adi. They give their Sheikhs access to their wives and (female) relatives, regarding this as a lawful, indeed pious act. They believe that Lalesh [Yezidi sacred site] is superior to the Ka'ba.[79]

The second fatwa that provides valuable information about Yezidis was written by the chief mufti of the Ottoman State, Ahmed ibn of Mustafa Abu al-Suud al-Imadi, better known as Ebussuud Efendi (1490–1574).[80] Ebussuud was a prominent religious figure during the reigns of Sultan Suleiman I (1520–1566) and Sultan Selim II (1566–1574), and he took a very active role during the ideological struggle with Shiite Safavid dynasty ruling Iran. He wrote numerous fatwas against the Safavid Empire and Shiites to justify the sultan's campaigns against them. I use the copy of the fatwa that Sami Said Ahmed used in his book, *The Yazidis and Their Life and Beliefs* (1975). The language of Ebussuud's fatwa seems much sharper and more zealous than al-Hakkari's fatwa. Ebussuud mentions similar actions of Yezidis related to God and Islam such as "mocking the glorious words of God and legal books, interpretations, the traditions, the denial of the judgement day and of the resurrection and the denial of the five pillars of religion."[81] Besides, Ebussuud mentions some other Yezidi activities to justify the killing of their men, capturing and enslaving Yezidi children and women like the other infidels, and having full rights to their virgin girls and wives.[82] Ebussuud Efendi also portrays Yezidis as a group of bandits. He writes, "[T]he reason for their required murder is their brigandage, terrorizing the nation by bloodshed and continuous plundering of possessions and cutting off the highways."[83] Similar to al-Hakkari, Ebussuud uses strong religious language to justify actions against Yezidis and emphasizes that their killing is permissible according to all four Sunni sects. For example, he states, "[T]he reason for their war is all the above-mentioned factors and they are more infidel than the original infidels and their killing is permissible according to the four schools of theology and their war is more correct and retributive than religious worship (obligations)."[84]

These two fatwas have provided important details about how the Yezidi population and their religion were received by the central and provincial muftis of the Ottoman Empire. They show that muftis did not denounce Yezidis only on religious grounds but referred to their perceptions of a group generating insecurity. Al-Hakkari knew much more about Yezidis and their practices in comparison with Ebussuud, but both agreed that plundering Yezidi properties was lawful.

Conclusion

Studies that highlight the relationship of Yezidis and the Ottoman Empire from the point of view of violence and persecution can be found through the use of a few sources without asking critical questions about the positionality of the author, reliability of the source, and context. Evliya Çelebi's *Seyahatname* is an especially important text for understanding how a loyal Sunni Ottoman servant from Istanbul perceived the Yezidi community and how he attempted to reconstruct a framing of Yezidis based on a critical moment in Islamic history, the Battle of Karbala, and denounced them as one of the perpetrators of the massacre.

Seyahatname is also one of the most well-known and used accounts to demonstrate the brutality of the Ottoman Empire against Yezidis. However, Çelebi not only provides details about violence but talks about the relationships between Yezidis and the state and other local groups. Moreover, Yezidis were not a passive and powerless community. The narratives that put Yezidis only in the mountains and far from civilization can be challenged by reading between lines. As stated, it is clear that sizable Yezidi communities could be seen in many areas of Ottoman Kurdistan. Sources like *Van Tarihi*, written by local individuals, reveal new dynamics related to the Yezidi community and their influence. Because of a lack of written sources from Yezidis we are able to see only the views of others about Yezidis. One of the common features of these accounts related to the Yezidi community is the justification of brutal actions and hostile attitudes against Yezidis through the use of religious elements, tales, and presenting Yezidis as an "uncivilized" group. Another reason behind the hostility toward and attacks against the Yezidi community was the wealth of the Yezidis. As we were able to see in different accounts, the question of wealth was an important component of justification in these historical writings. Consistent with what Güneş Murat Tezcür argues in his introduction, examining the history of Yezidis, not only from the perspective of constant violence, but also from a broader perspective and in conjunction with other actors on the ground, can open new avenues to understanding the role of Yezidis in Middle Eastern history and their connections with other communities in Ottoman Kurdistan.

Notes

1   Boyîk (2006); Torî (2000).
2   Allison (2001); Kreyenbroek (1995); Omerkhali (2017).
3   *Imam* is the person who leads prayers; *Hatip* is a preacher.
4   Dankoff (2006: 2).
5   Fuccaro (1994b).
6   MacLean (2019).
7   Dankoff (1990).
8   Dankoff (1991).
9   Dankoff (2006).
10   Van Bruinessen (1985: 31).
11   Van Bruinessen and Boeschoten (1988).
12   Van Bruinessen (2000).
13   Dankoff (1991: 15).
14   Ibid.
15   Evliya Çelebi Vol. 6 (2002: 82).
16   Evliya Çelebi Vol. 2 (1999: 146).
17   Ibid., 146.
18   Ibid.
19   Evliya Çelebi Vol. 4 (2001: 47).
20   Evliya Çelebi Vol. 3 (2001: 55).

21 Evliya Çelebi Vol. 4 (2001: 51).

22 Demirel (1991: 115).

23 Hyder (2006: 22).

24 Evliya Çelebi Vol. 4 (2001: 49). "İnşâallah bu Yezîdî mel'ûnlarından şehîdân-ı Deşt-i Kerbela'nın ve Hazreti Hüseyin'ın kanın alırız."

25 I am using this English part from Dankoff (1991: 170). "Cümlesi Abaza ve Çerkes ve Gürcî şehbâzları idi. Birbirlerinden hicâb edüp cengde asla zimâm-keşîdelik etmezler idi ve nâmûs-ı Muhammedî ne idüğün bilürler idi. Cümlesi derûn-ı dilden ve cân-ı gönülden cebel-i Saçlı'ya sarılup inşaallah bu Yezîdî mel'ûnlarından şehîdân-ı Deşt-ı Kerbela'nın ve Hazret-i Hüseyn'in kanın alırız."

26 Evliya Çelebi Vol. 6 (2002: 82). "Sincar dağının Yezîdî Kürdlerine bir sâtûr-ı Muhammedî urup on üç bin Saçlı Yezîdî Kürdleri katl olup şehîdân-ı Deşt-i Kerbela'nın intikâmların aldı."

27 Ibid., 50–1.

28 Dankoff (1991: 173).

29 Ibid., 172.

30 Ibid., 173.

31 Evliya Çelebi Vol. 4 (2001: 270). "Hemân Yezîd-i bî-mezîd Şâm diyârından ve Şâm-ı Tarablus dârlarından niçe bin kavm-i Dürzî ve Tımânî, Yezîdî, Hubârî ve aklı ve kızıllı Mervânî ve Hurûfî ve Nusayrî ve Türbedî ve Püsanî ve Zeydânî ve Zibânî ve Şehbâzî ve Kelbânî kavimlerin başına cem' etdi. Kürdistân'dan ve Sincârî ve Haltî ve Çekvânî ve Celüvî ve Bapırı ve Zıbarı ve kavm-I Dasni ve Cerdefilî ve'l-hâsıl yüz bin mikdârı Yezîdî asker cem' edüp Ubeydullah b. Ziyâd b. Ömer nâm abdullahı serdâr edüp Şâm'dan İrâk üzre gitmede."

32 Ibid., 51.

33 Ibid., 269.

34 Evliya Çelebi Vol. 5 (2001: 3). "Ve niçe yüz mel'ûnların hânelerinde mahfûz şehîdân-ı deşt-i Kerbela'nın esbâbları ve âlet-i silâhları vardır kim birbirlerinin mâbeynlerinde 'Atamız şu kadar Hüseynî katl etmişdir' deyü tefâhur kesb ederler."

35 Ibid., 314–15. "Hulusa-i kelam bu diyar-i Kürdistan 'da on bir sene seyhata edüp bu medrese-i Kophan gibi bî-misal görmedim."

36 Ibid., 330.

37 Ibid., 50.

38 Ibid., 325.

39 Ibid., 315.

40 Ibid., 306.

41 Ibid., 316–17.

42 Ibid., 316.

43 Ibid.

44 Ibid., 51.

45 Dankoff (1991: 167).

46 Dankoff (2006: 155–6).

47 Fuccaro (1999b: 10).

48 Guest (1987: 46–7).

49 Devlet Arşivleri Başkanlığı (Directorate of State Archives of the Republic of Turkey), March 10, 1556.

50 Bayatlı (1999).

51 Evliya Çelebi Vol. 4 (2001: 52).

52 Ibid., 327.

53 Guest (1987: 56–7).
54 Ibn-i Nuh (2003).
55 Ibid., 88.
56 Ibid., 87–91.
57 Ibid., 89. "Cânik'in düzünde bu kerb ve bela Oldu sahrâ sanki deşt-i Kerbela."
58 Ibid., 112.
59 Ibid., 113–14.
60 Bedlisi (2005: 33–4).
61 Ibid., 8.
62 Ibid., 42–4.
63 Ibid., 36.
64 Ibid., 36–8.
65 Bedlîsî (2014: 267).
66 Ibid., 63.
67 Ibid., 353.
68 Ibid., 161.
69 Ibid., 357.
70 Dehqan and Genç (2018).
71 Alsancaklı (2017b).
72 Sharaf Khan (1597: 9). MS. Elliott 332 at the Bodleian Libraries at the University of Oxford. I would like to thank Sacha Alsancakli for sharing this copy with me and Haidar Kherzi for his assistance with the translation. Alsancakli (2018: 172) writes that this copy could be the original manuscript.
73 Masud, Messick, and Powers (2005: 3).
74 Imber (1997: 80).
75 Dehqan (2008; 2015).
76 Dehqan (2008: 140).
77 Ibid., 149.
78 Ibid., 144–5.
79 Ibid., 146–7.
80 Ahmed (1975: 60). The fatwa was originally mentioned in al-Damaloji (1949).
81 Ibid., 386.
82 Ibid., 387.
83 Ibid., 386.
84 Ibid.

ORIENTALIST VIEWS OF KURDS AND KURDISTAN

Zeynep N. Kaya

Introduction

This chapter explores the Western perceptions of Kurdistan and Kurdish political agency in the late nineteenth and early twentieth centuries. These perceptions had an important impact on Kurdish political elite's pursuit of national legitimacy in this period and continue to remain to have an influence on Kurdish politics today. This chapter seeks to answer a number of questions: What were the underpinning ideas behind the orientalist and Western perceptions of the Kurds in the late nineteenth and early twentieth centuries? How did these influence Kurdish political elite's engagement with international actors and the Ottoman Empire? How did this engagement shape Kurdish political movements and their pursuit of political legitimacy? In addressing these questions, the chapter connects Western imperial powers' activities in the Ottoman territories with the construction of Kurdish national identity and the development of Kurdish politics since then. It shows that ethnographic maps of the region produced by Western geographers were adopted and used by Kurdish nationalists in the early twentieth century and onward and became key sources for mapping Kurdistan.

Orientalist perceptions of non-Western peoples had strong perennialist and civilizationist lenses. These perceptions were informed by the studies and observations of Western geographers, military officers, economic entrepreneurs, and missionary agents during their travels and engagements in non-Western territories. Eastern territories of the Ottoman Empire, especially eastern Anatolia and Mesopotamia, became a focus area for Western imperial states in the late nineteenth century. This was partly because of economic and political reasons, such as trade routes and increased Russian influence in the area, as well as the presence of Christian populations. The geographical and ethnographic studies undertaken by European travelers and how they informed imperialist powers' policies in the period leading up to, during and after the First World War, significantly influenced most of the territorial demarcations in the Middle East and the political fate of the Kurds. Even so, the resultant political and territorial settlement was also shaped by the strategic, economic, and political interests of the imperial powers and the rivalries between them.

This chapter focuses on the orientalist conceptions of the national identity of the non-Western peoples, the peoples of the Ottoman Empire in this case. Western travelers' and states' perceptions of nationality informed the construction of a retrospective view on Kurdish national identity and territoriality today. Western conception of national identity was based on views that for a community to be considered as a nation, it needs to have a certain level of development, unified political leadership, and a sense of shared identity and interest. However, Kurds were seen as a tribalistic, divided, and underdeveloped society. As discussed by Ekrem Karakoç and Ege Özen, such views exhibit uncanny resemblances to the Turkish views of the Kurds in the early twenty-first century.

Interestingly, the European ethnographic studies and cartographic depictions of the people of the region, including the Kurds, significantly informed the territorial conceptions of Kurdish national identity and the ways through which they constructed the Kurdish homeland. Indeed, European imperialism laid the groundwork for the world today and in this historical process geography played a significant role as "none of us is outside or beyond geography."[1] Cartography had huge power in the nineteenth and early twentieth centuries because it allowed for "achieving ideological supremacy over space."[2] Mapping reflects the wider ideological and political discourses and is the outcome of communication between cartographers, the goals of their study, the political offices, and wider society.[3] Neither territory nor its cartographic depictions can be taken for granted as static and ahistorical things. Maps are components of a "visual language" that communicates strategic interests and ideologies.[4] Even when the aim for the production of a map is not propaganda, maps reflect unconscious biases and assumptions situated in the particular values, ideologies, political interests of the producer, and the institutions and history they are situated in.[5] It is neither possible to escape geography nor the political and economic values and interests that shape its depictions and imaginations.

European Context That Affected Western States' View of Non-Western Peoples

Dominant political ideologies and the conceptions of development and political legitimacy in Europe in the nineteenth century framed European actors' perceptions of the Ottoman Empire and its peoples. Therefore, it is important to provide background for this historical European context and for the key political ideas that shaped this context.

Nineteenth- and early twentieth-century Europe is characterized by increased centralization of political and economic power and decision-making under militaristic nation-states. It also cultivated a form of imperialism that was driven by rivalry between these powerful states in most of the rest of the world.[6] In this world, nationalism was one of the most significant political forces and ideologies.[7]

In the late eighteenth century, the British colonies in North America rejected the monarchical authority of the British Empire and declared American independence based on the notion of national sovereignty. Similarly, in Europe, the French Revolution was based on the ideas of nationhood, republicanism, and liberty. Both revolutions saw the republican nation as the only legitimate form of political order to realize this latter goal of liberty.

Nationalism provided the collective ideology and legitimacy for the state to undertake the endeavor to accomplish individual freedom through institutional arrangements. Nationalists envisioned the possibility of a community bound together through common memories; therefore they saw nationalism as a benign force. In this context, the ideal of a nation and nation-state was perceived to be imbued with certain values such as liberalism, capitalism, democratic institutions, and popular sovereignty. In this model, the state could ensure a harmonious society and was seen as progressive if it embraced popular citizenship instead of imperial rule.[8] Collective governance, or democracy organized on national lines, defined as "the institutional arrangement for arriving at political decisions in which individuals acquire the power to decide by means of a competitive struggle for the people's vote"[9] emerged as the dominant form of governance over time.

Democracy and nationalism complement each other because nationalist groups or movements seeking self-determination see this goal as a democratic collective right.[10] By definition, the democratic enterprise has always been based on a defined group of people. As a result, constructing and defining a distinct nation came to be seen as a prerequisite for the formation of a democratic state. In turn, determining who belongs to "us" and who should form the nation is seen as a prerequisite for this democratic endeavor. Building a state based on a claimed distinct identity is perceived as a rational route due to the belief that it brings solutions to political problems. It also provides suitable political and social circumstances for the advancement of better governance and development. Yet history showed that the act to determine who belongs to the nation has also resulted in dictatorial or violent forms of nationalism utilizing suppressive and nondemocratic methods.[11]

A key outcome of this form of thinking in the nineteenth-century Europe was the emergence of self-determination, defined as the "nationality principle" or "self-governance" at the time. Self-determination has become one of the most crucial international norms in relation to nationalist claims to justify separation from empires in the nineteenth century, gaining independence through decolonization in the nineteenth and twentieth centuries, and in shaping borders during the dismemberment of communist states at the end of the Cold War, as well as secessionist, irredentist, or autonomist demands in other contexts.[12] Self-determination as a concept is widely discussed in the literature, and one thing that is agreed upon is the difficulty in defining this concept whether it is defined as a legal or political term. As a *principle* of international law, it is generally understood in a way that prioritizes the stability of the international system and protects the sovereignty of states. Alternatively, it is interpreted as a *political goal* to achieve the rights of people to determine their political future, as a people of a state or in the form of autonomy or secession. Nationalist groups and their supporters (lobby groups, diasporas, states or international organizations) are proponents of this meaning of self-determination. Lastly, self-determination as an *idea*, as an analytical concept, is utilized in the scholarly work on nations and nationalism to understand state formation, nation building, ethnic conflict, nationalist political movements, and other related issues.

In the nineteenth century, a civilizational interpretation of the "nationality principle" was dominant. This view was dominated by the Western orientalist thinking of the time and argued that not all peoples are ready for self-governance. Only when they reach a required level of civilizational development should the nationality principle apply to a people.[13] By the end of the nineteenth century, the idea of a national identity had become a common sensical idea and nationality principle became a principle used in liberation movements against the imperial powers, notably the Habsburgs and the Ottomans, and establishing a new state. It was believed that when an independence movement achieves separation, it would be deemed a nation and would be able to establish its popular sovereignty over a defined territory and thus realize the ideal of popular national sovereignty.[14] Especially after the First World War, nationalist ideology and self-determination became directly linked to popular sovereignty.[15]

Key characteristics of the logic of the state in nineteenth-century Europe were industrial capitalism/development and centralization, which coincided with the emerging nationalism in place of feudal and monarchical affiliations. This led to the perception that industrial development and nationalism go hand in hand, and a centralized economy, education system, military, police, and bureaucracy were seen as the outcomes or products of the consolidation of national integration. The reverse is also possible; nationalism could be considered as the outcome of these centralizing forces.[16] As a result of the coincidence of industrial capitalism, development, and nationalism, the ideas of development and civilization became associated with the nation, and its distinct identity, territory, culture, language, and values. In this context, racial and ethnic groups that appeared to constitute the majority in a particular society were perceived to overlap with such processes. If this perceived overlap was present, a nationalist movement was seen to be a legitimate force or an entity to be taken seriously. Envisioning a national ideal and its "essence" as a universal phenomenon (as autonomous, ahistorical, and natural) has become an integral component of explaining state-building processes or attempts to form a state in the nineteenth century. The success of the German and Italian unifications and the maturing of the British and French (and American) nationalisms legitimized and popularized the idea that the nation-state is the progressive and universal political unit.

What is important is that the conception of nationhood and statehood in nineteenth-century Europe and its overlap with development and industrial capitalism generated the lenses through which European colonial forces imagined the political future of non-European territories. They assumed that the consolidation of nation-states around specific identities within well-defined territories under a clear national leadership was an appropriate model for these areas as well. National communities were thought as entities with common identity traits and with a historical attachment to a defined territory and shared culture. This understanding of the nation was accompanied by the belief that nationalism and the nation-state are natural and progressive.[17] If such a people exist and if they have a nationalist leadership espousing these ideas, then they were seen to deserve being categorized as a national liberation movement. The lack of apparent shared identity or a nationalist leadership among a community or people was considered as indicators of backwardness. This rendered, in the orientalist perspective, these people as unable to govern themselves. European state officials, travelers, traders, and geographers often wrongly "projected upon local parochial communities the belief that national concerns not local issues should be at the forefront of local consciousness" and where that appeared to be missing, they were considered as being unready for national attainment.[18]

Western Imaginations of Ethnic Geographies in the Ottoman Empire and the Kurds[19]

European officers' and travelers' studies and observations about the peoples of the eastern territories of the Ottoman Empire, including the Kurds, had an impact on the way Western policies were developed toward the empire and its people during and after the world war. These views were both praising and critical of the Kurdish political elite and Kurdish society based on tribal structures. This highly biased view was an important factor in forming the perception that Kurds are not ready to attain statehood. For instance, the studies undertaken by British colonial officers and travelers visiting eastern territories of the Ottoman Empire, including writers, anthropologists, linguists, and geographers, saw the areas they explored and visited from this perspective, such as Mark Sykes' "The Kurdish Tribes of the Ottoman Empire" (1908), Francis Maunsell's "Kurdistan" (1894), and Fredrick Millingen's *Wild Life among the Koords* (1870). For instance, Millingen extensively discussed the role of tribal feuds and intertribal war and pointed to the primitive culture of the Kurds. Both Maunsell and Sykes reported on the intertribal fighting among Kurds, especially those that formed the Hamidiye regiments, and the negative impacts of this had on security in the region.[20] These writers also talked about the Hamidiye cavalry's oppression of the Armenians. For instance, Maunsell wrote that Kurds were bigoted and constantly quarreled with Christians.[21]

The European explorers' and travelers' explorations, activities, and studies in non-European territories in the nineteenth century informed the way their states exerted power to reshape the political division of the Middle East in the early twentieth century. Orientalist constructions of geography were shaped and informed by political and cultural values in the European context, as explained in the previous section, the interests of the states, and the different sources of information, including local informants and intercommunal perceptions on the ground. Such information and perceptions influenced the Western travelers' biases.

The Western Idea of a Territorially Contained Peoples

This section elaborates on the imaginations of ethnic territories by Western actors in their attempts to chart and map the East and its peoples and generate new political boundaries during and after the dissolution of the Ottoman Empire. The underpinning ideas and views behind the Western geographic study and mapping of non-Western territories and peoples in this period shaped the resultant imaginations. The Western perspective projected an understanding of the nation (as experienced, or thought to be experienced, in Europe) on rebel groups and the groups with distinct cultures and customs. In addition to this, accompanying the orientalist and colonial views on national identity and territoriality was the idea that the ability to form national unity around a specific identity and on a demarcated territory required a certain level of civilizational attainment, as explained in the previous section.

The relationship between mapping and the construction of a nation or a people has changed over history. This relationship in each period is framed by global and regional power configurations and ideas about the world pertaining to that historical period. Processes and structures of a particular long-term historical period, and the international order it generates, frame the assumptions, ideologies, perceptions, and interests that underlie territorial imaginations. Moreover, political and ideological discourses at international, regional, and local levels provide the supporting context for the production of geographical knowledge.[22] This means, the meaning of the territorial state (political entity) also differs in different international orders in which states can have distinct economic structures and different interstate dynamics.

Agnew identifies three such international orders in recent world history: 1815–1875, 1875–1945, and 1945–1990. The first and part of the second period are particularly relevant for this chapter.[23] In the 1815–1875 international order, according to Agnew, European states reached a period of balance of power in their relationship. The Concert of Europe that emerged after the Napoleonic wars and nationalism came to be seen as the most apt legitimizing ideology for states and as an indicator of more superior systems and values of the Western world vis-à-vis others. Agnew's second international order from 1875 to 1945 was one of intensified rivalry between imperialist powers over control of and access to areas, trade routes, and resources.[24] In both these periods, an orientalist view of the non-Western world and ideas of civilization and underdevelopment shaped the perspective of the European travelers and their states and informed perceptions about the peoples of the region and its mapping and study.

Looking at what was happening in the first period (1815–1875) in the eastern territories of the Ottoman Empire, we see that Western states, Italian, German and French travelers, missionaries, and states were already active, including in the areas where Kurdish communities resided alongside other communities. Britain's colonial power was on the rise and, as the century progressed, the British became increasingly more involved in the Middle East. European travelers were particularly interested in the fate of Christian populations. In the second period, especially until the end of the First World War, European explorations were made mainly for strategic purposes to promote and protect state interest against other European states' interests in the region. In this era, European powers were heavily involved in the demarcation of the territories of the new states and in identifying the specific colonial power's position and role in the governance of the new territory.[25]

The sociological thinking in the nineteenth century in Europe, as explained in the previous section, further reinforced the idea of a political territorial state.[26] Social science and geographers in the nineteenth and early twentieth century contributed to the study of "state-centred political geographies," which reinforced the idea that "the modern nation-state is natural and progressive."[27] Nationalism or national identity, in this period, was believed to have an essence, an origin, which the nationalist intelligentsia tried to revive—an idea contemporary perennialist and ethno-symbolist approaches in the nationalism studies have explained.[28] In nineteenth-century Europe, three geographical assumptions were crystallized: (1) state territories became fixed units of sovereign space, (2) binary divisions set in such as national/international or domestic/foreign, and (3) the state came to be seen as a prior to and a container of society.[29] Enabled by these assumptions, a link between spatially demarcated territories and state sovereignty led to the "territorial trap," and the fragmentation of the world into territorial states served as a justification for this trap.[30] The idea of the territorial state as the container of society became "common sensical" and was reproduced. Popular sovereignty over an inhabited territory created a people-territory relationship in which territory began to define the people.[31]

This ideal state unit was filled with values that represented progress, liberalism, development, and civilization. These values and ideals underpinned the colonial powers' perceptions of the other, their engagement with non-European contexts, and the way they interpreted their findings and information they gathered through their explorations and studies. Peoples that do not appear to be progressive, liberal, or civilized were deemed not ready to attain the status of nationhood and establish a state of their own. These values informed Western states' and their agents' visualization of the future of the Middle East and the Kurds in line with their strategic interests and the configurations shaped by the heightened imperial rivalry both leading up to and after the First World War.

The orientalist geographic studies and interpretations of this period were complex and multidimensional. The European philosophical thinking and perspectives on the ideal and most progressive form of governance and the political unit were integral to colonial geographical studies and map-making. Western cartography presented Europe as civilized and powerful, at the center of the earth, while the rest of the world was presented as uncivilized and weak. For instance, in the seventeenth- and eighteenth-century maps, Europe was put in a central and dominant position and it was even sometimes decorated into the physical shape of a queen stretching Europe's tentacles around the globe with the world submitting to it.[32] The European self-image presented in these maps, imbued with symbols, writings, and drawings of peoples, depicted Europe as "powerful, civilised, clothed, and cultured; the rest of the world [as] subdued, exotic, savage, half-naked and primitive."[33] This kind of iconography became less prominent in nineteenth-century maps. This was due to the switch to more "scientific"-looking maps and advancement in mapping techniques.[34] Despite the changes in mapping techniques, the orientalist view exemplified by such iconographies that informed earlier maps continued to exist in the studies of colonialist officers and travelers.

In the colonial era, European powers and their agents were heavily interested in objectifying, classifying, and charting/mapping.[35] Colonial explorers, officers, engineers, geographers, and anthropologists were driven to create rational and universal knowledge about the world. Therefore, map-making and geographic work even for purely exploratory and economic reasons tried to identify unifying or dominant identity markers such as language, customs, religion in their study of the peoples in the Middle East in Ottoman and Iranian imperial territories. They usually depicted the non-Western as underdeveloped, uncivilized, tribal and primitive, therefore, undeserving of national self-determination, which in their thinking justified colonization. When it comes to the Middle East, such perspectives were especially targeted at non-Christian communities. For instance, the Christian communities in these territories, such as Armenians, Assyrians, Nestorians, were depicted as less backward and with less degrading language. With regard to the Kurds, some travelers described Kurds more favorably compared to Arabs and Turkmans and blamed the underdeveloped and uncivilized life among the Kurds on their Ottoman and Persian rulers.[36] Others described Kurds as uncivilized and argued the Ottoman and Persian rulers have not managed to change them. They were also portrayed to be inferior to Christians in terms of intellect and to have savage characteristics.[37]

Kurds and Kurdistan in the Eyes of Western Travelers

European travelers and writers visited the Kurdish populated region as state agents, army officers, scientists, researchers, or journalists in the eighteenth, nineteenth, and early twentieth century, and they created numerous definitions and cartographic depictions of Kurdistan. They were interested in Kurdistan for several reasons and these reasons influenced their findings and the way they conducted research. Initially the Western interest in the region was for economic and religious purposes. Kurdistan is located on important communication and trade routes; therefore they produced a number of writings, reports, and maps for economic purposes, which included references to and observations about the Kurds and Kurdistan.

Italian merchants were among the earliest travelers to Kurdistan and they were interested in the trade routes going through the area and the region's economic potential. They wrote the oldest European accounts, including the first Kurdish grammar book and dictionary in 1789, and produced several other writings on the political structures and geographical location and features.[38] German travelers also had been writing about Kurdistan since the eighteenth century based on their study of the region and its features, particularly the transport routes. German engagement was further facilitated by its close relationship with the Ottoman Empire from the mid-nineteenth century onward.[39] Germans invested a big share of funding for the Baghdad Railway Project, whose construction, started in 1903, envisioned to go through Kurdistan. The British were also interested in trade and economic benefits initially; for instance, the East India Company was very active in the region. Similarly, the French were engaged in economic activities and had extensive economic links with the Ottoman Empire. The French had built railway lines in Ottoman territory[40] and had a 40 percent share in the Baghdad Railway Project. Russians produced the earliest accounts of the trade routes in the region.[41]

Western states, particularly Italy, France, and the United States, and later the British, were also heavily engaged in missionary activities in the eastern territories of the Ottoman Empire. They were particularly focused on the Christian communities. American missionaries, active in Kurdistan since the early nineteenth century, published several studies and reports on the Kurds. Italian and French Catholic missionaries carried out activities in the region, especially in the Mosul Province of the Ottoman Empire, and members of these missions wrote about different aspects of the Kurdish way of life, religion, and geography.[42] The missionaries' close focus on local Christians influenced their and other Westerner perspectives of Kurds and Muslims. It also played a role in the deterioration of intercommunal relations in the region. Westerners distinguished between local Christians and Muslims and perceived the former being more "civilised," while still maintaining a more pejorative view of all the locals in these territories, including Christians. The Russian and the French devoted particular attention to the Armenians in the late nineteenth and early twentieth century, which added to the tension in communal relations between Kurds and Armenians.[43] In turn, as discussed by Ohannes Kılıçdağı in his chapter in this volume, Armenian intellectuals perceived Kurds as "uncivilized" but argued that it was in the best interest of the Armenian community to help Kurds achieve a higher level of development.

The maps and reports the Europeans produced mainly relied on their studies and observations, but it is likely that they came across earlier descriptions of Kurdistan by Muslim historians and travelers such as Sharaf Khan, Evliya Çelebi, and Koyî. For instance, Rawlinson, a traveler and military officer, who visited the area's northern Mesopotamia and the Zagros mountains, read the *Sharafnama* (1596) written by the ruler of the Ottoman Emirate of Bitlis.[44] Yet there was limited writing and cartographic work on Kurdistan produced by local researchers in the nineteenth and early twentieth century. Therefore, it is safe to say that Europeans' cartographic study of the area and its people mainly relied on their orientalist point of view and colonial epistemologies and methodologies of geography. Such a perspective projected and interpreted information gathered through a colonial perspective, essentializing what is studied. For instance, European travelers and writers adopted the myth that Kurds were the descendants of the Medes despite the lack of historical evidence indicating such a lineage.[45]

In the second half of the nineteenth century and early twentieth century, the European states became even more interested in these areas due to intensified imperial rivalry. Therefore, their strategic interests played a significant role in their interpretations of the local context. Each imperial state wanted to gain political and economic supremacy in the region. Particularly the Baghdad Railway project increased the importance of the area and escalated imperial rivalry as each power wanted to enjoy the highest benefit from this new transport and communication route.[46] Russians further expanded their interests in Caucasia and its south due to increasing involvement by other European powers in the area. These Western powers as well as Ottoman and Iranian powers considered this a threat.[47] The imperial rivalries in the region shaped the future of most of the region, which in the long term led to the frustration of the Kurdish nationalist desire for statehood after the First World War.

European travelers produced several maps of the region, including maps depicting Kurdistan. One of the first maps produced by a Western traveler was that by English traveler Claudius Rich who visited the Middle Eastern territories of Ottoman and Iranian Empires in the first two decades of the nineteenth century.[48] The Germans in 1854 later produced an ethnographic map of Armenia, Azerbaijan, and Kurdistan, which illustrated trade routes.[49] Karstov, a Russian military officer, produced a map of Kurdish tribes in 1896 (O'Shea 2004: 112). The first map that specifically focused on Kurdistan was produced by Maunsell, a British military officer, after his travels in the region in 1892. The map provided detailed information on the geography of Kurdistan, Kurdish habitation, and habitation by other communities.[50] The British government used Maunsell's projections of the ethnographic composition of the area when strategic plans about the region were being made in the period before the First World War. The British Foreign Office's ethnographic map of the area, produced in 1919 (but relying on data from prior to the First World War), reflected the Foreign Office's position on the territorial extent of Armenian habitation. O'Shea states that this was because at the end of the war, the Allied forces wanted to weaken Ottoman territorial claims in eastern Anatolia and therefore produced a map that indicated large Christian habitation in the region.[51]

The colonial and imperial powers also took a direct role to influence boundary drawing in the eastern territories of the Ottoman Empire as early as the mid-nineteenth century. The boundary between the Ottomans and Persians was set in 1639 with the Zuhab Treaty and demarcated a wide border area (about 100 kilometers), in which several Kurdish tribes were located. The demarcation of this border between Turkey and Iran was not finalized until the 1910s.[52] This location provided the Kurds some degree of autonomy and they were able to change alliances between the two empires as it fit them. This location made the Kurds and other communities living in this zone vulnerable because they were easily manipulated by external imperial powers and their specific interests. The maps produced in this period played an important role in the drawing of boundaries before and after the First World War, including Maunsell's maps.[53]

The studies and explorations undertaken in Kurdistan and the reports and outputs produced by European travelers and their governments' officials in the nineteenth and early twentieth centuries were used to formulate European states' policy with regard to the Kurds before, during, and after the First World War. Ironically, the cartographic information on the Kurds and anthropological studies on their distinct features also constituted the foundation of Kurdish nationalist cartography and historiography later in the twentieth century. Kurdish nationalists replicated these maps or improvised on them to imagine the Kurdish homeland and its extent. Maunsell and other travelers' maps became widely accepted and used by Kurdish nationalists, who improvised on them and produced their own maps in the early twentieth century and later.[54]

For instance, Sherif Pasha's map included in the memorandum demanding Kurdish self-determination in 1919 at the Paris Peace Conference was constructed based on the maps produced by Western travelers, British and German armies, and entrepreneurs in the region.[55] The conference hosted many delegations representing different peoples and groups; however, not all these delegations were given official hearings, including the Kurdish delegation. Sherif Pasha,[56] an Ottoman diplomat in Paris, acted as the Kurdish representative to the British ambassador in Paris and as the head of the Kurdish Delegation to the Conference. The pasha prepared a Memorandum on the Claims of the Kurd People (Kurdish Memorandum) that included a map of Kurdistan that he produced. At the conference, maps were widely used by multiple different delegations as tools to persuade others of the existence of territorially identifiable peoples that should be considered as nations around the world[57] and the Kurdish representation was no exception to this. Sherif Pasha's memorandum demanded a free Kurdish state and its main goal was to show the soundness of Kurdish demands against Armenian claims. It argued that the districts claimed by the Armenians were actually within the boundaries of Turkish Kurdistan and stated that if contested districts were to be included in the new Armenia, disorder and irregular warfare would be inevitable.[58] It defined the ethnographic frontiers of Turkish Kurdistan as follows:

> in the North at Ziven, on the Caucasian frontier, and continue westwards to Erzéroum, Erzindjan, Kémah, Arabkir, Benismi, and Divick; in the South they follow the line from Haran, the Sindjihar Hills, Tel Asfar, Erbil. Kerkuk, Suléimanié, Akk-el-man, Sinna; in the East, Ravandiz, Bash-Kalé, Vizir-Kalé, that is to say the frontier of Persia as far as Mount Ararat.[59]

However, Sherif Pasha was not considered representative of the Kurds by the European powers and, despite pasha's efforts, eventually it was not taken seriously by the British.[60] The pasha was neither chosen nor supported by powerful local Kurdish leaders either and came to be seen as disconnected from the Kurdish masses and Kurdish leaders in Istanbul. The conference received a series of telegrams from Kurdish chieftains stating that they did not recognize Sherif Pasha as a legitimate representative and protested against his map of Kurdistan. Emin Ali Bedirxan, one of the leaders of the Society for the Advancement of the Kurds in Istanbul, vehemently opposed to pasha's plans, especially the extent of Kurdistan on his map.[61] Sherif Pasha's map left the Lake Van area, which was considered as the heart of the Armenian homeland, out of his map of Kurdistan. It is said that the pasha also made a secret arrangement with the Armenian Delegation for the formation of both Armenia and Kurdistan.[62] Some other Kurdish chieftains also sent telegraphs to the conference to condemn Sherif Pasha's initiative for a Kurdish state and to assert that they did not want separation from the Turks, emphasizing their fraternity instead.[63] The pasha resigned from his position as Kurdish representative in April 1920 and from this point on, the British interacted directly with local leaders.[64]

Post–First World War Settlement and the Kurds

In the early twentieth century and after, Western states continued to engage with the Kurds, to carry out their missions and interests in the region. However, they did not give full support to the idea of Kurdish state. European colonial officers' and travelers' projection of a European understanding of the nation and their perspectives on the peoples of the Ottoman Empire through these lenses contributed to the view that the Kurds did not have the characteristics of a nation and were not seen as a legitimate group to deserve national liberation because of the Kurdish society's "under-developed," tribal, and divided nature. The discussions about the Kurds during the First World War period are clear indicators of such perceptions.

Especially the British, who played a significant role in shaping the political fate of the Kurds in this period, perceived the fragmented and multiple Kurdish voices and rivalries between different leaders as a drawback and an impediment for forming a Kurdish state.[65] Lloyd George, the British prime minister between 1916 and 1922, wrote "no Kurds seemed to represent anything more than his own particular clan."[66] This was seen as a stark contrast to the coherent, stronger, and unified Armenian movement supported by an influential and well-organized Armenian representation.[67] Perceptions about the Kurdish dividedness and unreadiness to form their own state have continued to shape the political discourse about the Kurds until present. The role of the Kurds in the suppression of minorities and treatment of Armenians under Ottoman rule, especially through their involvement in the Hamidiye Cavalry under the Abdülhamid II's reign, also tainted the perceptions of Western actors toward the Kurds and weakened the case for a Kurdish state.[68]

During the Paris Peace Conference, it was decided that the Ottoman territories would be divided between the British, French, Italians, and the Greeks. However, these external actors had different expectations and plans for the territories. Rivalries and dynamics within this cohort of countries made it hard to decide the territorial boundaries of potential political entities. Each external actor wanted new political entities to help fulfill their own economic, political, and strategic plans in the region. In the end, European influence over the eastern territories of the Ottoman Empire remained limited even if territories south of these lands, which included the Mosul province with its significant Kurdish population, are divided and put under British and French mandates (later Iraq and Syria respectively).

The provisions of the Treaty of Sèvres pertaining to the Kurds showed that the nineteenth-century views that Kurds were considered as being unready for national attainment were still shaping the thinking of the European powers after the First World War. Signed in August 1920 between the Ottoman Empire and the victorious powers (but not ratified), the treaty set the terms for the partition of the Ottoman territories and its Articles 62–64 dealt with the status of the Kurds. The Kurdish nationalist historiography usually sees the Treaty of Sèvres as a legal guarantee for the establishment of a Kurdish state and argues that if it was implemented a Kurdish state would have been established. However, a closer look at the Sèvres document shows that the guarantee appears far more elusive than assumed. The Article 64 of the treaty makes reference to the capacity of the Kurds to become independent, implying civilizational and national attainment and readiness for forming a state:

> If within one year from the coming into force of the present Treaty the Kurdish peoples within the areas defined in Article 62 shall address themselves to the Council of the League of Nations in such a manner as to show that a majority of the population of these areas desires independence from Turkey, and if the Council then considers that these peoples are capable of such independence and recommends that it should be granted to them, Turkey hereby agrees to execute such a recommendation, and to renounce all rights and title over these areas.

The British had abandoned the idea of creating a Kurdish state during the 1919 Paris Conference, and Sèvres Treaty's relevant article was not only limited in allowing for the creation of a Kurdish state but also was not implemented. The only area where self-determination was implemented for Kurds, albeit in a very limited and a procedural form, was north Mesopotamia. In this area, the British created a semi-autonomous regional administration called Sulaymaniyah in 1918, in accordance with the ideals of President Wilson's Point 12.[69] However, this administrative rule came to a quick end when Sheikh Mahmoud Barzinji, the head of the administrative region, defied the British and rebelled against them.

Conclusion

Maps and geographic studies typically "reflect and recreate dominant geopolitical discourses" and in the nineteenth century these were linked to orientalist discourses.[70] In these orientalist discourses, national identity began to be geographically imagined and territorialized, which was the outcome of constructions of national identity and nationalism in the nineteenth century. Spatial categories began to be used to categorize peoples and their ethnic and linguistic characteristics. Such categories started to attain significant explanatory power in studying and mapping nationalism and ethnicity not only in Europe but in other parts of the world as well. Ethnographic maps produced by European travelers and geographers are excellent examples of this kind of thinking. The idea of national territory in the state-centered political geography became an essential and taken-for-granted entity, and its presence was seen as a stage (and component) in the social and national advancement and development of a people[71] to reach to the level of civilization as experienced in the European context. Such perspectives were ingrained into the nineteenth-century and early twentieth-century political geography and map-making by colonial geographers and officials.

European travelers' accounts reflect the values and perceptions of the travelers who were representatives of the states that ultimately decided the political future of the region. The orientalist view of the world perceiving non-European peoples as less civilized and underdeveloped informed these accounts. The civilizational understanding of nationalism that considers national consciousness, the degree of shared history, language, and culture as an indicator of readiness and criteria for being considered as candidates to join the family of nations constituted the lens through which the European travelers and officers saw the Kurds and other peoples of the region. These European cultural and political values were considered as universal and this perception of universality and superiority informed their views. In addition, their own relatively positive bias toward Christian and other non-Muslim communities also informed their accounts and their view of the Kurds.

The studies and explorations undertaken in Kurdistan and the reports produced by European travelers and their governments' officials were used to formulate European states' policy with regard to the Kurds before, during, and after the First World War. Crucially, the geographical information and anthropological studies about the Kurds constituted the foundation of Kurdish nationalist cartography and historiography in the following decades of the twentieth century. Kurdish nationalists replicated these maps or improvised on them to imagine the Kurdish homeland and its extent. Today the map of greater Kurdistan, extending from the Mediterranean to the Persian Gulf, produced by Kurdish nationalists has become a key symbol of Kurdish national identity and is being used widely by the Kurds. The idea of an independent Kurdistan at some point in the future when the circumstances allow resonates with many Kurds, both in the region and the diaspora.

Kurds have benefited from significant international and transnational opportunities over the twentieth century and early twenty-first century. For instance, international support for Kurdish self-governance in the form of autonomy within a federal Iraq continues. The United States and other Western countries have established a strategic and military alliance with Kurds in Syria in the fight against the Islamic State of Iraq and Syria, an alliance that received a fatal blow when the United States let a Turkish incursion into the Kurdish-controlled northeastern Syria in fall 2019. Kurdish political actors have engaged with contemporary dominant norms, such as democracy, human rights, minority rights and gender equality, and self-determination to solicit support for their political legitimacy. However, this does not mean that the international community is ready to support a Kurdish state. Neither the United States, the UK nor regional

Figure 7.1 The Erbil Citadel and the Kurdish independence referendum campaign (Erbil, September 2017)

countries consider Kurdish secession from Iraq as an acceptable option.[72] The lack of international support for the Kurdish independence referendum in October 2017 clearly showed this.

Notes

1   Said (1994: 6).
2   Wintle (1999: 137).
3   Ibid., 138.
4   Harley (1989).
5   Harley and Woodward (1987: 2); Tyner (1982).
6   Laughlin (1986: 322).
7   Although according to Freeden (1998) nationalism is not a full ideology, the way it was used to justify state formations and policies in the nineteenth century could qualify it as an ideology. In other contexts, nationalism can also be a sentiment or a movement.
8   Agnew (1994: 61–2).
9   Schumpeter (1976: 250).
10   Nodia (1994: 8–9).
11   Ibid., 58.

12 Whelan (1994: 99–100).
13 Mill (1872: 284–93).
14 Knight (1985: 252).
15 Diamond and Plattner (1994: xii).
16 Breuilly (1993); Tilly (1994).
17 Laughlin (1986: 300).
18 Ibid., 308.
19 This section uses O'Shea's excellent analysis of the European engagement with the Kurds and other peoples in the area, and her archival research on European mapping in eastern Ottoman territories in the nineteenth century.
20 Maunsell (1894: 166); Sykes (1904: 202). For an excellent analysis of the British travelers' accounts of the Kurds and Kurdistan in the nineteenth century, see Muhammad (2017).
21 Maunsell (1894: 166).
22 Crampton (2001: 235).
23 Agnew (1994: 67).
24 Ibid., 67.
25 The third international period Agnew refers to from 1945 to 1990 is outside the focus of this chapter. This period was one in which "interstate competition and conflict were largely transformed by the US reconstruction of the industrial capitalist state along liberal capitalist lines." Ibid.
26 Ibid., 64, 69.
27 Laughlin (1986: 301; 307–8).
28 Smith (2004).
29 Agnew (1994: 53–9).
30 Ibid., 60.
31 Knight (1985: 250–1).
32 Wintle (1999: 152).
33 Ibid., 160.
34 Black (2000).
35 Said (1994); Sidaway (2000: 592).
36 Rawlinson (1839); Rich (1836).
37 Mignan (1839).
38 O'Shea (2004: 109–14).
39 The railway connecting Berlin and Istanbul and the role of German military in the reformation of the Ottoman army were important factors.
40 1,266 km by the end of the nineteenth century.
41 O'Shea (2004: 114).
42 Meiselas (2008: 2–50).
43 O'Shea (2004: 108–13).
44 Alsancakli (2017b); Rawlinson (1839).
45 O'Shea (2004: 65).
46 McMurray (2001).
47 O'Shea (2004: 112–13).
48 Ibid.
49 Ibid., 108.
50 Ibid., 110.
51 Ibid., 48.
52 For the decades-long process of border demarcation, see Ateş (2013).
53 Ibid., 125.
54 Ibid., 107.

55 Ibid.

56 The pasha was raised in Istanbul and had Kurdish origins.

57 House and Seymour (1921: 14).

58 Kurdish Delegation to the Peace Conference (2019: 3).

59 Ibid., 12.

60 McDowall (1996: 122).

61 Bozarslan (2003: 169); Özoğlu (2004: 39–40). Sayyid Abdulkadir, the other leader of the SAK and rival to Emin Ali Bedirxan, supported Şerif Pasha's efforts at the Paris Peace Conference.

62 Bozarslan (2003: 169); Olson (1991: 399).

63 Bozarslan (2003: 172); Van Bruinessen (1992: 279).

64 O'Shea (2004: 129).

65 O'Shea (2004: 117–18). For the lack of international support for the Kurdish state in the post–First World War period, see Bajalan (2019).

66 Quoted in Macmillan (2002: 458), from Lloyd George's diary.

67 Helmreich (1974).

68 Klein (2007b).

69 Edmonds (1971: 92). Point 12 in Wilson's Fourteen Points: "The Turkish portion of the present Ottoman Empire should be assured a secure sovereignty, but the other nationalities which are now under Turkish rule should be assured an undoubted security of life and an absolutely unmolested opportunity, security of life and an absolutely unmolested opportunity of autonomous development, and the Dardanelles should be permanently opened as a free passage to the ships and commerce of all nations under international guarantees."

70 Culcasi (2006: 680).

71 Laughlin (1986: 321).

72 UK House of Commons, Foreign Affairs Committee (2018).

8

"WHITE MAN'S BURDEN" OR VICTIM'S HOPE(LESSNESS): ARMENO-KURDISH RELATIONS AND MUTUAL PERCEPTIONS BEFORE THE GENOCIDE

Ohannes Kılıçdağı

Introduction

Several centrifugal forces in the body of notables, *ayans*, emirs emerged both in the Ottoman-ruled Balkans and Anatolia through the eighteenth century. The modernization project of the Ottoman Empire, named after the Tanzimat Edict of 1839 but started earlier, involved the elimination of these provincial power figures and establishment of the central authority. As a part of this endeavor the Ottoman state organized military expeditions in 1830s against the Kurdish emirs who had founded de facto autonomous rule in the eastern provinces of Anatolia. Armenians, as another major community in the region, made different choices in this conflict. The Armenian Patriarchate of Constantinople instructed prelacies in the region to provide soldiers for the Ottoman army whereas some local Armenians supported Kurdish emirs against the central state.[1] By the late 1840s the Ottoman state achieved to curb the power of the Kurdish emirs to a large extent. However, it did not bring peace to the region as it left a power vacuum. Since Armenian peasants lost the feudal-like protection provided by the Kurdish emirs and no other overarching and reliable authority was formed instead to observe the law, they became vulnerable against assaults coming from "petit chieftains." Kurdish (and Turkish) local elites were displeased with the Tanzimat reforms that promised the security of life and property and equality for all subjects and perceived them favoring Armenians. Therefore, they sabotaged them by increasing the "dosage" of violence targeting Armenians. Also, they showed to the central government that it was powerless without their collaboration.[2]

This article was written during my fellowship at the Center for Middle Eastern Studies, Harvard University. Calouste Gulbenkian Foundation also kindly supported my research with its Armenian Studies Scholarship. I am thankful to both institutions for their support.

In this environment, some serious problems between Armenian and Kurdish groups that would last till the end of the empire started to be formed. This chapter, after giving an account of how Armeno-Kurdish relations were evolved and how policies and preferences of the Ottoman state influenced them in the nineteenth century, discusses the state of intercommunal relations and problems of these two groups in the Second Constitutional Period (1908–1913) in the Ottoman Empire. Land seizures and security problems will be handled as two major sources of intercommunal tension. The present text also tries to follow how these groups perceived each other in this social environment before the Armenian Genocide. It contends that, contrary to the conventional thinking, the Second Constitutional Period did not bring about equality and fraternity but prepared the ground for a new wave of violence since there were, on the one hand, rising expectations of Armenians (besides other non-Muslims) and, on the other hand, the resentment of Muslim groups, including Kurds, vis-à-vis Armenians. In this conflictual environment, Armenians ascribed themselves some cultural and moral superiority vis-à-vis Kurds just like colonizers did in the colonies. However, there were fundamental differences between Armenians and the Western "white man." Unlike colonizers, Armenians took this "civilizing mission" not to maintain and legitimize their domination over "the other," that is, Kurds, as they did not have such domination but to find a way of coexistence with Kurds in which they would protect their identity and honor. Eventually, however, the discrepancy or asymmetry between their self-perception and their actual sociopolitical situation turned detrimental to them.

From Tanzimat to the 1908 Revolution

Oppression that Armenians of the eastern provinces experienced became quite tense by the 1860s. Extortion of Armenians' lands, murder, robbery, abduction of Armenian women and girls, double taxation by the state and local despots, exploitation in the form of corvée, overwintering of Kurdish tribes for free in Armenian villages were the main problems. This does not mean that Armenians and Kurds were always in clash as two monolithic entities, or there was no intergroup collaboration or alliance. As relayed by Janet Klein, European observers in the eastern provinces reported examples of collaboration between Armenians and Kurds both in urban and rural areas through 1870s, 1880s, and even 1890s which was particularly a violent decade. For example, in Mardin, some Muslims entrusted their capital to their Christian neighbors who invested it and paid interest to Muslim capital owners. In rural areas of Bitlis, in one instance at least, an Armenian village was saved from starvation by their Kurdish neighbors. Besides, Kurds and Armenians wrote and submitted joint petitions to complain of corrupt officials or seek famine relief.[3] In some rural regions, the cultural practices of Armenians and Kurds were so intermeshed that some Armenian clerics alarmed about the assimilation of Armenian peasants into Kurdishness.[4]

On the other hand, in the 1860s and 1870s Armenian peasants in some regions such as Mush, Van, and Sason were living in a sort of serfdom under the Kurdish chieftains. It was reported that in some cases a whole Armenian village belonged to a local despot.[5] The 1860s witnessed uprisings of Armenians in Zeytun, Mush against Kurdish oppressors as well as some attempts to make their voice heard by the government. In 1864, Mush Armenians complained of the Kurdish attacks to the governor of Erzurum without any effect. A year later, they sent twenty-four delegates representing the twenty-four towns of Mush to the Ottoman capital. On March 31, 1865, they presented a petition to the government about the assaults they had faced. Instead of being offered a solution, they were prisoned for a week. Two years later in 1867, an Armenian delegation this time from Erzurum reached the capital to seek help. However, the Grand Vizier Ali Pasha turned them down by saying that "[i]f the Armenians do not like the things as they are in the provinces, they may leave the country; then we can populate these places with Circassians."[6]

The 1860s also witnessed some seemingly positive developments. With the 1856 Reform Edict (*Islahat Fermanı*), the Ottoman state promised to ameliorate the political status of the Christians and Jews. For that purpose, the state instructed each community to prepare a document to govern their internal civil affairs. After long negotiations between the Ottoman state and the Armenian community, the state ratified a document named as "constitution" by Armenians as "regulations" by the state itself in 1863. This was a quite detailed code (ninety-nine articles) that created an autonomous structure to direct the civil, religious, and educational affairs of the Armenian community. More importantly, it had a popular base as Armenian people, both in the capital and provinces, voted for deputies who constituted a general/national assembly with 140 members, although the seats were quite unjustly distributed among Istanbul and provincial Armenian communities. This assembly elected the patriarch as well as a religious and a civil council that executed the communal affairs and organized the relations with the government.[7] However, neither the Tanzimat reforms nor the Armenian constitution brought about any considerable improvement in the situation of Armenians in the eastern provinces. A special commission was appointed by the Armenian National Assembly on November 27, 1870, to examine and report the unlawful acts against Armenians in the eastern provinces. The commission produced and submitted its first report to the government on April 11, 1872. This report, which contained a summary of assaults and violations against Armenians and suggestions to remedy them, did not generate any result. A second and more detailed report was prepared on September 17, 1876, which listed oppressive acts in 320 locations from April 12, 1872, to the end of August 1876. A majority of these cases (272) were land usurpation by *aghas*, mullahs, and sheikhs. Any judicial process or punishment of perpetrators was rare. The commission showed the feeling of anger among Muslims, both people and officials, toward the idea of equality promised by the Tanzimat reforms. Kurdish chieftains were mentioned as responsible for most of these assaults besides Circassian immigrants, Avshar, and Turkish *derebeys*.[8]

The reign of Abdülhamid II, who ascended to the throne in late 1876, exacerbated the disappointment and anger of Armenians as he declined the principle of equality that had been promoted by the Tanzimat regime and pursued policies bolstering the political and social priority of Muslims. Accordingly, he allied with some Kurdish chieftains to suppress the Armenians in the eastern provinces. However, before going into details of his policy, one important development of the 1870s should be underlined; it is the internationalization of the Armenian Question.

When war broke out between the Ottoman Empire and Russia in April 1877 due to the stress in the Balkans, the Armenian Patriarch Nerses Varjabedian issued a letter calling his people "to work and pray for the victory of Ottoman arms." However, as the war unfolded and Russia openly triumphed over the Ottoman Empire it seemed as the only hope that may maintain stability and security for the Armenians living in the border regions.[9] As a matter of fact, the war concluded with an overwhelming Russian victory. The Article 16 of the Treaty of San Stefano that ended the war stipulated that the Sublime Porte would implement reforms in the Armenian provinces immediately and guarantee the security of Armenians from Kurds (and Circassians). Thus, Russia became the official guarantor and protector of Armenian rights in the Ottoman Empire. However, Great Britain decided that she could not let the Russian influence rise so much in the Balkans and in the Eastern Anatolia and called for another peace conference in Berlin. Article 16 of the Treaty of San Stefano became Article 61 of the Treaty of Berlin which repeated the same guarantee. Nevertheless, how the Ottoman state would apply reforms and what would happen if it did not were vague and abstract. As a matter of fact, the Ottoman state did not implement the reforms that she had promised. Despite some occasional mutterings, by the mid-1880s it became clear that neither Russia nor Great Britain was willing to take serious steps for the implementation of reforms that would alleviate the oppression of Armenians. However, both powers, especially Russia, retained their influence over regional developments. For example, it was seen that when Kurdish chieftains did not like any policy or decision of the central state they threatened to cross over the Russian side of the border, taking their people and cattle with them.[10]

Under these conditions, some Armenians thought that they could take their destiny at their own hand by armed resistance. Although there had been some short-lived previous examples, the first serious and long-lasted underground organization, which subsequently became a party, was the Armenakan Party established in Van by Mugırdich Portukalian in 1885. The other two Armenian parties that dominated the Armenian politics were the Hnchakian Revolutionary Party and the Armenian Revolutionary Federation (Tashnaksutiun), established in Geneva in 1887 and in Tbilisi in 1890, respectively. Although their ideologies exhibited parallels, and both accepted armed struggle as a method, the Hnchaks had more ambitious political goals. Two main objectives of the first Hnchakian program were the independence of Turkish Armenia and the establishment of socialism.[11] The Tashnaks, on the other hand, did not mention independence or autonomy in the 1892 party program. They aimed "the entrenchment of democratic liberties in Turkish Armenia and accepted armed resistance as a method to achieve this goal."[12] Besides local bands of resistance in the eastern Anatolia, those parties organized demonstrations in the capital to protest the oppression and massacre of Armenians in the provinces. In 1890, the Hnchakian Party organized a demonstration in Kumkapı quarter of Istanbul, where protestors and police clashed and some protestors were killed. In 1895 again the Hnchakian Party organized another rally in Bab-ı Ali, the site of government in the capital, to protest the massacre of Sasun taken place in the previous year. There were also killings in this protest. The next year, on August 26, 1896, this time a group of armed Tashnak militants occupied the Ottoman Bank in Galata of Istanbul and threatened to blow up the building. Their aim was to take the attention of Europe to the situation of the Ottoman Armenians. During the occupation, some of the militants and policemen were killed. The militants ended their occupation through the mediation of the Russian embassy and accepted to leave the country on a British boat while keeping their arms by their side. When they were still in the bank, an organized pogrom of ordinary Armenians of Istanbul by the Hamidian regime started and lasted for one and a half days. According to foreign observers around 5,000–6,000 Armenians were killed in almost thirty-six hours.[13]

One of the Hamidian responses to the foundation of Armenian "revolutionary" groups was to form the Hamidiye Regiments (*Hamidiye Alayları*) consisted of some Kurdish chief and their tribes in the eastern provinces in 1891. They officially became a part of the Ottoman army and those chiefs were given some military ranks. The aim was to counterbalance the Armenian political movement as well as strengthening the bonds between the Ottoman state and Muslim Kurds.[14] To put it bluntly, the establishment of the Hamidiye Regiments brought about more oppression, blood, and massacre for Armenians. In the summer of 1894, Sasun Armenians refused to pay double tax to the Kurdish despots and the Ottoman government and raised arms. The governor of Bitlis, Hasan Tahsin, sent a military force to assist Kurds in repressing those Armenians, who resisted for a month until they ran out of all their supplies. They agreed to surrender in the exchange of amnesty. But, after their surrender, almost 3,000 Sasun Armenians were massacred. This incident marked the beginning of a very bloody period. In fact, other massacres followed in September and October of 1895 in a vast area including Trebizond, Erzincan, Erzurum, Gumushane, Baiburt, Urfa, Bitlis, Diyarbekir, Sasun, Kharput, Malatia, Arapkir, Sivas, Amasia, Marsovan, Gurun, Kayseri, Aintab. The total death toll was far above 100,000.[15]

In sum, neither Ottoman reforms nor the great power involvement nor the Armenian Constitution of 1863 solved "the Armenian Question" once and for all in the nineteenth century. On the contrary, toward the end of the century, the situation worsened and intercommunal relations between Armenians and Kurds remained tense. Given this background, the Revolution of July 1908, restoring the constitution and parliament, which had been suspended thirty years ago by Abdülhamid II, arrived as a hope of peaceful ethnic and religious coexistence. A new era began under the domination of the Committee of Union and Progress (CUP) which led the revolution as the backbone of opposition against Abdülhamid II. The Armenian Revolutionary Federation (Tashnaksutyun) presented itself as the most important partner of the revolution and the CUP. Everybody was extremely optimistic. They thought that once all the evil that had been generated by the Hamidian regime ended, everything would be perfect. People from distinct religions were in a euphoria, jubilating hand in hand in the streets, shouting the principles of equality, liberty, fraternity, and justice.

The rest of the chapter examines the relations and intercommunal perceptions of Armenians and Kurds in the eastern provinces in this optimistic political environment and under the legacy of previous violence. It argues that despite the widespread optimism it generated, the 1908 Revolution and the restoration of the constitution did not solve the intercommunal problems. To the contrary, it produced more enmity, resentment, and frustration. Kurds, especially local elites and chieftains, were resentful with the idea of equality and feared the possibility of returning the lands they had seized from Armenians. This exacerbated their anger against Armenians and animosity toward the constitutional regime. Armenians, on the other hand, oscillated between the psychology of victimhood and regarding themselves as the carrier of civilization who would bring "enlightenment" and prosperity for both the Kurds and the rest of the country. They tried to overcome their political weakness and the psychology of victimhood by ascribing moral superiority to themselves. In this regard, there are both similarities and differences between the Armenian views of Kurds in the early twentieth century and Turkish views of Kurds in the early twenty-first century. As discussed by Ekrem Karakoç and Ege Özen in their chapter to this book, Turks, similar to Armenians of Anatolia a century ago, view themselves as being superior to Kurds. Yet the political and social structure in which the relations between Kurds and Turkish majority are shaped today are quite different than those between Armenians and Kurds before the Armenian Genocide. Before discussing the political positioning of Kurds and Armenians of the time in the last section, what follows is an account of major disputes between them.

Land Extortions

Maybe the most important source of mutual enmity was an age-old problem, namely the land grabbed from Armenians by various actors through various methods. Before going into some details of this problem it should be said that the tension due to the land problem was not peculiar to the relations between Armenians and Kurds as, for example, similar disputes occurred between Armenians and Muslim immigrants (muhajir) from the Caucasus or the Balkans. However, in any case, land disputes were a persistent problem increasing the tension between Armenian and Kurdish peoples. Members of these communities were living in close proximity to each other in many of the eastern provinces. Therefore, the frequency and intensity of land disputes between them were higher compared to the level of similar conflicts between Armenians and other groups in the eastern provinces. Although it is hard to quantify land disputes comprehensively and compare them on the basis of different variables such as the ethnicity of invader or the location of the conflict, a series of reports published by the Armenian Patriarchate between 1910 and 1912 gives the researcher an opportunity to observe some characteristics of land disputes.

These four booklets list the lands and other immovable properties across Anatolia belonging to either Armenian institutions, villages, or individuals that had been seized. The booklets[16] mention some invaders by name (e.g., Ahmet Agha, Sheikh Hussein) or refer to collectivities such as "Kurds," "Turks," and "Circassians." When the intruder is mentioned by name, it is difficult to detect his ethnicity unless there is a specification such as "Kurd Mehmed" or "Circassian Hasan." The total number of cases in the report is 982. In 256 of these it is possible to identify the ethnicity of intruders. In 68 percent of all detectable cases, the intruders are Kurdish individuals or anonymously "Kurds," "Kurdish peasants," and "Kurdish neighbors." The same ratio for "Turkish" invaders is 14 percent, whereas "Circassians" and "immigrants," as two other categories of intruders, each make 7.5 percent. Lastly, in 3 percent of all cases, the intruders are defined as "Muslims."

If one focuses on the six eastern provinces (Erzurum, Sivas, Mamuret-ül Aziz, Van, Bitlis, and Diyarbekir), epicenter of the Armenian Question, where Armenians and Kurds had been living in close proximity, this percentage goes even extremely higher as land disputes with immigrants from the Balkans or Caucasia mentioned in the report were usually in the western cities like Bursa, Izmid. Approximately 870 cases, which equals to almost 90 percent of all, were in one of these six provinces. Consequently, these numbers, despite being incomplete and partial, suggest that in the majority of cases land disputes were between Armenians and various Kurdish actors.

Another characteristic of the land conflicts was their longevity as there were cases lingering for decades since the 1890s, even the 1880s. It is unsurprising that this longevity contributed to the persistence and acceleration of intercommunal tension, given that new generations took over the problem from their fathers. One might easily say that the land problem was a factor continuously "poisoning" intercommunal relations between Kurds and Armenians.

In addition to these statistics, some incidents reported in the Armenian press of the time also reveal how the land problem deteriorated the Armeno-Kurdish relations and increased intercommunal tensions. Residents of a Kurdish village in Pasin (Erzurum) named Sheikh Yusuf had invaded some lands belonging to the neighboring Armenian village, Dodi. After the restoration of the constitution in July 1908, Kurds were supposed to give those lands back to Armenians, but some "dark forces" tried to provoke the enmity between two villages in order to prevent that and also "harm the constitutional regime." Someone opened the grave of a holy figure respected as a saint by the Kurds of Sheikh Yusuf and took his remaining body parts away. The Kurds thought that this act violating the sacredness of the grave was a deliberate hostile action by Armenians from Dodi. One of the Kurds, Esad Efendi, probably a notable, led others to complain to the governor. At the end of the investigation, it was understood that this was a plot organized by Esad Efendi himself in order to increase the tension and enmity between two villages and accordingly prevent the restitution of the aforementioned lands. He was arrested.[17]

An event in another village of Erzurum, reported in the newspaper *Haratch* on August 21, 1909, especially demonstrates the extent to which land disputes could generate horrific violence. There was a similar conflict as those mentioned above between some local Kurdish despots and Armenian inhabitants of the village called Kakarlu. Upon the appeal of the Armenian villagers, the government took back the lands from a Kurdish *agha* and gave it back to the villagers. Afterward, *agha*'s son decided to take revenge. With his men, he crept into the village one night and beheaded a certain Khachadur Safarian who had been the son of one of the petitioners to the government. Murderers were not caught, and they spread the rumor that who killed the young one was Armenian *fedais*.[18] According to the correspondent, the local government did not show enough effort and enthusiasm to arrest the perpetrators. Armenians protested and complained, but for no avail.[19]

Contemporary observers were also aware of and underlined the stress accumulated due to the land conflicts. For example, Gerald Henry Fitzmaurice, Chief Dragoman and First Secretary at the British Embassy, explains the situation in 1913 as such:

> After the revival of the Constitution in 1908, large numbers of Armenians returned, especially from the Caucasus, and though the Committee of Union and Progress repeatedly promised to deal with the matter, especially in the case of Armenians who are in possession of the title-deeds of their lands, nothing has been done … This failure to settle the usurped lands question has been interpreted by the Armenians as evidence of bad faith on the part of the Committee [of Union and Progress], and of their secret intention to persist in the old methods of breaking up the peasantry.[20]

Similarly, Ahmet Şerif, a journalist who traveled across Anatolia after the revolution and wrote his impressions for the newspaper *Tanin*, stated that the Armenians of the eastern provinces felt sad and desperate because of continuous stall in land usurpations. He warned that hopelessness and sorrow might turn into an important force. So the government had to understand that it had already been time, even late, to solve this problem once and for all. Otherwise, he adds, within a short time there would be no sign of government in the eastern provinces.[21]

The restitution of lands was one of the issues brought to the fore also by Armenian political parties just after the 1908 Revolution. Both the Tashnaks and Hnchaks demanded the return of the seized lands belonging to Armenians by separate declarations on August 3 and November 24, 1908, respectively.[22] These demands must have been discussed also in Turkish political circles as Cemal Pasha states in his memoirs that before the mutiny of March 31, 1909, the CUP had intended to form a special commission and sent it to the eastern provinces to solve land disputes between Armenians and others.[23] However, this attempt faced harsh opposition from the Muslim deputies from those regions. Indeed, whenever Armenian MPs tried to open discussion about this topic in the general assembly,

Muslim deputies of the eastern provinces formed a bloc against these attempts.[24] Mostly because of this opposition and partially because of the rebellion of March 31, the CUP completely shelved this project.[25]

Security Problems

In addition to land seizures, assaults threatening the security of life, movable properties, and honor of Armenians were another factor that deteriorated the intercommunal relations. Like land seizures, these attacks had lasted for decades before the 1908 Revolution and were not peculiar to Armeno-Kurdish relations. Kurdish despots or groups were not the only ones attacking the Armenian life and property. However, just like land seizures, they were a reality of daily life in the eastern provinces where Armenians and Kurds were living side by side. The contemporary Armenian press frequently reported one or more such assaults taking place in various locations. Although one can argue that at those times a general lack of security and absence of rule of law were prevailing across Anatolia, Armenians thought that the political authorities exhibited systematic indifference if victims were Armenians. According to the narratives of assaults against Armenians reported in the Armenian press, in nine out of ten cases, attackers were either not detected or not caught or not prosecuted justly. A newspaper asked, upon reporting about assaults on Armenians in Harput and Siirt, whether there will be an end to the "agony and martyrdom of poor Armenians," especially those living in the inner towns of provinces.[26] For instance, reportedly a notable from the Kurdish Bedri tribe led an attack against the Armenians of Bitlis and killed eight of them, including a priest. Upon this event, the Armenian Patriarchate once again applied to the Supreme Port for the punishment of Kurdish beys who became "a calamity over Anatolia." Otherwise, the Patriarchate claimed, it would not have been possible to reestablish peace.[27]

Similarly, Erzurum newspaper *Haratch* reported assaults in different districts of the province. A telegram from Eleshkirt reported that in the village of Hıdır (Karakilise, Beyazıt) a certain Molla Huseyin and his men, by the encouragement of Hamidiye captain Rızvan Beg, raided Avedis Hovhannesian's house on June 3, 1909, and wounded him and seven of his relatives seriously. Because of indifference and inactivity of the sub-governor, criminals did not face any prosecution. Encouraged by this impunity, more than 100 Kurds re-assaulted the aforementioned man's house. Upon this, Armenians applied to the local commander to send military force, and the prelate petitioned the government. During the same days, three Armenians grazing their herd were also assaulted in Pakasic, one of the villages of Tercan, by six Muslims. One was killed; two were seriously wounded. Four of the criminals were caught. The correspondent reports that people were impatiently waiting to see how justice would work in a constitutional regime.[28]

Another incident especially illustrates the impotence and reluctance of the security forces to provide public order. On June 10, 1909, Krikor Babikian from Hekebad (Pasin, Erzurum) village was assaulted by three Kurds and beaten severely; his three pairs of oxen were also stolen. The Armenian villagers urged the sub-governor of Hasankale to arrest perpetrators. Gendarmeries searched them for a while but could not find them. They then advised the villagers that they should catch and punish the criminals by themselves. Upon this event, *Haratch*, the newspaper reporting the event, commented: "Many villages of Pasin are still under the pressure of Kurdish tribes. The word freedom has not been heard here yet. Armenians are not living freely even within the limits of their own village."[29]

In sum, perennial problems of land disputes, public security, and absence of rule of law continued to be the biggest impediments for peaceful cohabitation of communities. The promulgation of the constitution did not alleviate these issues. The longer these problems remained unsolved, the more Armenians lost their trust in the new constitutional regime. These problems had been lasting for a long time and the revolution created optimism for their final solution. Therefore, the failure of the new regime to address them brought about deeper frustration. If the anticipated revolution could not solve these problems and establish peace, then what or who would do that? For the peaceful cohabitation of communities, it was also critical how they perceived and positioned each other. The next section focuses on this theme.

Armenian Self-Perceptions and Perceptions about Kurds

While facing these problems Armenian intellectuals reflected about the Kurds and Armeno-Kurdish relations. The question of "what shall we do with Kurds?" was one of the frequent topics of their articles or debates. In most of these analyses, Armenian authors[30] depicted Kurds as "semi-savage," "barbaric," or at best "uneducated" people. According to these commentaries, Kurds were still living in a feudal order which did harm not only themselves but also Armenians. According to this perspective, as long as Kurds remained in ignorance and feudalism, Armenians would continue to suffer from them. Therefore, Armenian commentators suggested helping Kurds in coming out of "dark ages" which would be beneficial for both Armenians and the rest of the country. One commentator from Hınıs, Erzurum, says in Hartach newspaper dated August 25, 1909, that the majority of Kurds were so ignorant that they did not even know reading and writing. Their ignorance was also a risk for the future of the new regime since it was not possible to make uneducated people understand important political principles and concepts such as constitution, equality, and justice. It would be unrealistic to expect them to contribute to the development of the Ottoman fatherland. "Give them light, education; within a decade or two, they [the Kurds], as a brisk and strong race, will be able to contribute to our fatherland."[31]

Another author writing from Van in the same paper on November 10, 1909, made similar arguments. He claims Kurds were uneducated, ignorant, and accustomed to living through pillage, so they had a natural affinity to sword and blood. As long as they remained uneducated and "uncivilized," they would continue killing and plundering Armenians. Moreover, he claims, the encouragement they saw from the tyrant (Abdülhamid II) convinced them that peaceful, hard-working people had to feed them for free and forever. It was unacceptable for Kurdish *aghas* that the constitution brought equality for Christians. In those circumstances, ordinary Kurds, who were always ready to assault Armenians, were a very convenient tool for those who wanted to continue their despotic rule. He foresees that although some Young Turks had sincerely tried to establish the constitutional regime, it would not be possible to entrench the constitutional regime on firm and stable grounds unless they considered the problem of "the Kurdish enlightenment" seriously. He continues: "Let us educate Kurds, improve their knightly characteristic, eliminate their negative instincts, and try to sow the seed of virtue, goodness, and beauty. Then we can be sure that the Kurd, who become decent by heart and soul, will present real services to his fatherland."[32]

According to many commentators, Armenians should have taken the responsibility of enlightening and helping Kurds. For example, Armenians could assist them in overcoming illiteracy which was a major problem among Kurds. As a matter of fact, an Armenian named Hrachia from Hınıs, Erzurum, prepared a primer to teach Kurds reading Kurdish in Armenian scripts, whose topics were derived from "pure Kurdish life," and *Haratch* newspaper would publish and distribute it in hope of helping the expansion of education among the Kurds and "putting them on the way of civilization."[33]

Indeed, Armenians ascribed themselves as a general mission of civilization for the whole Ottoman land. In the division of labor among communities, most of the Armenians regarded their own community as a mediator between the modern and civilized world and Muslim communities of the Ottoman Empire. This view originated from their better education and more close relations with Europe, as articulated in the words of an Armenian commentator in Sivas newspaper *Antranik* on May 23, 1909:

> Due to our position and occupation, we have had more opportunity to contact with Europeans and their civilization. Therefore, the Armenians should first provide their inner harmony and later perform the duty of mediating between European nations and our Turkish brothers. This is, besides being a mission, also a glory for us. The fate of our nation is so inscribed that we should live agreeably and gladly with the Turks and also other communities living in Turkey ... Only through this way that we can have the best position in the economic and moral life of this beautiful country.[34]

An Interpretation

In the light of contemporary texts, the social relations between Armenians and Kurds during the second constitutional period cannot be described as peaceful, harmonious, although there had been examples of interethnic collaboration and solidarity. People from distinct ethnoreligious communities celebrated the constitution with a shared sense of euphoria, but persistent structural-legal problems, legacy of previous generations, strained the intercommunal relations. It is quite clear that these unsolved problems increased the intercommunal tensions and amplified negative feelings among Armenians against neighboring communities. Security problems and especially land disputes became main cleavages along which social tension accumulated. These disputes created "open accounts" which were to be settled at the first opportunity, that is, war, banishment, or massacre. What becomes critical and determinative at those times of crisis is not relations among individuals from different communities, but the social, political, and legal structure in which these relations are shaped. As a matter of fact, Ahmet Şerif, reflecting upon his observations in the eastern provinces in 1911, argued that although there was not a clash between communities on daily basis, if the land and security problems had not been solved it might have turned into a "fight of nations" in the near future. He described land problems as "lava flow" which could ruin everything on its way.[35] Therefore, when examining the relations between Armenians and other communities, land and security problems should be given a central role.

Moreover, in conflicts born out of land disputes, Armenians' distinct ethnic and religious identity made them easy targets. Usurpers tried to legitimize their unlawful deeds by emphasizing the cultural difference and "inferiority" of the victim. As Michael Mann states, whenever ethnic differences intertwine with other social distinctions and where ethnonationalism can capitalize on other sources of exploitation, conflict becomes stronger.[36] After a point, it becomes almost impossible to differentiate whether it is an economic or cultural/religious conflict, or which one is the cause, which one is the effect. In other words, the land question as a material question became an occasion to insult or humiliate the Armenian identity and faith whereas the cultural and moral inferiority of Armenians in the eyes of Kurds and other Muslims provides a justification for and normalized their oppression and the seizure of their rights. Kurdish notables or chiefs in the eastern provinces perceived the revolution as a threat because it promised to bring an end to this sociopolitical justification mechanism.

This absence of the rule of law and justice created certain mentalities and perceptions on both sides of Armenians and Muslims, including Kurds. As Stephan Astourian says, unpunished and continuous crimes against Armenians from the 1850s onward made Armenians "fair game" in the eyes of neighboring communities. This atmosphere of impunity created a social setting in which violence against a target group was routinized and normalized.[37] At the same time, Armenians developed a psychology of victimhood and vulnerability. They saw themselves under a systematic attack from the state and its agents. Due to their collective memory shaped by past oppressions and massacres, they regarded every single assault as made not just against Armenian individuals but against Armenianness and their Christian identity. Even after the establishment of the constitutional order, they could not completely get rid of the fear of being massacred. Leaving aside the actual massacres of Adana, one can observe through the Armenian press that Armenians felt this risk, real or perceived, in other places like Harput, Sivas, and Erzurum.

However, Armenians' self-image did not consist of only everlasting victimhood, an important distinction from the Yezidi self-perceptions discussed in Tutku Ayhan's chapter in this volume. They, especially intellectuals, ascribed a "civilizing mission" to the Armenian community, especially in their relations with Kurds. As in examples mentioned above, they described Kurds as "uncivilized savages" who had accustomed to living on others' labor and blood. According to this approach, Armenians could and should have assisted them in their endeavor of getting civilized. This was the Armenians' responsibility for the benefit of not only Kurds but also Armenians themselves. At the same time, however, one could come across some statements in the Armenian press of the time that depicted Kurds as having heroic and noble characteristics. Indeed, Kurds might have been very helpful for the country, if they had had enough education.

One can easily notice the similarity between Armenians' approach and discourse about Kurds and the Western colonialist approach and discourse that put into effect to legitimize Western domination in colonies, as discussed in Zeynep Kaya in her chapter. Just like Europeans had ascribed themselves a civilizing mission by the phrase of "white man's burden," Armenian did so for themselves, and just like Europeans had defined native people of the colonies as "noble savages," Armenian defined Kurds in a very similar way. However, there were also crucial differences between Europeans in colonies and Armenians in Anatolia. First of all, obviously, Armenians were not outsiders or invaders in Anatolia unlike the Westerners in colonies, but one of indigenous people. Secondly, the colonialists held the indisputable political and military power in colonies, whereas Armenians, except for very limited territories, were the weak and vulnerable party in Anatolia. As a result of their political weakness, they could only complain or prepare reports and petition the Ottoman authorities to end the injustices they faced in daily life due to land usurpations and other exploitations. The armed struggle initiated by the Armenian parties in late 1880s on was sporadic, uncoordinated, and small in capacity, therefore, far from making any fundamental change. Similarly, the involvement of European powers did not better the situation of Armenians since they had avoided taking any measure that may have demolished the Ottoman Empire which they had seen as a barrier holding the Russian sway.

Consequently, Armenians' civilizing discourse was not an attempt to legitimize their political domination since they did not have such a domination, but an attempt to compromise with the stronger party, that is, Turks/Kurds/Muslims. As they knew very well that they could not get rid of Kurds, they tried to formulate a way of cohabitation. According to this equation, they ascribed themselves moral superiority, and this was a way of saving their honor. They put themselves in white man's shoes, but indeed, they were "the Indians" in the scene, which they would learn soon.

Notes

1   Derderian (2016: 92).
2   Astourian (2011: 62, 63).
3   For the detail of these examples and some more see Klein (2007a: 156–7).
4   Derderian (2016: 101).
5   Barsoumian (1997: 199).
6   Nalbandian (1963: 73, 79).
7   For how the events led up the "Armenian constitution" and its content, see Artinian (1970); Koçunyan (2014).
8   Astourian (2011: 59–60).
9   Hovannisian (1997: 207).
10   Klein (2007a: 161).
11   Nalbandian (1963: 112).
12   Ter Minassian (1992: 27).
13   Hovannisian (1997: 225–6).
14   Klein (2007a: 159).
15   Hovannisian (1997: 219–23).
16   Armenian Church (1910; 1911; 1912a; 1912b).
17   *Haratch*, December 18, 1909: 3.
18   A name given to the Armenian members of armed bands.
19   Pet (1909: 2).
20   Relayed from official correspondence of Foreign Office by Astourian (1992: 66–7).
21   Şerif (1999: 332).
22   Avagyan and Minassian (2005: 34, 43).
23   Kaligian (2009: 59).
24   Avagyan and Minassian (2005: 53).
25   Kaligian (2009: 60).
26   *Iris*, June 1, 1911: 7.
27   *Iris*, June 15, 1911: 5.
28   *Haratch*, June 9, 1909: 4.
29   *Haratch*, July 3, 1909: 4.
30   Mostly, they were editors, college professors and students, lawyers, doctors, politicians, and literary figures.
31   Tutuncian (1909: 3).
32   Adrag (1909: 2–3).
33   *Haratch*, June 12, 1909: 4.
34   Metzadurian (1909: 2).
35   Şerif (1999: 338, 344).
36   Mann (2004: 5).
37   Astourian (1992: 61).

TURKISH PUBLIC OPINION AND CULTURAL AND POLITICAL DEMANDS OF THE "KURDISH STREET"

Ekrem Karakoç and H. Ege Özen

Introduction

Does Turkish public opinion facilitate or impede a resolution to the Kurdish conflict in Turkey? Despite the fact that ordinary Turks[1] are, along with Kurds, at the center of the Kurdish conflict, scholarly knowledge about what ordinary Turks think about the social and cultural rights of Kurds and their demand of political equality remains limited. Most works have focused on the state and the insurgency as primary actors of the conflict.[2] Although a growing number of studies provide important empirical insights about Turkish perceptions of Kurds, they have various limitations such as lacking representative sampling or more detailed focus on attitudes toward Kurds and their political and cultural demands.[3] This chapter contends that the way that Turks perceive the origins of the conflict and respond to the cultural and political demands of Kurds carries crucial importance for conflict resolution. Analyzing the public opinion of the dominant ethnic majority toward the Kurdish conflict enables scholars to gauge to what extent public opinion constraints or facilitates conflict resolution.

This study aims to contribute to this unexplored relationship between the Turkish public and the Kurdish conflict by examining an original public opinion survey intended to gauge ordinary Turks' opinion toward the Kurdish conflict. The survey was conducted in April 2015, several months before the collapse of the Kurdish opening. The nationwide public opinion survey includes 7,099 citizens of Turkey; more than 5,300 individuals that identify themselves as Turkish ethnic identity and about 1,170 individuals that identify themselves as ethnic Kurds.[4]

The findings suggest that Turks have developed resentment toward all aspects of the cultural and political demands of Kurds, ranging from education in their mother tongue to Friday sermons in Kurdish and to attitudes toward the Kurdish political actors. Most significantly, Turks overwhelmingly oppose not only the linguistic and cultural rights of Kurds but also the constitutional recognition of Kurds, let alone the right to political autonomy and other political demands. They view Kurds not as their political equals, but subordinates who should be content with the social, economic, and political status quo. In the imagination of the vast majority of Turks, Kurdish identity is reduced to a folkloric construct with no political significance. Except for the regions where Turkish and Kurdish populations are mixed, all regions show a similar level of opposition to Kurdish demands. In particular, people from the Black Sea and Mediterranean regions present the most adverse reactions to such demands. In addition, neither religiosity nor party affiliation significantly affects Turks' hostility toward minority rights. Overall, these findings depict a pessimistic view of the longevity of the coexistence between Turks and Kurds and suggest that their shared religion and culture neither helps Turks develop positive attitudes toward cultural and political demands of Kurds nor makes Kurds content with the current social and political status quo.

Constructing national identity on the basis of one ethnic group, and thus dismissing cultural and political rights of subordinate groups, aims to legitimize the dominant ethnic position in socioeconomic, cultural, and political spheres. This pattern is not unique to Turkey, but also observable, to varying degrees, across many ethnically divided countries such as Iraq, Switzerland, Israel, Spain, Bulgaria, and China.[5] An ethnic majority's opposition to minority rights such as mother tongue education in public schools, or the giving of ethnic minority names to children or places, is not primarily about preserving linguistic homogeneity. It is more about preserving a long-established and institutionalized social and political group hierarchy.[6] Such hierarchies are also observable in long-standing democracies even if the level of discrimination and repression of minority demands may be indirect and constrained.[7] Exploring the determinants of stereotyping, lynching, and discrimination of minorities mostly in the US context, scholars of social dominance and racial threat theories present similar findings.[8] Social dominance theory proponents[9] argue that the members of dominant ethnic groups are not willing to give up their hegemonic position when subordinate groups demand progressive change or some rights. This applies whether the majority benefits from the status quo either consciously or unconsciously. What makes the Kurdish case unique, however, is that outgroup antagonism among Turks is exceptionally high; none of the mainstream parties or their supporters present any empathetic position toward Kurdish minority rights. Social status or economic competition does not necessarily foster anti-minority rights; antagonism toward such rights reflects the desire of a dominant ethnic group (Turks) to maintain hierarchical socioeconomic and political power relations between themselves and a subordinate ethnic group (Kurds).[10]

To understand the historical roots of the Turkish opposition toward the cultural and political rights of Kurds as well as social and political group inequality, we have to analyze group hierarchy-enhancing discourse and policies of the Turkish state between Turks and Kurds from the foundation of Turkish republic to present. For this purpose, the next section explores change in discourse and policies toward the Kurdish conflict in the post-1990 era, along with hierarchy-attenuating policies such as the rhetorical recognition of the Kurdish identity, broadcasting in

Kurdish, optional Kurdish-language courses at the fifth grade, and other reforms. Having discussed the Kurdish conflict along with its major actors, we present our survey data and show how ordinary Turks' views of the Kurdish conflict as well as linguistic, cultural, and political rights of Kurds differ from those of Kurds. We conclude by a discussion of various factors that may impact these views.

The Turkish State and the Kurds

Although the Kurdish conflict did not start with the formation of the Turkish nation-state but instead dates back to the centralization policies under the Ottoman Empire,[11] this chapter focuses on policies and dominant discourses the Turkish state has pursued since its foundation. The ruling elites of the new republic, mostly former generals or bureaucrats originally from the Western provinces of the Ottoman Empire, shared the belief that adopting political reforms for (religious) minorities or giving political autonomy to them in the nineteenth century had not stopped the disintegration of the empire.[12] Having spent their formative years witnessing the dismantling of the empire, the founding elites of the republic strategically appeared open to the idea of Kurdish autonomy during the Independence War (1919–1923), before vehemently opposing it. Consequently, they developed policies that viewed Kurdish ethnicity as an existential security threat that must be either assimilated or repressed.[13]

The nascent Republic of Turkey with its secular nationalism did not acknowledge Kurds as a separate ethnic group, but rather as a group of people who required civilizing and assimilation through public policies. This denial dominated the political discourses of both Turkish actors and institutions.[14] The causes of this denial lie, to a certain extent, in the (inherent) colonial/hierarchical mindset of Turkish elites, derived from the institutionalized belief that to catch up to the "civilized world," a modern nation-state must be created around a secular Sunni Turkish identity. This colonialist mindset saw people on the periphery, and especially Kurds mostly residing in the countryside, as requiring assimilation into the chosen identity as "prospective Turks."[15] The official discourse and popularized public perception were that Kurds were not a distinct ethnic group; these Easterners (*Doğulular*) were "mountain Turks," who had lost the norms and values of the rest of the population and would benefit from the modernizing hand of the state.[16] In an attempt to create a national identity based on Turkishness, the regime banned the Kurdish language and replaced Kurdish names of places and Kurdish names of children.[17] The state's modernization policies aimed to re-acculturate this ethnic group so that it could catch up with the western parts of the country, and the country as a whole could, in turn, catch up with the civilized Western world.[18] The inferiority complex toward the West reflected itself as a superiority complex toward Kurds, along with the right to control and assimilate these less-developed people into Turkish society and culture. In this framework, the conflict becomes a struggle between a modernizing state and the culturally backward periphery. As

Tutku Ayhan's contribution to this book shows, similar statist civilizing missions, involving mass atrocities and assertive assimilation policies, were also observed toward Kurds and Yezidis in post-independence Iraq, especially under the Ba'th party.[19]

After Turkey transitioned to a multiparty system in the post-1946 era, intellectuals and political elites of the Turkish state have (in)voluntarily internalized and agreed to "the Turkish contract" and thus overlooked the assimilationist policies toward Kurds.[20] The brutal suppression of numerous Kurdish rebellions and the overall state control over Kurds led to the denial of the saliency of the Kurdish identity. Instead, political elites focused on other significant political cleavages like the conflict between religious and secular ideological outlooks, and that between socialism and capitalism, in line with the zeitgeist of the post–Second World War era. Except for small socialist movements that incorporated the Kurds into their discourse of class struggle and anti-imperialism, mainstream parties, movements, and political figures were silent about the Turkish state's denial of an ethnic group's existence, and its ban on the Kurdish language, music, and culture.

The DP (*Demokrat Partisi*), which came to power in 1950, criticized the repressive policies of the single-party era on Kurds, allowed the return of exiled Kurds, and made influential Kurdish personalities of the region MPs. Nonetheless, its discourse of "our Eastern citizens" or "citizens in the East" fell short of recognizing Kurds as a distinct ethnic group. In this multiparty period, the state and its ideological tools, ranging from textbooks to newspapers and journals, associated the "Eastern problem" with cultural and economic backwardness. They identified the language spoken as a primitive one, the combination of mostly Turkish, Arabic, and some Persians. "Citizen, Speak Turkish" policies of the single-party era, in various forms, did continue to shape public opinion, whose effects are still visible in the twenty-first century.[21] Newspapers, reports, and books produced under the state institutions including the Ministries of Education and Interior reinforced this pejorative perception of Kurdish language and culture. In many official reports, Kurds are defined as a group of tribal people living in economic and cultural backwardness and the ones that lost their Turkish identity into this tribal/Kurdish identity.[22] The first party that openly recognized Kurds as an ethnic group in Turkey was a leading socialist party at that time, the TİP (*Türkiye İşçi Partisi*), a politically audacious act that later contributed to the party's ban in 1971. That would serve as a warning to other parties.

Recognition with a Stick and Its Discourse

The denial policy finally ended in 1991 when the government removed the ban on speaking "languages other than Turkish" that was imposed after the 1980 coup. Until this era, using social dominance theory's conceptualization, one can argue that the supremacy of hierarchy-enhancing discourses policies of the Turkish state already indoctrinated much of the Turkish population: social values attributed to being part of the Turkish identity were associated with highly positive ones while other identities, in particular, Kurdish, Christian and Jewish, were associated with pejorative social values. The non-Muslim groups with their declining numbers, no longer viewed as a threat to territorial integrity of the Turkish state, did not face intensive assimilationist policies as much as Kurds', but surely faced discriminatory policies, despite the protections offered by the Lausanne Treaty of 1923.[23]

The change in the denial policy was the result of the intense fight between the PKK (Kurdistan Workers' Party) and the security forces that erupted in 1984 as well as Turgut Özal's realization after he became the president in 1989 that the conflict could not be solved through military means. The PKK emerged as a formidable force against exploitative landlords and the military, proving itself a resilient resistance movement, compared to the relatively easily crushed Kurdish rebellions in the 1920s and 1930s. Özal and some civilian elites were aware of a growing threat to the integrity and economic development of the state. He contemplated various policies to end the conflict, including an amnesty to the PKK. Süleyman Demirel (prime minister from 1991 to 1993 and president from 1993 to 2000) mentioned the possibility of constitutional citizenship in 1992, and Tansu Çiller (prime minister from 1993 to 1996) briefly suggested the "Basque model" as a possible solution.[24] However, the Kemalist military and bureaucracy, the guardians of the then-secular republican regime, rebuffed these ideas, clearly signaling to elected politicians that they may not pursue a different policy solution other than the denial one.

Amidst the prevalence of unstable coalition governments, the continuing guardianship role of the military, and the lack of public support for peaceful solution to the Kurdish conflict, elected politicians were unwilling and incapable of pursuing platforms more inclusive of Kurdish identity after 1993. The civil war escalated with heavy causalities on both sides with the return of the securitization policies that perceived the problem exclusively from a terrorism perspective and emphasized military means to end it. While rhetorically recognizing the Kurdish identity in 1991, the Turkish political actors had moved from the denial to recognition with a stick in which they define the Kurdish cultural and political demands as "separatism/terrorism."

The political discourse of social, political, and economic elites as well as the Turkish public followed the example of the Turkish military and state institutions. In this telling, the Kurdish conflict does not emanate from the denial policies that rejected the existence of Kurds in Turkey and condoned and justified gross human rights violations against Kurds, but rather from violence/terrorism, supported by foreign powers that have sought Turkey's division since the Sèvres Treaty of 1920. According to this narrative, the state is again under siege by imperialist powers, and the PKK is a terrorist organization used by those powers to brainwash the poor and ignorant people or to kidnap their children. Kurds or *Doğulular* (Easterners) are poor and uneducated, easily deceived by the "terrorist" organizations and foreign powers.[25] Mainstream Turkish media, pro-government or not, have popularized the state narrative and worked to discredit Kurdish political movements.[26] Before the 1990s, newspapers rarely used phrases like "Kurds" or "Kurdish" in news reports or columns. In the 1990s, newspapers began using those terms, primarily because of the formation of a de facto Kurdish autonomous zone in northern Iraq in 1992, implicitly acknowledging the Kurdish reality also in Turkey while still aligning with the state discourse. Yet they employed these terms in a pejorative sense and portrayed Kurdish as a language cobbled from Arabic, Persian, and Turkish, and too primitive to cultivate sophisticated literary, cultural, or political expressions. Furthermore, the newspapers kept mimicking the state discourse by citing public opinion surveys as evidence that Kurds were primarily concerned about employment opportunities and were relatively unconcerned about learning or speaking Kurdish.[27]

The AKP Era

When the AKP came to power in 2002, it initially received the benefit of the doubt from Kurds. The capture of the PKK leader Abdullah Öcalan in Kenya in 1999, the EU Accession process, along with the abolition of the death penalty and other changes paved the way for the AKP to launch new reforms about Kurdish language and culture, eventually going beyond the EU-induced reforms of the previous government between 1999 and 2002. While the hierarchy-attenuating policies were launched in the initial AKP years (2002–2007), more substantial ones came later, especially between 2013 and 2015 era. Being slow in the first years, the post-2009 and especially 2013 AKP governments restored Kurdish names to Kurdish villages, offered the Kurdish language as an optional course at the fifth grade, permitted broadcasting Kurdish in public and private channels, and developed a repatriation program for Kurdish citizens forcefully evacuated from their villages.[28]

Like the Milli Görüş (National Outlook) movement and other Turkish religious communities, the AKP leader Recep Tayyip Erdoğan saw secularism as a cause of division between Turks and Kurds and "highlighted the value of unification and brotherhood on the basis of 'common citizenship' in the Republic of Turkey."[29] In Erdoğan's discourse or other major Turkish Islamic movements, Kurds have never been identified as citizens with cultural and political rights equal to that of Turks. Rather, Erdoğan expressed the idea of "Türkiyelilik," belonging to the citizenship of Turkey, in the early years of the AKP rule, but such references became sporadic over time. In addition to the reforms of previous coalition government (1999–2002), such as allowing "languages other than Turkish" in broadcasting as well as learning in private institutions, the AKP continued to launch a second wave of administrative reforms such as a Kurdish public TV channel, the possibility of electoral campaigning in Kurdish, the use of Kurdish in courts, and others. However, these reforms were tangential to what has been negotiated with the Kurdish movement between 2009 and 2011, and especially between 2013 and 2015 (e.g., the constitutional recognition of Kurds, decentralization, and education in the Kurdish language).[30] In addition, the bureaucratic apparatus, including security forces, the judiciary, or state bureaucratic ministries, either hindered the implementation of reforms or did not implement those reforms at their discretion.

During the Kurdish opening process that lasted from late 2012 to mid-2015, the AKP's policies did not positively transform Turks' attitudes toward Kurds and Kurdish rights. To the contrary, the process was likely to amplify nationalist impulses and votes among Turks, reflected especially in the June 2015 elections. The growing authoritarianism of Turkey under Erdoğan, especially since the Gezi protests that started in late May 2013, concurrent with the Kurdish opening, aggravated resentment against anything related to the Kurdish identity and conflict. Even before then, anti-Kurdish sentiments became gradually but progressively prevalent in public discourse and media along with ubiquitous anti-Kurdish attitudes and stereotypes.[31] In addition to politically charged "terrorist discourse," ordinary Turks associated Kurdish identity with negative moral characteristics.[32] As Saraçoğlu argued, not only people with the low socioeconomic class affiliations but also middle-class people openly expressed their prejudices against Kurds.[33] The dominant discourse among Turks has still been portraying Kurds as non-modern, separatist hate-mongers, and potential terrorists while also explicitly stating their resentments against higher-status Kurds such as business owners. These types of prejudicial attitudes toward Kurds further intensified in reaction to the somewhat hierarchy-attenuating policies of the Kurdish opening. Riding the popular resentment, ultra-secular nationalists and conservative nationalists have mobilized significant support for undermining the opening policies pursued by the AKP government.

In sum, state policies that fostered an ethnic hierarchy, especially between Turks and Kurds, continued to increase prejudices across ethnic lines.[34] This prejudice was especially high among Turks who feel that they "own" the state and hold an internalized latent view that Kurds are subordinate citizens.[35]

Do all Turks oppose right and equality demands of Kurds? How do demographic, political, and socioeconomic characteristics affect Turkish views of Kurds? After discussing the sample and content of public opinion survey conducted in 2015 to gauge Turkish political opinion on Kurdish conflict, the rest of this chapter will (a) show in detail the extent to which Turks share with or differ from Kurds in their view toward minority rights and (b) discuss how political identities, religious identities, and factors associated with the contact (with Kurds) affect Turks' attitudes toward cultural and political rights of Kurds.

Survey Data

The data come from a nationwide public opinion poll conducted in Turkey in April 2015, with around 7,099 individuals; a short time before the Kurdish opening was officially over and the fight between the PKK and Turkish security forces erupted again.[36] The nationally representative survey utilized a multistage, stratified, cluster-sampling procedure, along with age and gender quotas. The survey asked several questions that aim to capture the ethnic identity of a respondent. They included self-identification with a particular ethnic identity (e.g., Turk, Kurd, Zaza, Arab, Armenian, and others), mother tongue, the language spoken at home, ethnic identity of parents. In this chapter, we utilized the last one, whether any one of parents, Kurds or both Turks or Kurds, to measure ethnic identity. As a result, four categories emerged out of this categorization: Both parents are Turks (76 percent), both parents are Kurds (16 percent), only mother is Kurdish (5 percent), only father is Kurdish (3 percent). The empirical analysis only includes respondents whose parents are from the same ethnic identity, Turks, or Kurds. Using other categories does not change the substantive interpretation of the results.[37]

Before presenting the cross-tabulations of cultural and political rights by ethnicity, our first task is to explore whether Kurds and Turks share a similar opinion on the nature and origins of Kurdish problems in Turkey. The survey asks whether there is state discrimination against Kurds, whether Turks and Kurds are equal in terms of social and economic rights, and whether Kurds and Turks are equal in civil rights and liberties. Putting aside "I do not know" or "No response" for the sake of simplicity,[38] Figure 9.1 shows that among Turks, 11 percent agree that there is state discrimination against Kurds; 78 and 82 percent believe that they are citizens with equal rights and liberties and with social and economic rights, respectively.[39] In contrast, 57 percent of Kurdish respondents, five times more than Turks, agree that Kurds suffer from state discrimination. Moreover, only 35 percent of Kurds think that both groups are citizens with the same rights and liberties.

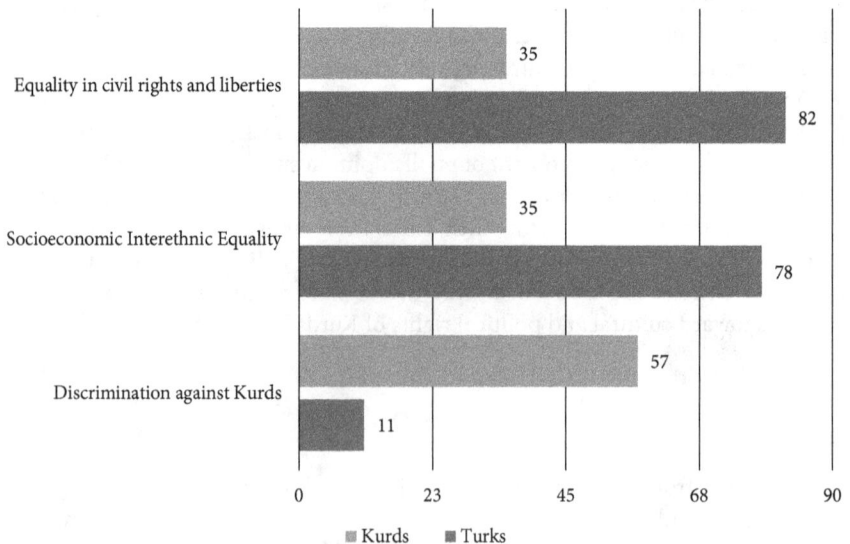

Figure 9.1 Attitudes toward Interethnic Inequality and Discrimination (%)

Note: N is 5,383 for Turks and 1,340 for Kurds. A series of t-tests suggests that there is a statistically significant relationship between ethnic identity and issues above. The percentages reflect "Yes" answers to the questions that ask whether interethnic equality in first two issues and discrimination against Kurds.

In terms of perceptions of linguistic/cultural and political rights of Kurds, Figure 9.2 suggests that there is, indeed, a great divide between Turks and Kurds. Turks are not willing to grant linguistic and cultural rights to Kurds. Only one-third of Turks approve of the availability of optional Kurdish language courses in the public education system; a meager 14 percent support education in the Kurdish language. The support for Kurdish names for geographical places, Friday sermon in Kurdish, and support for Kurdish service in public institutions such as municipalities, courts, and hospitals also remain low among Turks, ranging from 18 percent to 27 percent. There is almost no support for Kurdish as a second official language (6 percent), a regional flag (4 percent), autonomy (5 percent). Interestingly, those who say that Kurds can have their state is 10 percent, significantly higher than those who approve Kurdish autonomy. The higher support for the former comes from CHP and MHP supporters, some of whom show strong dislike toward Kurds, as reflected by an infamous MHP slogan, "love (accept the status quo) or leave."

Around 87–90 percent of Kurdish respondents agree with the idea that Kurds should possess the following rights: optional Kurdish courses in schools, Kurdish

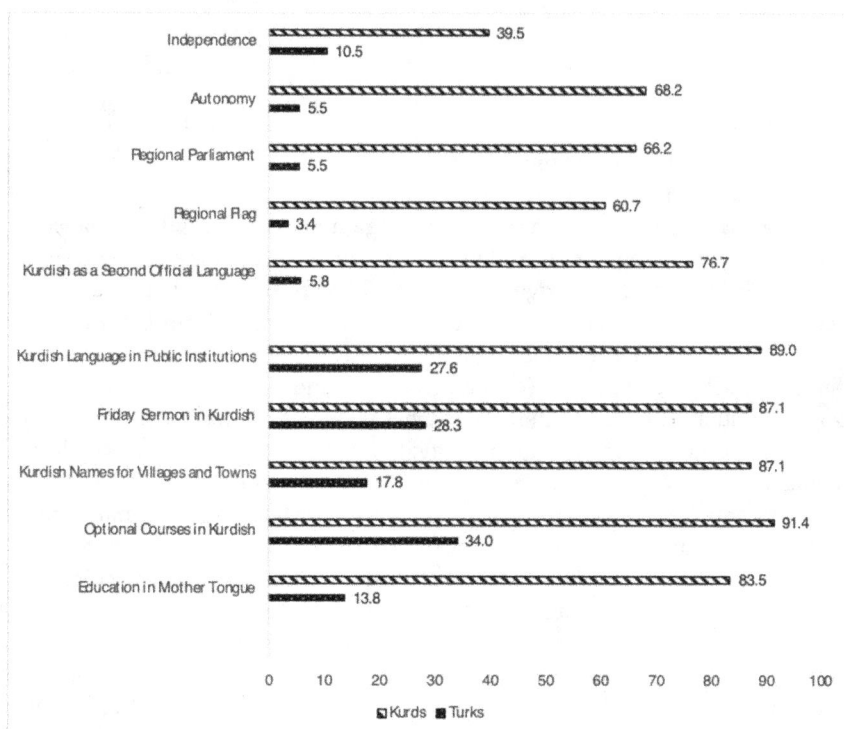

Figure 9.2 Support for Cultural and Political Rights by Turks and Kurds (%)

Note: A series of t-tests suggests that there is a statistically significant relationship between ethnic identity and all issues above.

names for locations (e.g., keeping Kurdish names for villages, towns, mountains), Friday sermons in Kurdish. As for education in Kurdish, it gets 83 percent support from Kurds. Heavy majorities of Kurds demand Kurdish to be recognized as an official language, Kurdish flag, parliament, and autonomy. The ratio of those who demand secession from Turkey is lower but still substantial, about 39 percent.

The difference in support for Kurdish cultural and political rights across regions is substantial. As Table 9.1 shows, confirming social contact theory,[40] Turks residing in ethnically mixed Eastern and Southeast Anatolia are more supportive of cultural rights. Around 48 percent of those from Eastern Anatolia and 75 percent of those from Southeast Anatolia are fine with about optional courses in Kurdish. The percentages are 36 and 40 percent for Kurdish names for locations; 45 and 39 percent for Friday sermons in Kurdish; and 48 and 65 for Kurdish service in municipalities, hospitals, and courts. Moving to political rights, 20 percent in the Eastern Anatolia and 31 percent in the Southeast regions support Kurdish as a second official language. As for a regional flag and parliament, the support is lower: 7 and 8 percent among Turks in the Eastern Anatolia, and 19 and 35 percent among Turks in the Southeastern Anatolia. Support for independence is 11 percent in the Eastern, but 30 percent in the Southeastern Anatolia.

Turks in the Marmara region exhibit significant support for cultural rights, but not much for political rights. Their support for education in mother language, optional Kurdish courses, Kurdish names, Friday sermon, and Kurdish in institutions are about 20, 47, 25, 43, and 38 percent, respectively. Support for political rights such as the recognition of Kurdish as an official language or Kurdish autonomy remains much lower (around 6 percent). Support for cultural rights remains very low in other regions, in the 10s and 20s. The Aegean, Central Anatolia, Mediterranean, and Black Sea regions also show little variance in support for cultural and political rights. Turks in the Mediterranean region shows a strong dislike for political rights for Kurds, followed by Turks in the Black Sea. Support for the regional flag, parliament is very low, ranging from 1 to 4 percent. Support for autonomy remains negligible, around 2 percent (Mediterranean), 3 percent (Black Sea), 4 percent (Central Anatolia), and 8 percent (Aegean). Rather ironically, support for independence reaches to 16 percent in the Mediterranean and 15 percent in Aegean regions, which seems to reflect the "love or leave" mentality (indicating Kurds could leave and have their state somewhere else). The Central Anatolia and Black Sea regions show a similar but more moderate trend: 8 and 9 percent support for independence.

One may argue that this descriptive analysis may not reflect the heterogeneity of attitudes toward the Kurdish conflict in Turkish society, which may vary across political affiliation, religiosity, ideology, the location of their residence, and other factors.[41] However, the decades-old dominant social and political state discourse and practices of ethnic hierarchies seem to have created similar attitudes. Popular support for these issues is low even among supporters of the AKP that launched the opening policies.

Neither the center-left nor right-wing parties challenged the state discourse on Kurds, with the limited exceptions of the TİP and smaller socialist groups.

Table 9.1 Support for Cultural and Political Rights among Turks by Regions (%)

Support for	Marmara	Mediterranean	Aegean	Central Anatolia	Black Sea	Eastern Anatolia	Southeast Anatolia
Education in Mother Tongue	20.1	4.8	14.2	7.2	6.8	31.3	43.9
Optional Courses in Kurdish	46.7	17.6	24.4	29.3	26.3	48.3	74.6
Kurdish Names for Villages and Towns	25.4	7.7	13.3	13.7	12.3	35.6	40.4
Friday Sermon in Kurdish	42.7	12.8	14.9	23.3	24.8	45.1	39.5
Kurdish Language in Municipalities Hospitals and Courts	37.7	10.2	23.2	22.3	21.3	48.0	64.9
Kurdish as a Second Official Language	6.2	2.1	8.0	3.5	1.9	20.0	30.7
Regional Flag	3.5	1.4	4.9	2.0	1.6	7.4	19.3
Regional Parliament	6.4	1.7	7.4	3.2	2.8	8.0	35.1
Autonomy	5.5	1.9	8.4	3.6	2.6	14.3	29.5
Independence	6.5	16.5	15.2	8.4	8.8	10.7	30.1
N	1,768	707	834	1,053	685	181	114

Note: Pearson chi-square values show that the relationship among categories above is not random; there are statistically significant regional differences in support for minority rights issues.

For the Kemalist left, the SHP/CHP, the problem was socioeconomic. The solutions they offered remained limited to the eradication of poverty, ignorance, underdevelopment, and feudalism.[42] Neither the center-right parties of the 1950s and 1970s, the DP and the AP, nor their successors in the 1980s and 1990s, the DYP and the ANAP developed comprehensive platforms challenging the military's views. In rare cases when they tried to pursue alternative policies, their reforms were rebuked by the military on grounds that "terrorism" could be only dealt with security measures.[43] The policies do not change, but the reasons for denying rights have been conveniently varied. As for the Turkish nationalist, the MHP, its official position for decades has followed the state's official line and asserted that Kurds are either mountainous Turks or sub-ethnic/cultural group.

In comparison, the (Turkish) Islamist movements, including the Welfare Party (RP) and their successors, have long been attributing the Kurdish problem to *laïcité* and the Kemalist ideology, believing that the republican secularist policies weakened the religious ties between Turks and Kurds. While they recognized Kurds as a distinct group with its language and culture, they also wanted to keep them subordinated to a supranational Islamic identity.[44] They often highlighted human rights violations in the region but were careful not to offend the sensibilities of the nationalist state, emphasizing the integrity of the Turkish state under one flag and motherland.[45]

The AKP, offshoot of the Welfare Party and its successors, did not diverge from this tradition. Erdoğan's discourse and reform policies always emphasized the cultural rights of Kurds, which might resonate among conservative Turks who feel alienated from the Kemalist regime, even if they were enthusiastic about supporting Kurdish cultural and political rights. The AKP passed legislation that allowed the broadcasting of a Kurdish public TV channel, Kurdish radios, optional courses in Kurdish courses, and opening of several programs on the Kurdish language in several universities. The implementation of such reforms was pushed back and delayed by the courts, bureaucracy, and other agencies. But more importantly, neither these laws nor any Constitutional amendments mentioned or recognized Kurds. As the AKP has subdued its secularist rivals in the political and bureaucratic spheres in Turkish politics by the 2010s, it lost its reformist agenda and became a status-quo party with some religious makeup regarding the Kurdish issue.

Socialist movements, which remain on the fringes of political power, did not embrace the denial policies but neither were they enthusiastic about cultural and political rights of Kurds. Like "Islam is the solution," the socialists believed that "socialism is the solution" and social class identity supersedes all others, including ethnicity, in the struggle against the exploitative bourgeoisie/imperialism. Yeğen describes the 1990s as the years of rupture between the Kurdish movement and the Turkish left.[46] For instance, one of the most prominent leftist parties of the 1990s, the Party of Freedom and Solidarity (ÖDP), spoke about the need to solve the Kurdish problem but refrained from making it an essential element of the party's platform.[47] Two other parties representing the Turkish left in the 1990s, the Communist Party of Turkey (TKP) and the Labor Party (IP), failed even more thoroughly to recognize the autonomous position of the Kurdish movement. For the TKP, for instance, the Kurdish issue is merely an indicator of a class conflict. The IP, under the leadership of Doğu Perinçek, completely changed its position on the Kurdish movement over time. In 2005, the party declared that the Kurdish issue was resolved because democratic rights that Kurds had been demanding were now granted.[48] In the following years, Perinçek went even further by denying the Kurdish problem, supporting military operations and the closure of Kurdish parties and imprisonment of their leaders.

Do supporters reflect these parties' position on the Kurdish issue as well? Do we see major differences across party supporters toward the Kurdish demands? In order to gauge supporters of parties, we utilize a question in the survey, "which party they intend to vote in the June 7, 2015 elections?" Table 9.2 shows that a higher ratio of AKP supporters support cultural rights, compared to MHP and CHP supporters. MHP supporters are dismissive of giving linguistic

Table 9.2 Support for Cultural and Political Rights by Party Choice

Support for	AKP %	MHP %	CHP %	HDP %	Saadet/BBP %
Education in Mother Tongue	15.1	3.9	12.4	77.0	17.6
Optional Courses in Kurdish	37.2	16.2	32.4	92.0	53.7
Kurdish Names for Villages and Towns	19.2	5.9	16.0	82.8	33.3
Friday Sermon in Kurdish	32.5	15.5	24.8	79.3	46.3
Kurdish Language in Municipalities Hospitals and Courts	30.5	13.5	26.3	83.9	44.4
Kurdish as a Second Official Language	5.2	1.8	4.8	60.9	8.3
Regional Flag	2.5	1.1	3.4	46.5	0.0
Regional Parliament	4.8	1.9	6.3	48.3	3.7
Autonomy	5.5	1.2	4.7	51.8	5.6
Independence	8.7	13.5	10.5	33.7	5.6
N	2,240	862	1,584	87	109

Note: Pearson chi-square values show that the relationship among categories above is not random; there is a statistically significant relationship party choice and support for minority rights issues.

and cultural rights to Kurds, followed by CHP supporters. While 15 percent of AKP supporters support education in mother language, only 4 percent of MHP and 12 percent of CHP supporters do so. The difference is much more visible regarding other linguistic and cultural rights. For example, significant numbers of AKP supporters endorse optional Kurdish courses (37 percent), Friday sermon in Kurdish (32 percent), or receiving service in Kurdish in public institutions (30 percent). Support for these initiatives drops to 32, 25, and 26 percent among CHP and 16, 15, and 13 percent among MHP supporters, respectively. Restoring Kurdish names for geographical locations receives very low support among MHP supporters (6 percent), but higher among CHP (16 percent) and AKP supporters (19 percent).

However, party affiliation ceases to be an important factor when considering support for Kurdish political rights. Only 5 percent of AKP and CHP and 2 percent of MHP voters positively affirm the Kurdish language as a second official language. Similarly, the support for the autonomy of the Kurdish populated region remains around 5 percent among AKP and only 1 percent among MHP voters. Similarly, there is basically no support at all for the regional flag and parliament among MHP supporters. AKP, CHP, and MHP voters show higher support for secession/independence, reaching 9, 10, and 13 percent, respectively. This difference between support for independence and autonomy is likely to reflect the so-called "accept the status quo or leave" mentality among a small but non-negligible segment of the Turkish society.

The Saadet Party and the BBP, two small right-wing parties, formed an electoral coalition in the parliamentary elections. That's why we could not single out supporters of each party. Supporters of Saadet, which is the official successor of the Welfare Party, and BBP, which is a more religious version of ultra-nationalist MHP, exhibit relatively higher support for cultural rights: 54 percent of them support Kurdish optional courses and around 45 percent support Friday sermon in Kurdish and Kurdish service language in state institutions. Yet, similar to AKP supporters, only 5 percent of the Saadet and BBP supporters support autonomy and independence, and 8 percent of them support Kurdish as an official language.

Finally, a very low ratio of Turks are HDP supporters (around 1.6 percent). About 77 percent of Turks who vote for HDP, the main Kurdish political party in Turkey, support education in mother tongue and 92 percent of them endorse optional courses in Kurdish. Moving to political rights, 61 percent of them support Kurdish as a second official language, 52 percent of them support autonomy, and around 47 percent support a regional flag and parliament.

It is also insightful to consider if religiosity is associated with different views of the Kurdish issue among Turks. Several studies emphasized the role of religion affecting one's attitude toward the Kurdish conflict, while recent studies argue that shared religion is not a panacea.[49] However, all these studies focus on how religious Kurds form opinion toward the Kurdish conflict. Even though the AKP's religious discourse was heavily used in Kurdish-dominant cities, the intensity of such discourse was thin and sporadic in the western part of the country. Erdoğan and the AKP blamed the Kemalist policies on religion to divide between Turks and Kurds and labeled Kurds as the victims of the repressive policies under the single-party rule. One may expect that those who are religious espouse more sympathy toward Kurds and their linguistic and cultural rights (Erdoğan frequently cites the Quranic verse, God "created different ethnicities/ nations so that they should know one another") if not for their political rights. To test this expectation, we employ two survey questions, whether one prays five times a day and whether one fasts during Ramadan: those who do both are called "pious" while those do neither "non-pious."[50]

Figure 9.3 suggests that the non-pious Turks hold relatively higher positive attitudes toward cultural and political rights of Kurds, but the difference is minimal. For example, pious respondents hold 14 percent support for education in the mother language compared to 16 percent of non-pious respondents. Differences between two types of respondents regarding other cultural rights are also very low. Support for political rights declines significantly for both categories, with non-pious respondents exhibiting slightly higher support. The support for Kurdish as an official language and autonomy are 6 and 7 percent, respectively, among non-pious respondents, and 5 percent for both among the pious. Around 12 percent of non-pious respondents support independence, and 8.5 percent of pious ones.

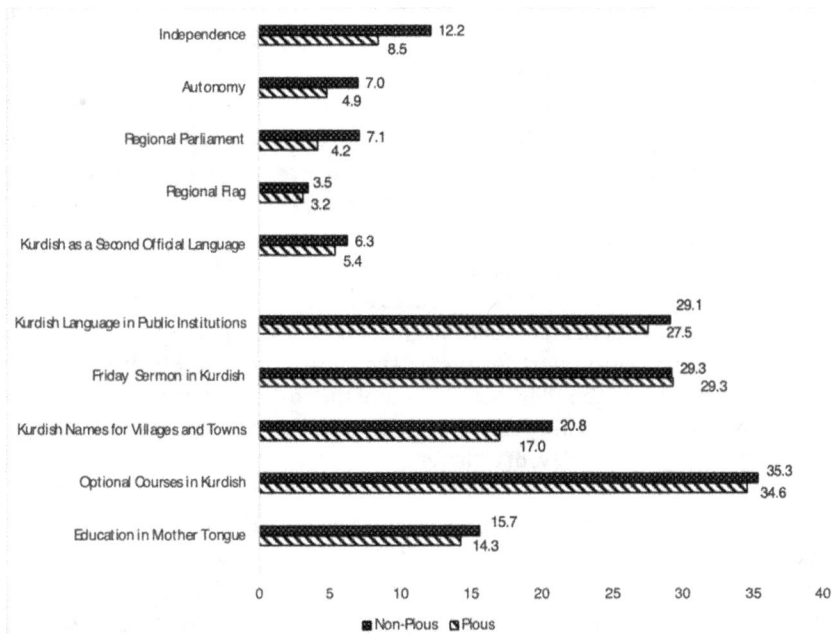

Figure 9.3 Support for Cultural and Political Rights among Turks by Religiosity (%)

Note: A series of t-tests suggests that there is a statistically significant relationship pious/ non-pious and issues above only for Independence, Regional Parliament, and Kurdish Names for Places.

Why does religion not matter? Recent studies[51] give some clues on ethnic identity and the Kurdish conflict. Türkmen (2018) discusses statist/nationalist intrinsic values that make Turkish citizens reluctant to recognize Kurdish ethnicity as a separate identity entitled to full cultural and political rights.[52] She argues that religious Turks develop "ethno-religious" identity even when they espouse the unity of *ummah* and recall Quranic principles (i.e., all races are equal before the God / all believers are brethren).[53] While arguing for the brotherhood of Turks and Kurds, they do not articulate support for policies that would reform the current ethnocratic Turkish political system. As the AKP has consolidated its power, Kurds are no longer perceived as the allies of the Islamic actors like in the 1990s when Turkish Islamic actors were seeking to change the secularist political status quo. Once religious Turks have replaced secular Turks as the new owners of the state, they view political Kurdish actors continuing to challenge the political status quo as hostile forces.

Conclusion

The nation-state formation process across the world, especially in multiethnic countries, results in the formation of intractable ethnic political hierarchies. Along these lines, this chapter suggests that the Turkish-dominant ethnic group does not want to share the political identity of the state with Kurds and prefers to preserve the hierarchical socioeconomic and political status quo. The widespread Turkish opposition to education in Kurdish and recognition of Kurdish as a second official language are the reflections of such preferences.[54] Turkish ethnocracy has changed over time in the way it operates but persists in most Turks' minds.[55] At the same time, they are less reluctant to grant second-order rights such as using the Kurdish language in public institutions like hospitals, courts, and municipalities while receiving service.

One can argue that an important reason for the failure of the Kurdish opening in 2015 was that Turkish public opinion opposed any reform that would reform the social and political hierarchy between Turks and Kurds. While this is a plausible argument, it overlooks the fact that the AKP started the opening policies when there was already low support for them. The support for the Kurdish opening policies in Turkey was about 46 percent before the so-called Habur events in fall 2009 but declined to 35 percent in the immediate aftermath and then 27 percent shortly after.[56] The Habur events, the entrance of a group of PKK militants at Habur Border Gate as part of the opening policies, created a nationalist backlash whose lingering effects persisted long after the events. The subsequent opening policies were conducted in an already hostile political context.

Second, the failure of the opening policies cannot be solely attributed to public opinion. The fact that the AKP incorporated neither civil society organizations nor other political parties into the political process facilitated the formation of a broad coalition of nationalist groups vehemently opposing the Kurdish opening policies.[57] For instance, the CHP, a party that initiated the Kurdish openings in the early 1990s, opposed the AKP's Kurdish opening. Despite these forms of opposition, the AKP launched the opening policies and received tacit public support. It does not mean that the AKP's electoral concerns did not play a role in the failure of the opening policies,[58] but there are other factors that need to be taken into consideration while judging the failure of the opening policies. The high distrust between the state and the Kurdish political movement significantly increased after the formation of de facto Kurdish autonomy in Syria. Moreover, the presence of various factions with different positions on the Kurdish issue within the state and the PKK and the absence of third parties that further diminished trust between the two actors all contributed to the failure.

Importantly, the elites posed a major problem for the success of the opening policies. Somer and Liaras found the low support among elites for the opening policies, in particular, support for education and broadcasting in Kurdish. As a lasting solution to the Kurdish problem, which is primarily about political rights, not only public but also elite support has to substantially change their position toward the conflict.[59] Zaller, Dalton, and many other political behavior scholars showed that the public receives cues from their trusted elites.[60] In the Turkish context, political elites could shape the public opinion and bridge gaps between the two ethnic groups at least in the middle and long run. Unfortunately, this did not happen. Social, political, and economic elites, while diverging in their positions on social, economic, and political issues, converge on their positions when it comes to the Kurdish conflict, pursuing the statist policies. This convergence is a great legacy of the Turkish state, which has not only facilitated anti-Kurdish sentiments and hate crimes against Kurds in Turkish society but has also made the peaceful coexistence of Turks and Kurds improbable.

Notes

1   Turks here refers to those who accept Turkish identity as their primary ethnic identity. See the data section for the survey questions that capture Turkish and Kurdish identity.
2   Çelik and Blum (2007: 67); Heper (2007); Tezcür (2010).
3   For further detail on those studies that provide empirical insights about Turkish perceptions of Kurds, please check the following: Bilali (2014); Çelebi et al. (2016); Dixon and Ergin (2010).
4   We used several questions to capture ethnic Turks and ethnic Kurds identifications, as discussed in the data section.
5   Hechter (2000); Wimmer (2002); Yiftachel (2006).
6   Wimmer (2002).
7   Sidanius and Pratto (2001: 46).
8   Blalock (1962); Jost et al. (2004); Pratto, Sidanius, and Levin (2006).
9   Pratto et al. (1994); Sidanius and Pratto (1991).
10   Sidanius and Pratto (2001).
11   Özok-Gündoğan (2014); Yadırgı (2017); see also Ohannes Kılıçdağı's mention in this book of the Ottoman military expeditions in the 1830s against the Kurdish emirs.
12   For an interesting take on the relations between Armenians and Kurds in the context of centralization reforms applied by the Ottoman administration, please see Ohannes Kılıçdağı's chapter in this book.

13 Buzan et al. (1998); Roe (2004); Yeğen (2009).
14 Aslan (2011).
15 Yeğen (2009); and also, for how and why Westerners and Armenians viewed Kurds through the orientalists lens, see Zeynep Kaya's and Ohannes Kılıçdağı's chapters in this book.
16 Firat (1983); Sılan (2010).
17 Zeydanlıoğlu (2012).
18 Heper (2007).
19 Ayhan also makes an argument that Yezidi identity was compressed not only by pro-Arab policies under the Ba'th Party but also by pro-Kurdish identity under KRG.
20 Ünlü (2016).
21 Aslan (2007).
22 E.g., Sılan (2010).
23 Güven (2005); Oran (2013).
24 Bahcheli and Noel (2011).
25 Uluğ and Cohrs (2016); see Ayhan in this volume and Karakoç (2013) for the reasons why Yezidis and Kurds have higher confidence in international organizations than national ones.
26 Aktan (2012).
27 Sezgin and Wall (2005).
28 Tezcür 2014; Weiss (2016: 577).
29 Somer and Glüpker-Kesebir (2016: 8).
30 Tezcür (2014: 176–80).
31 Dixon and Ergin (2010).
32 Ergin (2012).
33 Saraçoğlu (2010).
34 Çelebi et al. (2016).
35 Sarıgil and Karakoç (2016a).
36 We are grateful for Zeki Sarıgil who provided the public opinion survey used in this study.
37 Hosgor and Smith (2002), using intermarriage data collected as part of the Turkish Demographic and Health Surveys, show that Turks and Kurds are more likely to form mixed marriages in regions where either of them is minority. They also found that a Kurdish man is more likely to marry a Turkish woman; the educational level of the former is higher than the latter. Our findings, not shown here, suggest that those with a Kurdish mother are less likely to demand cultural and political rights than those with a Kurdish father (50 percent versus 69 percent for cultural rights and 25 percent versus 40 for political rights). This suggests that nationalistic identity is likely to derive from fathers than mothers.
38 Including these categories does not change the substantive interpretation of the results.
39 Both conservative and secular political elites usually claim that discrimination by officials or institutions are isolated cases that cannot be generalized to the state.
40 The social contact theory argues that intergroup contact successfully hinders prejudice and increases tolerance. Yet further research shows that the positive effects of social contact are in fact conditional on the nature of the contact itself. For instance, when people have common goals, when they are not in competition, and are in relatively equal class or status, the likelihood of positive interactions increases (Cook 1962, 1978; Forbes 1997; Pettigrew 1986, 1997).

41 Gidengil and Karakoç (2016).
42 Yeğen (2016).
43 Loizides (2008).
44 Bahcheli and Noel (2011).
45 Sakallioglu (1998).
46 Yeğen (2007).
47 Yeğen (2016).
48 Yeğen (2007: 1230).
49 Some of those studies are the following: Gurses (2018); Karakoç and Sarıgil (2020); Sarıgil (2018).
50 For the sake of simplicity, the results of other religiosity categories are not shown here.
51 Gurses (2018); Sarıgil (2018).
52 Türkmen (2018).
53 Ibid.
54 An earlier survey (2013) that asked the same questions does not display a significant difference on the same issues (Sarıgil and Karakoç 2016b).
55 Bilici (2017).
56 Kayhan Pusane (2014).
57 Çiçek (2018); Kayhan Pusane (2014).
58 Tezcür (2014).
59 Somer and Liaras (2010).
60 Dalton (2013); Zaller (1992).

"WE ARE YEZIDI, BEING OTHERWISE NEVER STOPPED OUR PERSECUTION": YEZIDI PERCEPTIONS OF KURDS AND KURDISH IDENTITY

Tutku Ayhan

Introduction

The nature of Yezidi identity, as well as the origins of the Yezidi religion, has long been contested. The question of the ethnic identity of this religious minority has carried significant political implications since the establishment of the new Iraqi State. While Kurdish nationalist leaders increased over time their claims on the Kurdish origins of the Yezidis, the Ba'th regime adopted a discourse, which appraised them as Arabs. The fact that most Yezidi settlements in Iraq fall under the territories disputed between the central Iraqi and the Kurdish Regional Government (KRG)—a topic that has become even more critical after 2003—reinforced the relevance of ethnic belonging of the Yezidi minority. The KRG thus far adopted various strategies to have the support of religious minorities in the northern Nineveh region, strategies including economic support, co-option, and coercion. When it comes to the Yezidis, the distinct religious group whose members mostly speak the Kurmanji dialect of Kurdish, it has endorsed the rhetoric, which asserts that the Yezidis are ethnic Kurds and an inseparable part of Kurdistan.

The Yezidis and Kurds, who have coexisted in the same region, have a long history of tribal relations and social interaction. In contemporary times, the Yezidi-Kurdish relations in Iraq had different dynamics than in the post-2003 era, and it took a completely different momentum after the 2014 Islamic State (IS) attacks against the Yezidis. In this chapter, I aim to analyze, in a historical context, the perception of the Yezidis, who had been labeled as "double minority" for their precarious existence in Iraq and Syria,[1] of the Kurds and Kurdish identity. While my focus is on Yezidis of Iraq, I also touch upon the Yezidi perceptions of the Kurds in Caucasia, Germany, and North America.

The fieldwork informing this chapter has received an approval from IRB at UCF (#SBE-18-13819).

We currently observe a (re)construction of a separate ethnoreligious Yezidi identity where Yezidis from different backgrounds define themselves as a distinct ethnic group. Also, the word "Kurd" is associated with "Muslim" for most of the Yezidis in Iraq as well as in diaspora. I argue that a rather fixed, primordialist self-interpretation of their identity as a historically victimized and marginalized minority group contributes to the recent (re)construction efforts of identity. This fixed perception, on the other hand, stems from three main factors: first of all, the Yezidi myth of genesis attributes separate origins for Yezidis than the rest of the humankind. The community practices endogenous marriage to preserve the purity of their "race."[2] Although borders between the Yezidis and the Kurds have been historically porous, there has been a distance in intercommunal relations since the late Ottoman period when ethnic and religious identities started to gain greater significance. Secondly, the IS's genocidal campaign, based on its Salafi jihadist ideology, which considers the Yezidis an "apostate" group that should be eradicated, is perceived as a continuation of other anti-Yezidi attacks in history.[3] Lastly, there is a widespread Yezidi feeling of powerlessness and being pawns in the wider Arab-Kurdish conflict. All these factors lead to a fixed self-interpretation of the Yezidi identity as members of a historically persecuted group, which, in turn, contributes to the (re)construction of an ethnoreligious identity, a phenomenon we observe among the community since 2014. According to this perception, the Kurds are identified primarily as Muslims and have the same status as the Muslim Arabs and Turks who have been persecuting them for ages.

In that sense, the Yezidi views of the Kurds significantly differ from Turkish, Western or Armenian views of Kurds as suggested respectively by Ekrem Karakoç and Ege Özen, Zeynep Kaya, and Ohannes Kılıçdağı in this book. While Karakoç and Özen suggest that the Turks, as a dominant ethnic group, consider the Kurds in Turkey as their subordinate, Kaya shows that most of the Western orientalists who traveled to Kurdish regions depicted them as backward and tribal. Interestingly, according to Kılıçdağı, the Armenians, who hold a religious minority status in the Ottoman Empire, considered the latter as barbaric and uneducated who were living under feudal kinships, and even took on a mission to "educate" their Kurdish neighbors. The Yezidis on the other hand, who mostly speak the same language as the Kurds and who longtime lived in similar tribe systems with even higher illiteracy rates, may perceive the Kurds as violent, but certainly not as "backward."[4]

For this chapter, I utilize historical and contemporary documents (i.e., reports by international associations and local organizations) as well as dozens of face-to-face interviews I have conducted in May 2018 and May 2019 in Duhok, Iraqi Kurdistan among Yezidis, and also several online interviews with Yezidis of Iraq and Turkey who are currently living in diaspora. I conducted 116 in-depth semi-structured interviews in total with a wide range of individuals including religious and political leaders, displaced persons living in camps, survivors of IS genocidal attacks, activists, social workers, professionals, and also Kurdish authorities. These interviews develop a comprehensive view of the Yezidi population with regard to social caste, economic class, gender, age, and geographical location.

Contested Origins of the Yezidi Identity

Historically, outside attitudes of the Yezidis usually center around their consideration as an eccentric, backward community that worships the devil. Although there have been plenty of writings about the Yezidis over the centuries, Yezidi self-representations have been rare until recently. There are different views in the literature about the origins of the Yezidis who had been living in areas spread between northern Iraq, southeastern Turkey, and northwestern Syria[5] as a traditional, close-knit community. Some views seek the origins of the Yezidis in Assyrian or Sumerian civilizations; others represent the Yezidi faith a deviation from Islam.[6] There is today a scholarly consensus on the fact that Sheikh Adi, who has a very central place in Yezidi teachings, was the Adi b. Musafir who established the Sufi Adawiya order in twelfth century.[7] As a matter of fact, some Yezidi Sheikh families are reported to claim to be descendants of the Umayyad caliph Marwan b. al-Hakam[8] or even of Muawiya I.[9]

Another prevalent view on Yezidi ethnic origins considers them as the Kurds[10] and their religion as a modern incarnation of Zoroastrianism, the believed ancestral religion of the Kurds. The idea seems to be first theorized by Bedirxan brothers, an illustrious family whose members committed to the Kurdish nationalist cause, in the 1930s in their efforts to build a Kurdish national identity. Based on the writings of European travelers, they argued that Zoroastrianism, which was still practiced by Kurdish peasants, was the original religion of Kurdish people and the Yezidis were the representatives of this ancient belief.[11] As the Kurdish nationalist movement rose in the 1960s, Kurdish political elites, as well as certain Yezidis, started to espouse this view.

Despite internal divisions in the community about their origins, most Yezidis agree on the ancient roots of their religion. During my fieldwork, I was told many contrasting views on the ancestry by community leaders or "old savants" (ordinary, and especially young, Yezidis did not seem to know much about the origins of their religion), from Assyrian roots to Sumerian forefathers, or the Zoroastrian past.[12] However, even when they acknowledged Zoroastrian origin and claimed themselves as the original Kurds, most Yezidis would not necessarily embrace the Kurdish identity, as after all, "Kurds are today Muslims and not Yezidis anymore."

According to the Yezidi theology, the Yezidis are descendants of Adam's son who was conceived in a jar, whereas the rest of humanity are descendants of Adam and Eve.[13] The ban on outside marriage and expulsion from the faith of those who marry outsiders stem from the idea of keeping the purity and distinctiveness of the community safe. Language wise, the Iraqi Yezidis speak the Kurmanji dialect of Kurdish, although the Sinjari Yezidis have a heavy accent, which easily differentiate them from the Muslim Kurds. Only those in Bashiqa and Bahzani, predominantly Yezidi villages near Mosul, speak Arabic as their primary language.

At the same time, it should be emphasized that the Yezidis were not as isolated as it has been long argued. Throughout history, they had social and economic interactions with the Kurds, the Arabs, and other non-Muslim communities, especially the Christians. There were even periods between the sixteenth and nineteenth centuries when their tribal associations with the Kurds prevailed their religious differences.[14] However, at the turn of the twentieth century, the Yezidis found themselves in the midst of newly emerging nation-states in which ethnic identities increasingly became the core of national identities. From then on, they would try to survive in the ethnically heterogeneous environment of northern Iraq.

Yezidi Communities across Regions

Before proceeding with historical analysis, it is important to summarize persistent structural conditions characterizing the Yezidis' existence in Iraq. First of all, we see *exemption from conscription* as one of the key demands of the Yezidis throughout the Tanzimat period in the nineteenth century, also continuing into the twentieth century. They mainly oppose military service for the fears of assimilation and conversion to Islam.[15] Their demands fail for good when the Iraqi state passes a law on compulsory military service in 1934.[16]

Land tenureship is another ongoing problem. Most Sinjari Yezidis have not possessed land titles since the Ottoman rule. When they were resettled in collective towns (*mujammaʿat*) in the 1970s, they were still not given any land titles, and the ownership of land in Sinjar has been one of the most controversial topics in the region since 2003.[17] Hence, competition with other communities (both in Sinjar and Sheikhan) over scarce land and water is a considerable structural issue. Related to this, *the precariousness* of Nineveh, especially Sinjar, is another problem that should be taken into consideration. According to the UNDP Report in 2006, the overall deprivation in Sinjar is "very extreme" and Sinjar is one of the least developed districts in Iraq. Of special concern is the lack of infrastructure, supply of potable water, health care, housing, and education.[18] Another factor contributing to their marginalized status in Iraq is their lack of any significant political power. Moreover, prejudices about their religious identity is widespread among not only Muslims, but the whole Iraqi society. Given these circumstances, the Yezidis are concerned with their survival in their relations with other ethnic groups.

One last point that needs attention is the *intra-community differences in shifting self-perceptions* of ethnic identity. This chapter focuses on the Iraqi Yezidis, who mainly live in Sinjar and Sheikhan regions. In the Iraqi context, we can speak of a difference in ethnic identity perceptions between these two communities. The Yezidis living in areas of Sheikhan that mostly fell under Kurdish control after 1992 have been more willing to embrace a Kurdish identity compared to the Sinjari Yezidis who were controlled by the Iraqi government until the fall of Saddam. Sheikhan also happens to be where religious and political leaders of the community reside and these leaders have been co-opted by various patronage mechanisms into the Kurdish political system.

For the Yezidis of Caucasus, dominant tendency has been to self-identify as Yezidis and not Kurds.[19] The Armenian state, recognizing Yezidis and Kurds as two distinct minority groups, grants them each a minority seat at the parliament.[20] According to Maisel,[21] the Yezidis in Syria were influenced by the cultural, socioeconomic, and political conditions of their environment while shaping self-perceptions of identity: the Yezidis in Afrin (northwest Syria) are better integrated to the larger society and face less discrimination, they speak Arabic, and they don't prohibit exogenous marriage.[22] The Yezidis of Jazira (northeastern part), on the other hand, are affected to a larger extent from border politics, assimilation, and persecution, which made victimhood an important aspect of their identity building. Maisel also argues that, for the Yezidis of Jazira, espousing a Kurdish identity and supporting policies of the predominant Kurdish political group (PYD) brought protection and moved them up in the ethnic hierarchical ladder.

In Germany, where the biggest Yezidi diaspora lives,[23] we see an increasing sympathy, especially among the young and educated Yezidis, toward the Kurdish nationalist movement and the idea that Yezidis are the original Kurds and followers of Zoroastraniasm in German diaspora in the 1990s.[24] This is conceivably related to the fact that most Yezidi and Kurdish immigrants in Germany originated from Turkey, which leads them to share an experience of Turkish victimization.[25] What also plays a role is the efforts of PKK offshoots in Germany to allure Yezidis to the Kurdish independence movement.[26] While some of my Yezidi respondents from Turkey who are living in Germany also espoused the view that Yezidis and Kurds share a common ethnic identity,[27] others claimed a separate ethnoreligious identity for Yezidis.

Finally, there are around 10,000 Yezidis in North America, with the largest community being based in Nebraska, Lincoln (around 3,000). The first wave of immigration to Nebraska took place in the 1990s. Some of the Yezidis who escaped the Iran-Iraq war and were living in the refugee camps in Syria, started settling in the United States in the 1990s. The second wave was after 2003 when the Yezidis who worked for the US army during the war as interpreters, and their families, applied for asylum and were resettled in Nebraska. The third wave was after the 2014 genocide. The Yezidi NGOs and cultural centers were soon established after the IS atrocities in Sinjar, and today they engage in awareness raising, lobbying, and fundraising for the community. My interview participants who worked in these centers also described the Yezidis as a distinct ethnoreligious group.[28]

A Historical Glance at the Yezidi-Kurdish Relations

The Yezidis, as not being considered "People of the Book," lacked any protection under Islamic law during the Ottoman rule. Their relationship with the state had largely been characterized by the tension between Yezidi demands for being exempt from conscription and government efforts to establish greater control over the community.[29] Although forced conversion of Yezidis was attempted during Abdülhamid's reign, it was not a constant concern for the Ottomans. On the other hand, in her depiction of the social interaction between the Yezidi and Kurdish tribes in Sinjar since the sixteenth century, Nelida Fuccaro[30] convincingly argues against the misconception that the Yezidis were historically isolated. To give an example of this interaction, in *Sharafnama*, a famous source of Kurdish history written by the emir of Bitlis, seven prominent Kurdish tribes are described as Yezidi.[31] Yet, despite the Yezidi-Kurdish tribal bonds and the widespread connections of Yezidis in Sheikhan to Kurds, the marginalized status of the Yezidis under the Ottoman rule and suspicions about expansionist desires of Kurdish leaders kept most of the Yezidis on guard against their Muslim neighbors. Moreover, the accounts by travelers to the region reflect Yezidis' perception of the distinctiveness of their identity.[32]

As a matter of fact, the nineteenth century witnessed a series of anti-Yezidi attacks not only by Ottoman forces but also by Kurdish tribal *aghas*, who were, in some cases, supported by government officials.[33] In the collective Yezidi memory, the attacks of Kurdish Mir of Rowanduz, Mohammad Kor, who killed more than half of the Yezidis in Sheikhan in 1832, are almost as central as the Omar Wehbi Pasha's campaigns in 1892. Nonetheless, the main Ottoman concerns in its administration of the "Yezidi question" appear to be related to their conscription, tax debts, and the banditry around Mount Sinjar targeting the trade caravans. The religious aspect seems to get in the picture as a factor shaping the form anti-Yezidi violence takes (i.e., enslavement of women and children, mass killings). Also, in the case of Mohammed Kor, tribal conflicts shaped the dynamics of violence. Yet the common Yezidi understanding of the violence against their community in history perceives each of these episodes as the Yezidis being targeted by Muslims for religious reasons. It does not much matter whether the Muslim is a Kurd, Arab, Turk, or Persian. This perception has been only reinforced since the Islamic State's genocidal campaigns.

As the British colonial administration accelerated the establishment of a modern nation-state in Iraq after the First World War, the ethnic/national identities gained prominence over religious identities. As stated by Fuccaro,[34] the leaders of Kurdish nationalism (Sheikh Mahmud and Sheik Ahmad of Barzan, and Sheikh Said) adopted predominantly a Sunni/Islamist discourse in the 1920s, and their ideas of Kurdish self-determination and their emphasis on national identity over tribal identities did not appeal much to Yezidis. Accordingly, Kurdish leading intellectuals' proposal in 1929 about the establishment of a Kurdish administrative unit did not even mention Sheikhan or Sinjar. Even though the Sinjari Yezidis were considered as part of Kurdistan in the petition of the Society for the Independence of Kurdistan, published two months later than the first proposal, we can speak of a lack of a sustained interest on the part of Kurdish nationalists about the Yezidis until 1960s.[35]

Overall, one might argue that the relatively modern and Western concepts of national ethnic identity took time to disseminate among the traditional Yezidi society. However, even when not using these terms in their modern sense, they have always been cognizant of the categorical difference between themselves and Kurds. While the social distance between the two communities seems to vary throughout history, the Yezidi practice of endogamy and the myth on their distinct origins have strongly contributed to their sense of being a distinct community. For instance, in the letter written by a group of Yezidi leaders to the Ottoman administration in 1872 asking for exemption from compulsory recruitment based on religious reasons, they mention how the Yezidis need to pray two times a day without the presence of a Muslim, Christian, or Jewish; or how they are not allowed to use a spoon of a Muslim, drink from the cup of a Muslim, or use a comb or razor, which has been previously used by a Muslim.[36] In a similar document, written by Ismail Chol Beg from the Mir family in 1908, he notes: "It is forbidden for Yezidis to enter into relations with those who belong to other nations. Otherwise they incur the curse of God."[37]

Ba'th Rule and the Establishment of Kurdish Autonomy

After the establishment of the British mandate over Iraq, the Yezidis had declared their request for protection from the British authorities.[38] A letter written by a Yezidi tribe leader to the British Ambassador in 1941 asking for protection against Iraqi government and conscription suggests that Yezidi demands of external/ international protection persisted even after the official end of the mandate in 1932.[39] These requests yielded no results while the pressure by the Iraqi government became more tangible by time, especially in Sheikhan, such that Bayazid Beg, Mir Tahseen Beg's cousin, claimed Umayyad descent for Sheikh Adi, and as his followers, for the Yezidis. As discussed by Majid Hassan Ali in his chapter in this book, under the influence of rising Arab nationalism, Bayazid Beg emphasized similarities between Yezidism and Islam and he organized the "Yezidi Umayyad" movement in Baghdad in 1964.[40]

The 1960s were also years the Kurdish intellectuals and leaders increased their efforts in building a national identity. Gathering all Kurdish-speaking communities under Kurdish identity and referring to a national religious myth dating back to Islam were parts of these efforts. According to this narrative, Zoroastrianism is considered as the original religion of Kurds who had long been inhabitants of Mesopotamia, and Yezidism reflects its current survival. Inasmuch as there were Sinjari Yezidis who joined peshmerga in the 1970s, it suggests a degree of success of Kurdish mobilization efforts.[41]

As the conflict intensified between the Iraqi government and the peshmerga, Ba'th regime engaged in a more systematic Arabization policy in northern Iraq, targeting religious minorities in particular. Thousands of Yezidis were deported from their ancestral lands on Sinjar Mountain to be resettled in collective villages in open plains, where the Iraqi army had better control. State services failed to provide basic needs of those villages, and Yezidis, who were earning their livelihoods out of trucking and livestock on the mountain, could find no other

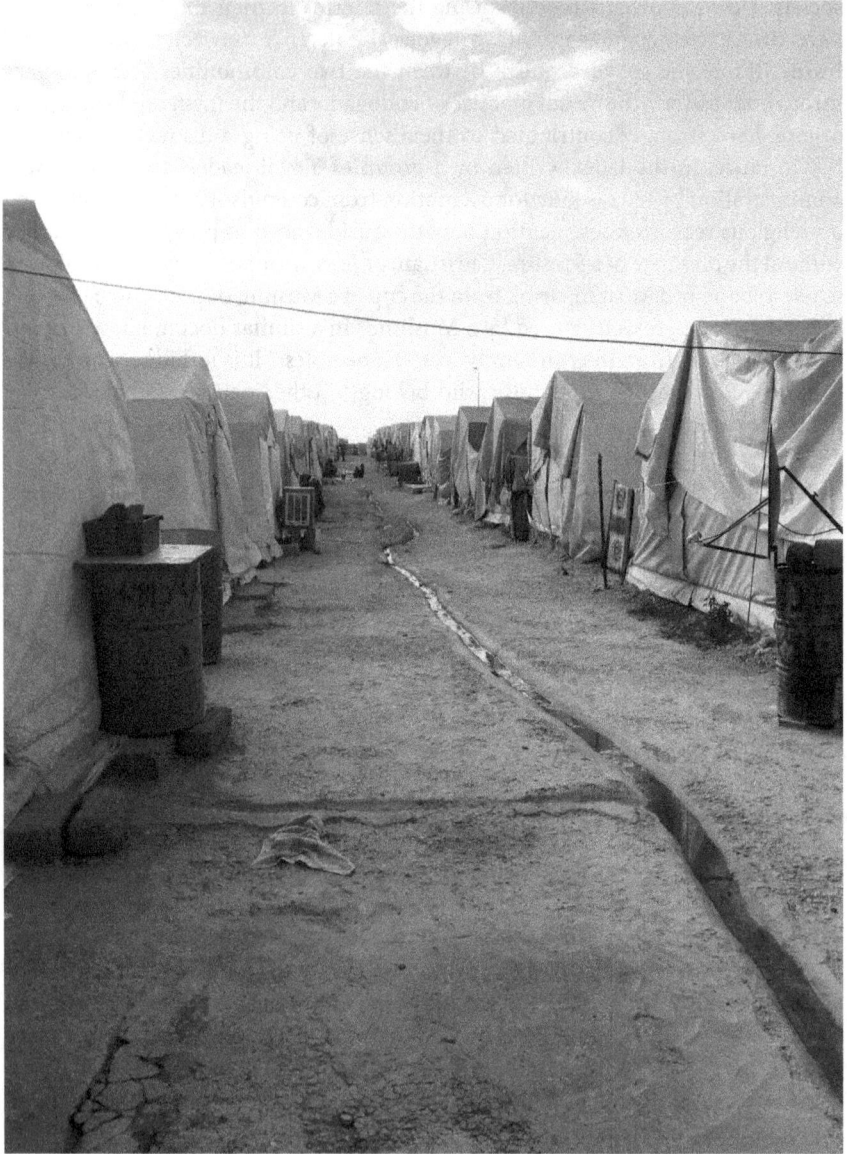

Figure 10.1 A view of the tents in the Sharya camp populated by displaced Yezidis (Duhok, May 2018)

alternative in the plains than to work in Arab landowners' farms or to work as laborers in construction in several Arab cities. One other alternative would be enlisting in the Iraqi army. Despite their low levels of education, Yezidis had their first generation of college graduates by 1970s.[42] Coming to the 1980s, some sources cite several thousand Yezidis who were massacred alongside Kurds during the Anfal massacres in 1988.[43] There are also accounts about Yezidi soldiers' involvement in the campaign on the Iraqi army's side.[44]

At the end of the First Gulf War, Yezidi villages like Khanke and Sharya in Duhok governorate, and Lalish in Sheikhan stayed under Kurdish administration, whereas Sinjar was still controlled by the central government. After 1992, Kurdish political entrepreneurs addressed Yezidis as part of the Kurdish nation and attended Yezidi religious celebrations.[45] However, these gestures and discourses at the political level failed to transform intercommunal perceptions between Yezidis and Muslim Kurds. Even today, among middle-class, secular Kurds who believe in Zoroastrian roots of Kurds and Yezidis, prejudices about Yezidis and the "devil-worshippers" stigma run deep. The kind of views on the community as eccentric and ignorant are still held by many Kurds.[46] On the part of Yezidis, Kurdish identity and the idea that Yezidis are the original Kurds are welcomed by many who live in the KRG. Nonetheless, Yezidi prejudices and negative perceptions about Muslims also run deep. Most Yezidi-Kurdish interaction, which does not go beyond formal friendships and limited contact, is characterized by Yezidi feelings of distrust, fears of assimilation or persecution, and Muslim feelings of aversion.[47]

The Post-2003 Chaos and Yezidis

As sectarian conflict and insecurity prevail over the country after the US invasion in 2003, the Sinjari Yezidis, who are deeply affected by the ethnic violence spiral, have had divided ideological and political attitudes toward Kurdish authorities. When anti-Yezidi violence by radical groups becomes more frequent and Baghdad and Mosul become "no-go areas" for Yezidis[48] Sinjaris start migrating to Kurdish cities such as Duhok, Erbil, and Sulaymaniyah to work as laborers. The Yezidis—especially the middle class—in Kurdish Regional Government (KRG) engage in closer relationships with the Kurdistan Democratic Party (KDP), preferring the stable and secular Kurdish regime to the rest of Iraq.[49] In Sinjar, those who support a separate Yezidi identity and an independent Yezidi political movement established a party called "Yezidi Movement for Reform and Progress," which would win the Yezidi quota seat in Iraqi parliament in 2005, 2010, and 2014. One of the party leaders, Ameen Farhan Jejo, actually engages in ideological theorization to build a national identity and writes books about Yezidi language and "Yezidi nation."[50] The party would win only 20 percent of the vote share in Sinjar in the 2005 provincial elections whereas Kurdish Alliance received 60 percent of votes.

In August 2007, two trucks loaded with bombs are detonated in Yezidi towns of Siba Sheik Xidir and Til Ezer, killing more than 300 civilians in what would become the worst attack in the country against civilians since 2003. After the attacks, KDP increased its control over the Sinjar area, establishing party offices, checkpoints, and administrative buildings with KRG flags. With Islamist groups' siege on Sinjar,

Figure 10.2 A visualization of the Yezidi displacement in Sinjar in August 2014 (Artist: Olgu Ergin)

the region got completely cut off from Mosul and depended entirely on the KRG. Lacking any health services or education, Yezidis did not have any other option than to accept Kurdish authority. After 2007, Duhok governorate started providing fuel and other supplies to Sinjar.[51]

In short, Yezidis find themselves as pawns in the larger Kurdish-Arab conflict in Nineveh after in the post-2003 Iraq. The Kurdish government pushes religious minorities in Nineveh (including Christians, Assyrians, Shabaks, Yezidis, and Turkmens) to align with its policies—at times by patronage and networks,[52] other times by repression[53]—in order to claim rights on disputed territories. The Kurdish territorial expansion led Arabs to desert their land in fear of Kurdish aggression and contributed to deterioration of Arab-Yezidi relations in Sinjar. In the 2009 provincial elections, Kurdish parties, while losing most of their seats to Arab parties, increased their vote share in Sinjar.[54] Nonetheless, it would be wiser to interpret Yezidi political behavior in 2009 as a search for a realistic promise of protection when concerns for insecurity peak, rather than their assimilation into Kurdish politics and identity. Hence, we can say that physical security and economic survival outweighed ethnic considerations for much of the Sinjari Yezidis. As a matter of fact, we do see certain strata of the Yezidi community getting a level of economic prosperity after 2007; some families could afford to buy or construct fancy houses; young Yezidis invested in cars; more people were able to send their children to school in Sinjar. However, economic disadvantage and discrimination continued to shape the experience of most of the Yezidis in Sinjar, who are employed in precarious, low-paying jobs.[55] In 2009, the Yezidis of Sheikhan described their social position to International Crisis Group as "second-class citizens" compared to Muslim Kurds.[56] The Sinjari Yezidis claimed services and compensations to be allocated only to party members. Unlike Christians and Turkmens, Yezidis also lacked any quota or minority seats in the Kurdish parliament, as they are considered ethnic Kurds.[57]

Overall, patronage relations in Sinjar led to a reaction from community members who opposed "assimilation in return for protection." As of 2009, even though some Yezidis considered peshmerga existence in Sinjar as a vital protection against a future attack, others emphasized their demand for a locally recruited, politically independent security force on the ground.[58] As the majority group in Sinjar, they expressed their claim to have the majority in the administration of Sinjar. The UN report also mentions that most Yezidis, even those who advocated peshmerga protection on Sinjar, when in total privacy, asserted the need for a law, which would protect Yezidis as a distinct ethnoreligious group. Regarding Yezidi leadership, Mir Tahseen declared Yezidis as ethnic Kurds who had the right to protect their particularity and asked Kurdish politicians not to gentrify Yezidi settlements.[59]

After the 74th Firman

Yezidi fears about a future attack were dramatically realized when the so-called Islamic State targeted the community in a genocidal campaign in August 2014. The Yezidis of Sinjar became an open prey to the IS fighters when peshmerga forces retreated from the area only hours before the attack, without any notice. Peshmerga's failure to protect Sinjar, as well as participation of some Arab tribal leaders—including Tayy, Khawatina, and Mitewta tribes—in the attacks,[60] has had a major influence on Yezidi self-perceptions and their perceptions of Kurds and Kurdish identity.

The reasons for peshmerga retreat remain unknown, yet it has clearly led to a massive feeling of betrayal among Yezidis who have witnessed their Muslim neighbors and *kreef*,[61] killing Yezidi men, kidnapping women and children. Many no longer see their future in safety in Iraq. Though Yezidi officials working for KRG or those who have economic ties to the regime refrain from openly criticizing Kurdish authorities, at the community level, a general level of distrust and belief in the idea that their survival depends on international protection is very dominant. The same can be said for many Yezidis who are involved with the Patriotic Union of Kurdistan (YNK), the Sulaymaniyah-based political party, rival of Masoud Barzani's KDP.[62]

However, the reality on the ground further complicates the picture. Today, almost 350,000 Yezidis are displaced in KRG territory, living in camps or in unfinished buildings.[63] Duhok governorate has hosted thousands of Internally Displaced Persons (IDPs) since 2014, pushing its infrastructural and economic capacity to limit despite the international aid. Moreover, although it is not much voiced to outsiders, host communities may hold resentments against Yezidi IDPs. Hence, their dependence on KDP for survival as well as the political intimidations they face put Yezidis once again in a vulnerable situation. During my fieldwork, participants (especially camp habitants) expressed their fears of speaking out, some even admitting their fear of arrestment. Yet the question of their ethnic identity has become all the more relevant today. As the topic of disputed territories remains unsolved between the two governments, the Kurdish authorities, which lost their control over Sinjar in October 2017, still need the support and loyalty of minority groups in northern Iraq to further its claims on the territory, which, in turn, increases the pressure and control on Yezidis.

In such a context, my own identity as a researcher posed challenges at times. In many cases, one of the first question my respondents ask would be about my country of origin, which hid the implicit question of whether I was a Muslim. Some finished the interview saying that they would never speak the way they did if I was to be a Muslim. During my visit to the field in 2019, I decided not to direct at all the question on ethnic identity to camp residents. Even starting a topic on current politics was usually enough to scare the respondents to tell me that they didn't know anything about politics. Activists and community leaders in general were less timid to touch on the subject. Some of the activists I talked to asserted being threatened by Kurdish authorities for criticizing government policies and that they were being forced to either leave the country or to keep quiet.

Another thing I observed during the interviews was how my respondents were presenting the community as a single, monolithic block, pretty much hiding any internal dissent or conflict. There are, however, significant intra-communal differences on the ethnic identity question. As mentioned above, while ordinary Yezidis from Sinjar tend to consider themselves as a distinct ethnic group, government employees in KRG, some politicians, or those serving the peshmerga, are more open to accept a Kurdish identity, for obvious reasons. According to Nicolaus and Yuce,[64] while one reason for this cooperation can be traced to personal interests or patronage networks, another reason (especially on the part of religious and political leaders) can be found in the search for support and protection for the community. That is why, for the authors, Hazim Tahseen Said who became the Mir after his father's death in 2019 thanks Masoud Barzani "for representing Kurdish Yezidis" but says on another media outlet that Yezidis are not aligned with any political parties. Furthermore, Mir's other son, Breen Tahseen Said, criticizes KDP for not caring about Yezidis but only for its political and territorial control.[65]

Almost none of the narratives in my interview data makes a differentiation between "Kurds" and "Muslims,"[66] and the word "Kurd" is associated with the word "Muslim." This obviously does not mean Yezidis hold hostile feelings against all Muslims; I was told many times of cases where Muslims helped their Yezidi neighbors to flee IS's attack. Yet the data I gathered, what I heard from other researchers and experts, as well as the majority of journalistic accounts, all point to the fact that Yezidis do not (once again) feel safe in a Muslim majority country.

While the increased contact and interaction between displaced Sinjaris in Duhok and the Kurdish host community give hope for the future of social cohesion, and some local Kurds are indeed openly welcoming of the Yezidi IDPs, deep-seated prejudices are not easily worn away on both sides. Some of my respondents mentioned abstaining from going to the doctor only because of how doctors and nurses looked down on them. A 2017 USCIRF report argued that some of the more conservative members of the host community even approved violence against Yezidi.[67] During our interview, a Yezidi woman working in a local university pointed to the current economic depression in the KRG and the high unemployment levels as exacerbating factors for negative host community reactions to the IDPs.

> So, with the Arab they cannot recognize if I'm Muslim or not. But with Kurdish it was obvious, like my accent. So sometimes it was risky for me to say that I'm Yezidi. They were saying "Oh, so you are Yezidi" and they were saying, because they were really hating the Yezidi people in Duhok. [Masoud Barzani] He advocates for Yezidi rights and stuff. So, the community cannot do anything, they cannot ask us to leave the city you know. But you know, when, when they see Yezidi people living within their community, they were not happy about that. That was really obvious.[68]

In the words of another Yezidi living in a camp in Duhok, "Yezidis are under pressure in the Middle East. They are under the pressure of Islamic Sharia. They live under the symbol of 'AllahuAkbar'. Life is no longer possible here, here in the Middle East."[69]

Reconstruction(s) of Yezidi Identity

On a final note, a (re)construction of a distinct Yezidi ethnoreligious identity has been taking place at a greater speed since 2014, both in Iraq and in diaspora. Newly established Yezidi NGOs, social media platforms, and activists, as well as young and educated Yezidis, play a significant role in this construction.[70] A respondent born in Sinjar, who first migrated with her family to Syria during the Anfal campaigns in the late 1980s and then to the United States, replied to my question about her perceptions of her ethnic identity:

> In Syrian refugee camps, we would not think of ourselves as Kurds, we were just Yezidis. But in general, what would stop our persecution, we would go with it. In Sinjar, they wrote as Arabs, we did not have a choice. Now, we say we are Kurds not to get any hassle. If we could have our land, maintain our heritage, we would have our own identity. If Yezidis are Kurds because of a common history, many of our persecutors in history were Kurd, if it is about common language, some Yezidis speak Arabic, and as a Kurmanji speaker, I don't understand Sorani or Zazaki. If I am Kurd, then so are Armenians.[71]

There also seems to be a greater interest in Yezidi history and religious practices among youth. Other respondents from Sinjar said:

> Before the attack, for young Yezidis, even for educated ones who knew about the history, their religious identity was not that strong—they would say I am Yezidi and that was it. The attack was a kind of slap on the face. People thought "we are attacked because of our identity." It brought a new kind of awareness. Now they participate even more in the religious practices and try to bring help.[72]
>
> Back then, I did not care about identity, or labels. But all of a sudden, these issues became more sensitive. When they would say, Kurdish people, or Kurdish students, I now say—no, Yezidi students. I am embracing all of it way more, while so many things are trying to erase it, I am constantly searching for ways to preserve it.[73]

Yet, of course, it is not possible to speak of a homogenous but multiple formations of Yezidi identity. As already mentioned, some Yezidis trace the origins of their religion and identity back to Assyrians or Sumerians; others consider their society as a completely separate, distinct community of believers. Some acknowledge a Zoroastrian history for their beliefs all the while denying any Kurdish attribute to their ethnicity. Still others, especially my respondents from Germany, remarked their sincere assumption on the Kurdish ethnicity of Yezidi people. Some Yezidis greatly respect Sheikh Adi ibn Musafir, while others blame him for the "Arabization" of the Yezidi religion. Finally, there are those who support a strict adhesion to traditions while modernists question the validity of certain rules in the Yezidi faith.

Conclusion

Over time, Yezidis have developed a primordialist self-interpretation of their identity as a historically persecuted and marginalized religious minority. As I have tried to demonstrate throughout the chapter, the myths about their origins in the

Yezidi theology appear as one of the reasons leading to such a perception. The histories of attacks and persecutions by outsiders do obviously contribute to this perception as well. However, the victimization of the community at the hands of imperial rulers and local pashas only because of their religion stands out more as a Yezidi self-perception than reality since most of the Ottoman expeditions targeting Sinjar were actually motivated by geopolitical and governance concerns, a point also made by Kerborani in his chapter. Furthermore, Yezidis were not passive victims neither in their relations with the central government nor in their interactions with local tribes. They formed alliances, made war with rival tribes and for a long time, robbed and plundered caravans passing through Sinjar. Yet the vicious campaigns of 2014 in which Yezidis were indeed targeted for their religious identity naturally reinforced the preexisting Yezidi self-perceptions. Last but not least, the disempowerment of the community in a general sense and its lack of self-representation or self-governance emerge as other factors contributing to such a self-identification.

I argue that the perception of Yezidi identity as continuously persecuted plays an important role in the reconstruction of a separate ethnoreligious Yezidi identity we currently observe among the community. In this reconstruction, Kurdish identity equals to nothing more than "Muslim" and is regarded the same as all other Muslim ethnicities. For even those Yezidis who endorse the idea that all Kurds were once Yezidi, hence, as Yezidis, they are "the original Kurds"; Kurdish and Yezidi identities are as distinct as they can be.

Finally, we can presumably expect the recent reconstructions of Yezidi identity to have a significant impact on the Yezidi diaspora, which is currently scattered around the world with post-2014 mass migrations. These efforts can create favorable conditions for the survival of the Yezidi identity, which is facing a risk of assimilation with future generations. On the other hand, the future is— once again—ambivalent for Yezidis of homeland who will most probably have to navigate in the near future the political pressures, internal divisions, and the obstacles for a safe return to Sinjar and communal empowerment. We have yet to observe what the newly constructed Yezidi *ethos* will bring for those in Iraq.

Notes

1   Maisel (2016).
2   There are exceptions to the rule among the Yezidis of Syria and Turkey (Adsay 2014; Maisel 2016).
3   Yezidis call the 2014 attacks the 74th *firman*, the 74th of mass-scale persecutions targeting the community.
4   As a matter of fact, Allison argues Yezidis to be considered by Kurdish Muslims as an outdated, premodern community, which belongs to the ancient Iraqi folklore: Allison (2001).
5   After the Russo-Turkish War of 1877–8, Yezidis started to immigrate to areas, which are today in Armenia, Georgia, and Russia. Yezidis in Turkey migrated to Western European countries, namely Germany, in mass waves, especially after the 1960s.

Today, Yezidis are scattered all around the world, living in countries as far as New Zealand, Australia, and Canada.

6   Lescot (1975).
7   Kreyenbroek acknowledges the influence Musafir's teachings had on Yezidi beliefs, yet he argues this influence to be somewhat limited. According to him, Yezidi religion is shaped by an interaction between Islam, Zoroastrianism, and a pre-Zoroastrian Iranian belief. Kreyenbroek (1995).
8   Guest (1993: 15).
9   Fuccaro (1999b: 174).
10   Fuccaro (1999b), for instance, speaks of the community as "Yezidi Kurds."
11   Strohmeier (2003: 167).
12   Gökçen mentions hearing about even Indian and Pakistani origins of Yezidi religion during his fieldwork among Yezidis in Turkey. Gökçen and Tee (2010).
13   The 72 *firmans* Yezidis believed to have suffered in their history could be interpreted as an allegory to seventy-two nations thought to make up the world.
14   Fuccaro (1999b).
15   Gökçen (2012).
16   Along with serving in the Iraqi army, Yezidis also started joining peshmerga in the 1960s: Dinç (2017).
17   UNHABITAT (2015).
18   UNAMI (2009).
19   Dalalyan (2011).
20   Nicolaus and Yuce (2019: 89).
21   Maisel (2016).
22   After the Turkish invasion in March 2018, Kurds, Yezidis, and Christians of the Syrian city of Afrin were reported to leave the city due to the threats and intimidations by the Turkish backed, proxy Sunni militias: Ahmado (2019).
23   They are estimated to number between 100,000 to 120,000 (Nicolaus and Yuce 2019).
24   Kreyenbroek (2009).
25   Nicolaus and Yuce (2019).
26   PKK would adopt a similar strategy in Sinjar when its local branch YBŞ established a permanent presence in the region after rescuing trapped Yezidi from the mountain during the IS attacks.
27   We need further research to see if the genocidal campaigns in 2014 have led to any changes in the perceptions of the Yezidi diaspora in Germany.
28   One of the biggest Yezidi NGOs, Yazda, who has a branch office in Nebraska, defines Yezidis as an ethnoreligious minority (https://www.yazda.org/genocide-recognition). Another Lincoln-based Yezidi NGO, Yezidis International, notes the Yezidi religious calendar to date back to 6000 BCE and claims that Yezidi religion is the oldest religion on earth: "During and after a great flood around 4000 BCE, the Yezidis dispersed to many countries in Asia, including India, Afghanistan, Armenia, and Morocco and possibly India. Returning from their adoptive countries around 2000 BCE, the Yezidis played an important role in the development of the Assyrian, Babylonian and Jewish civilizations of the Middle East. Ultimately, the Yezidis amalgamated elements of all these civilizations into Yezidism, including certain features of the Zoroastrian religion of Persia." (http://www.yezidisinternational.org/abouttheyezidipeople/)
29   In 1872, Yezidis write a petition to the Ottoman government explaining how Yezidi religion is different from Islam and why Yezidis cannot serve in the army (Gökçen 2012).

30 Ibid.
31 Spät (2018).
32 Spät (2005).
33 Guest (1993).
34 Ibid.
35 Fuccaro (1999b: 125–6).
36 Kreyenbroek (1995).
37 Ibid., 8.
38 League of Nations (1925).
39 Gökçen (2012: 452).
40 Fuccaro (1999b).
41 Allison (2001).
42 Ibid.
43 Hardi (2016).
44 Dinç (2017). There were actually a large number of ethnic Kurds who took part in the Anfal campaigns, who are derisively called *jash*.
45 Allison notes the KDP leader Masoud Barzani's visit to the acting Yezidi Mir in Lalish in summer 1992. Both Barzani and the YNK leader Jalal Talabani declare Yezidis as "the original Kurds" (2001: 38).
46 Allison (2001) who has conducted fieldwork in Iraqi Kurdistan in 1992 indicates observing Muslim and Christian prejudices against Yezidis, including their beliefs that the Yezidis never washed and eat dirt. During my own fieldwork in 2018, I had two Yezidi respondents who told me when they were at college; their Muslim roommates were surprised to see that they were taking showers each morning.
47 Allison (2001); Spät (2005).
48 UNAMI (2009).
49 Spät (2005).
50 Ali (2019c).
51 UNAMI (2009).
52 From 2007 onward, civil servants in Sheikhan receive their salary from the KRG. In Sinjar, KDP opens new posts and employs Yezidis in these offices. It also establishes pro-KDP Yezidi civil society organizations (i.e., Lalish Cultural Center) and undermines or challenges those who oppose its policies. Also, similar to *ta'rib* policy of the Ba'th government, KDP resettles Sunni Kurds in areas including Sheikhan to change the demographics in favor of Kurds. Kane (2011).
53 In a 2009 Human Rights Watch Report, some activists from Yezidi Movement for Reform and Progress claim being arrested and tortured by peshmerga for their political activities. Also mentioned in the same report is a flyer distributed in Sinjar that reads: "Shengal [Sinjar] is a cemetery for those who want it to be dismembered from Kurdistan," HRW (2009).
54 Kurdish parties get 77 percent of the votes while Yezidi parties' share drops to 6 percent.
55 Savelsberg, Hajo, and Dulz (2010).
56 International Crisis Group (2009).
57 Spät (2018).
58 UNAMI (2009).
59 Ali (2019c: 13–14).
60 Dinç (2017); Tezcür (2017).

61 According to the tradition longtime practiced between Yezidis and Muslims, a Muslim/Yezidi man, called *kreef* (godfather), would hold a Yezidi/Muslim boy on his lap during his circumcision and the two families would be bonded by blood.
62 Ali (2019c).
63 Dulz (2016).
64 Nicolaus and Yuce (2019).
65 Salloum (2016).
66 Some respondents were using the word *kreef* when talking about Muslims in general.
67 Smith and Shadarevian (2017).
68 Interview, May 28, 2018.
69 Interview, May 26, 2018.
70 To give an example, a recent tweet by a Yezidi activist living in the United States read: "Yezidis are Yezidis. They are a race. They are a religion. And any Yezidi's nationality is where he is a legal citizen, usually in the country where he was born. Iraqi Yezidis— yes, Kurdish Yezidis, no! Kurdistan is not a recognized nation. Therefore, there are no Yezidi Kurds and no Kurdish Yezidis."
71 Interview, November 27, 2018.
72 Interview, April 20, 2018.
73 Interview, October 4, 2018.

BIBLIOGRAPHY

Books, Book Chapters, and Articles

Açıkyıldız, Birgül. *The Yezidis: The History of a Community, Culture and Religion*. London: I.B. Tauris, 2010.

Adrag, "Calamity of A(di)lcevaz," *Haratch*, Nov. 10, 1909, No. 47, pp. 2, 3.

Adsay, Fahriye. *Yezidi Kadınlar: Kültürel Sınırların Edilgen Taşıyıcıları*. Istanbul: Avesta, 2014.

Agnew, John. "The Territorial Trap: The Geographical Assumptions of International Relations Theory." *Review of International Political Economy* 1, no. 1 (1994): 53–80.

Ahmed, Sami Said. *The Yazidis and Their Life and Beliefs*. Miami: Field Research Project, 1975.

Aktan, Hamza. *Kürt Vatandaş*. İstanbul: İletişim Yayınları, 2012.

Al-Damaloji, Sadiq. *Al-Yezidiyyah [the Yezidis]*. Mosul: Al-Itihad Printing, 1949.

Ali, Majid Hassan. "Religious Minorities in Early Republican Iraq (1958–1968): Between Granting Rights and Discrimination, a Sociopolitical and Historical Study." PhD diss., Bamberg University, Germany, 2017.

Ali, Majid Hassan. "Aspirations for Ethnonationalist Identities among Religious Minorities in Iraq: The Case of Yazidi Identity in the Period of Kurdish and Arab Nationalism, 1963–2003." *Nationalities Papers* (2019a): 1–15. https://doi.org/10.1017/nps.2018.20.

Ali, Majid Hassan. "Genocidal campaigns during the Ottoman Era: The Firmān of Mīr-i-Kura against the Yezidi Religion in 1832–1834." *Genocide Studies International* 13, no. 1 (2019b): 77–91.

Ali, Majid Hassan. "The Identity Controversy of Religious Minorities in Iraq: The Crystallization of the Yazidi Identity after 2003." *British Journal of Middle Eastern Studies* (2019c): 1–15. https://doi.org/10.1080/13530194.2019.1577129.

Ali, Majid Hassan, Dmitry Pirbari, and Rustam Rzgoyan. "The Reformation and Development of the Yezidi Identity from Theoretical and Historical Perspectives." Working Paper; Димитрий Пирбари & Рустам Рзгоян "К вопросу об идентичности езидов" (Кавказский этнологический сборник [(Papers of Caucasian Ethnology]) 4 (2014). http://institutehist.ucoz.net/_ld/1/151_KEK-XV.pdf.

Allison, Christine. *The Yezidi Oral Tradition in Iraqi Kurdistan*. New York: Routledge, 2001.

Allison, Christine. "'Unbelievable Slowness of Mind': Yezidi Studies, From Nineteenth to Twenty-First Century." *The Journal of Kurdish Studies* 6 (2008): 1–23.

Alsancakli, Sacha. "Matrimonial Alliances and the Transmission of Dynastic Power in Kurdistan: The Case of the Diyādīnids of Bidlīs in the Fifteenth to Seventeenth Centuries." *Eurasian Studies* 15 (2017a): 222–49.

Alsancaklı, Sacha. "What Is Old Is New Again: A Study of Sources in the Šarafnama of Šaraf Xan Bidlisi (1005-7/1596-99)." *Kurdish Studies* 5, no. 1 (2017b): 11–31.

Alsancaklı, Sacha. "Historiography and Language in 17th Century Ottoman Kurdistan: A Study of Two Turkish Translations of Sharafnama." *Kurdish Studies* 6, no. 2 (2018): 171–96.

Anonymous. *Kongra-Gel Kürdistan Halk Kongresi Demokratik Kuruluş Belgeleri*. İstanbul: Çetin Yayınları, 2003.

Arakelova, Victoria. "Ethno-Religious Communities: To the Problem of Identity Markers." *Iran and the Caucasus* 14, no. 1 (2010): 1–17.

Artinian, Vartan. "A Study of the Historical Development of the Armenian Constitutional System in the Ottoman Empire, 1839–1863." PhD diss., Brandeis University (1970).

Aslan, Senem. "'Citizen, Speak Turkish!': A Nation in the Making." *Nationalism and Ethnic Politics* 13, no. 2 (2007): 245–72.

Aslan, Senem. "Everyday Forms of State Power and the Kurds in the Early Turkish Republic." *International Journal of Middle East Studies* 43, no. 1 (2011): 75–93.

Aslan, Senem. *Nation Building in Turkey and Morocco: Governing Kurdish and Berber Dissent*. New York: Cambridge University Press, 2014.

Astourian, Stephan H. "Genocidal Process: Reflections on the Armeno-Turkish Polarization." In *The Armenian Genocide: History, Politics, Ethics*, edited by Richard G. Hovannisian, 53–79. New York: St. Martin's Press, 1992.

Astourian, Stephan H. "The Silence of the Land: Agrarian Relations, Ethnicity and Power." In *A Question of Genocide: Armenians and Turks at the End of the Ottoman Empire*, edited by Ronald Grigor Suny, Fatma Muge Göçek, and Norman M. Naimark, 55–81. Oxford; New York: Oxford University Press, 2011.

Ateş, Sabri. *Ottoman-Iranian Borderlands: Making a Boundary, 1843–1914*. New York: Cambridge University Press, 2013.

Ateş, Sabri. "Treaty of Zohab, 1639: Foundational Myth or Foundational Document?" *Iranian Studies* 52, no. 3–2 (2019): 397–423.

Avagyan, Arsen, and Gaidz F. Minassian. *Ermeniler ve İttihat ve Terakki: İşbirliğinden Çatışmaya*. İstanbul: Aras, 2005.

Aziz, Mahir A. *The Kurds of Iraq: Ethnonationalism and National Identity in Iraqi Kurdistan*. London: I.B. Tauris, 2011.

Bahcheli, Tozun, and Sid Noel. "The Justice and Development Party and the Kurdish Question." In *Nationalisms and Politics in Turkey: Political Islam, Kemalism and the Kurdish Issue*, edited by Marlies Casier and Joost Jongerden, 101–20. London: Routledge, 2011.

Bajalan, Djene Rhys. "The First World War, the End of the Ottoman Empire, and Question of Kurdish Statehood: A 'Missed' Opportunity?" *Ethnopolitics* 18, no. 1 (2019): 13–28.

Barsoumian, Hagop. "The Eastern Question and the Tanzimat Era." In *The Armenian People from Ancient to Modern Times*, edited by Richard G. Hovannisian, 175–201. New York: St. Martin's Press, 1997.

Bedlisi, Sharaf Khan. *The Sharafnama or the History of the Kurdish Nation, 1597, Book One*. Translated by M. R. Izady Costa. Mesa: Mazda, 2005.

Bedlîsî, Şerefxanê. *Şerefname: Dîroka Kurdistanê*. Translated by Ziya Avci. Mersin: Azad, 2014.

Baser, Bahar, and Mari Toivanen. "The Politics of Genocide Recognition: Kurdish Nation-Building and Commemoration in the Post-Saddam Era." *Journal of Genocide Research* 19, no. 3 (2017): 404–42.

Batatu, Hanna. *The Old Social Classes and the Revolutionary Movements of Iraq*. Princeton: Princeton University Press, 1978.

Bayatlı, Nilüfer. *XVI Yüzyılda Musul Eyaleti*. Ankara: Türk Tarih Kurumu, 1999.

Belge, Ceren. "Civilian Victimization and the Politics of Information in the Kurdish Conflict in Turkey." *World Politics* 68, no. 2 (2016): 275–306.

Bennigsen, Alexandre. "Islamic or Local Consciousness among Soviet Nationalism." In *Soviet Nationality Problems*, edited by Edward Allworth. New York: Columbia University Press, 1971.

Bilali, Rezarta. "The Downsides of National Identification for Minority Groups in Intergroup Conflicts in Assimilationist Societies." *British Journal of Social Psychology* 53, no. 1 (2014): 21–38.

Bilici, Mücahit. *Hamal Kürt: Türk islamı ve Kürt sorunu*. Istanbul: Avesta, 2017.

Black, Jeremy. *Maps and Politics*. London: University of Chicago Press, 2000.

Blalock, Hubert M. "Occupational Discrimination: Some Theoretical Propositions." *Social Problems* 9, no. 3 (1962): 240–7.

Boyîk, Eskerê. *Êzîdiyatî, Mîrzikê Zaza, Fermanên Reş*. Oldenburg: Weşengeha Dengê Êzîdiyan, 2006.

Bozarslan, Hamit. "Kurdish Nationalism in Turkey: From Tacit Contract to Rebellion." In *Essays on the Origins of Kurdish Nationalism*, edited by Abbas Vali, 163–90. California: Mazda Publishers, 2003.

Breuilly, John. *Nationalism and the State*. Manchester: Manchester University Press, 1993.

Brubaker, Roger. "Ethnicity without Groups." *European Journal of Sociology* 43, no. 2 (2004): 163–89.

Bulut, Faik. *Ehmedê Xanî'nin Kaleminden Kürtlerin Bilinmeyen Dünyasi* [The Unknown World of the Kurds in Ehmedê Xanî's Writings]. Berfin Yayinlari, 2011.

Buzan, Barry, Ole Wæver, and Jaap De Wilde. *Security: A New Framework for Analysis*. Boulder: Lynne Rienner Publishers, 1998.

Capoccia, Giovanni, and R. Daniel Kelemen. "The Study of Critical Junctures: Theory, Narrative, and Counterfactuals in Historical Institutionalism." *World Politics* 59, no. 3 (2017): 341–69.

Celîl, Ordîxanê, and Celîlê Celîl. *Zargotina Kurda*. Vienna: Institut für Kurdologie, 2014.

Cetorelli, Valeria et al. "Mortality and Kidnapping Estimates for the Yazidi Population in the Area of Mount Sinjar, Iraq, in August 2014: A Retrospective Household Survey." *PLoS Medicine* 14, no. 5 (2017): 1–10.

Cindî Reşo, Xelîl. "Mîrgeha: Şêxan û Şingal û Kilîs." *Kürt Tarihi Dergisi* 15 (2014).

Cook, Stuart. "The Systematic Analysis of Socially Significant Events: A Strategy for Social Research." *Journal of Social Issues* 18, no. 2 (1962): 66–84.

Cook, Stuart. "Interpersonal and Attitudinal Outcomes in Cooperating Interracial Groups." *Journal of Research and Development in Education* 12, no. 1 (1978): 97–113.

Çelebi, Elif, Maykel Verkuyten, and Natasa Smyrnioti. "Support for Kurdish Language Rights in Turkey: The Roles of Ethnic Group, Group Identifications, Contact, and Intergroup Perceptions." *Ethnic and Racial Studies* 39, no. 6 (2016): 1034–51.

Çelik, Ayşe Betül, and Andrew Blum. "Track II Interventions and the Kurdish Question in Turkey: An Analysis Using a Theories of Change Approach." *International Journal of Peace Studies* 12, no. 2 (2007): 51–81.

Chatty, Dawn. *Syria: The Making and Unmaking of a Refugee State*. New York: Oxford University Press, 2018.

Chyet, Michael. "'And a Thornbush Sprang Up between Them': Studies on *Mem û Zîn* a Kurdish Romance." PhD diss., University of California, 1991.

Çiçek, Cuma. *Süreç: Kürt Çatışması ve Çözüm Arayışları*. Istanbul: İletişim Yayınları, 2018.

Ciwan, Murad. *Çaldıran Savaşı'nda Osmanlılar, Safeviler ve Kürtler: İlk Kürt-Osmanlı İttifak ı(1514)*. Istanbul: Avesta, 2015.

Crampton, Jeremy W. "Maps as Social Constructions: Power, Communication and Visualisation." *Progress in Human Geography* 25, no. 2 (2001): 235–52.

Crampton, Jeremy W., and John Krygier. "An Introduction to Critical Cartography."
  ACME: An International E-Journal for Critical Geographies 4, no. 1 (2006): 11–33.
Culcasi, Karen. "Cartographically Constructing Kurdistan within Geopolitical and
  Orientalist Discourses." *Political Geography* 25, no. 6 (2006): 680–706.
Сталин ИВ [Stalin I. V.], Как понимает социал-демократия национальный вопрос?
  [How does social democracy understand the national question?]. Moscow, 1953.
Dalalyan, Tork. "Construction of Kurdish and Yezidi Identities among the Kurmanji-
  Speaking Population of the Republic of Armenia." In *Changing Identities: Armenia,
  Azerbaijan, Georgia*, edited by Viktor Voronkov, 177–202. Heinrich Boell Foundation
  South Caucasus Regional Office, 2011.
Dale, Stephen. *The Muslim Empires of the Ottomans, Safavids, and Mughals*. Cambridge:
  Cambridge University Press, 2010.
Dalton, Russell J. *Citizen Politics: Public Opinion and Political Parties in Advanced
  Industrial Democracies*: Washington DC: CQ Press, 2013.
Dankoff, Robert. *Evliya Çelebi in Bitlis: The Relevant Section of the Seyahatname*. New
  York: Leiden, 1990.
Dankoff, Robert. *Intimate Life of an Ottoman Statesman: Melek Ahmed Pasha, 1588–1662*.
  Leiden: Brill, 1991.
Dankoff, Robert. *An Ottoman Mentality: The World Evliya Çelebi*. Leiden: Brill, 2006.
Davies, Sara E., and Jacqui True. "Reframing Conflict-Related Sexual and Gender-Based
  Violence: Bringing Gender Analysis Back In." *Security Dialogue* 46, no. 6 (2015):
  495–512.
Dehqan, Mustafa. "The Fatwa of Mala Salih al-Kurdi al-Hakkari: An Arabic Manuscript
  on the Yezidi Religion." *The Journal of Kurdish Studies* VI (2008): 140–62.
Dehqan, Mustafa. "A Yezidi Commentary by Mawlana Muhammad al-Barqal'i." *Nûbihar
  Akademî* 3 (2015): 137–51.
Dehqan, Mustafa, and Vural Genç, "Kurds as Spies: Information-Gathering on the
  16th Century Ottoman-Safavid Frontier." *Acta Orientalia Academiae Scientiarum
  Hungaricae* 71, no. 2 (2018): 197–230.
Demirel, Hamide. *The Poet Fuzûli: His Works, Study of His Turkish, Persians and Arabic
  Divans*. Ankara: Ministry of Culture, 1991.
Derderian, Dzovinar. "Shaping Subjectivities and Contesting Power through the Image
  of Kurds, 1860s." In *The Ottoman East in the Nineteenth Century: Societies, Identities
  and Politics*, edited by Ali Sipahi, Yaşar Tolga Cora, and Dzovinar Derderian, 91–108.
  London: New York: I.B. Tauris, 2016.
Deringil, Selim. *The Well-Protected Domains: Ideology and the Legitimation of Power in the
  Ottoman Empire, 1876–1909*. London: I.B. Tauris, 1999.
Diamond, Larry, and Marc F. Plattner. *Nationalism, Ethnic Conflict and Democracy*.
  Baltimore: Johns Hopkins University Press, 1994.
Dinç, Namık K. *Ezidilerin 73. Fermanı: Şengal Soykırımı*. İstanbul: Zan Vakfı, 2017.
Dixon, Jeffrey C., and Murat Ergin. "Explaining Anti-Kurdish Beliefs in Turkey: Group
  Competition, Identity, and Globalization." *Social Science Quarterly* 91, no. 5 (2010):
  1329–48.
Dulz, Irene. "The Displacement of the Yezidis after the Rise of ISIS in Northern Iraq."
  Kurdish Studies 4, no. 2 (2016): 131–47.
Edmonds, Cecil J. "Kurdish Nationalism." *Journal of Contemporary History* 6, no. 1 (1971):
  87–106.
El-Rouayheb, Khaled. "The Myth of 'the Triumph of Fanaticism' in the Seventeenth-
  Century Ottoman Empire," *Die Welt des Islams* 48 (2008): 196–221.

El-Rouayheb, Khaled. *Islamic Intellectual History in the Seventeenth-Century: Scholarly Currents in the Ottoman Empire and the Maghreb.* New York: Cambridge University Press, 2015.

Eppel, Michael. *A People without a State: The Kurds from the Rise of Islam to the Dawn of Nationalism.* Austin: University of Texas Press, 2016.

Erdem, Hakan Y. *Slavery in the Ottoman Empire and Its Demise, 1800–1909.* New York: St. Martin's Press, 1996.

Erdener, Eda. "The Ways of Coping with Post-War Trauma of Yezidi Refugee Women in Turkey." *Women's Studies International Forum* 65 (2017): 60–70.

Ergin, Murat. "The Racialization of Kurdish Identity in Turkey." *Ethnic and Racial Studies* 37, no. 2 (2012): 322–41.

Evliya Çelebi. *Evliyâ Çelebi Seyahatnâmesi.* Edited and transliterated by Zekeriya Kurşun, Seyit Ali Kahraman, and Yücel Dağlı. Vol. 2. Istanbul: Yapı Kredi Yayınları, 1999.

Evliya Çelebi. *Evliyâ Çelebi Seyahatnâmesi.* Edited and transliterated by Seyit Ali Kahraman and Yücel Dağlı. Vol. 3-4. Istanbul: Yapı Kredi Yayınları, 2001.

Evliya Çelebi. *Evliyâ Çelebi Seyahatnâmesi.* Edited and transliterated by Yücel Dağlı, Seyit Ali Kahraman, and Ibrahim Sezgin. Vol. 5. Istanbul: Yapı Kredi Yayınları, 2001.

Evliya Çelebi. *Evliyâ Çelebi Seyahatnâmesi.* Edited and transliterated by Seyit Ali Kahraman and Yücel Dağlı. Vol. 6. Istanbul: Yapı Kredi Yayınları, 2002.

Evliya Çelebi. *Günümüz Türkçesiyle Evliyâ Çelebi Seyahatnâmesi.* Edited and transliterated by Seyit Ali Kahraman and Yücel Dağlı. Istanbul: Yapı Kredi Yayınları, 2013.

Firat, M. Şerif. *Doğu İlleri ve Varto Tarihi.* Ankara: Tandoğan Yayınları, 1983.

Forbes, Frederick. "A Visit to the Sinjar Hills in 1838, with Some Account of the Sect of Yezidis, and of Various Places in the Mesopotamian Desert, between the Rivers Tigris and Khabur." *Journal of the Royal Geographical Society of London* 9 (1839): 409–30.

Forbes, Hugh D. *Ethnic Conflict.* New Haven, CT: Yale University Press, 1997.

Freeden, Michael. *Ideologies and Political Theory: A Conceptual Approach.* Oxford: Clarendon Press. 1998.

Fuccaro, Nelida. "Aspects of the Social and Political History of the Yezidi Enclave of Jabal Sinjar (Iraq) under the British Mandate, 1919–1932." PhD diss., University of Durham, 1994a.

Fuccaro, Nelida. "A 17th Century Travel Account on the Yazidis: Implications for a Socio-Religious History." *Annali dell'Istituto Orientale di Napoli*, 53 no. 3 (1994b): 241–53.

Fuccaro, Nelida. "Ethnicity, State Formation, and Conscription in Postcolonial Iraq: The Case of the Yazidi Kurds of Jabal Sinjar." *International Journal of Middle East Studies* 29, no. 4 (1997): 559–80.

Fuccaro, Nelida. "Communalism and the State in Iraq: the Yazidi Kurds, c. 1869–1940." *Middle Eastern Studies* 35, no. 2 (1999a): 1–26.

Fuccaro, Nelida. *The Other Kurds, Yezidis in Colonial Iraq.* London, New York: I.B. Tauris & Co Ltd, 1999b.

Fuccaro, Nelida. "The Ottoman Frontier in Kurdistan in the Sixteenth and Seventeenth Centuries." In *The Ottoman World*, edited by Christine Woodhead, 237–50. London: Routledge, 2012.

Giddens, Anthony. *Consequences of Modernity.* Cambridge: Polity Press, 1990.

Gidengil, Elisabeth, and Ekrem Karakoç. "Which Matters More in the Electoral Success of Islamist (Successor) Parties–Religion or Performance? The Turkish Case." *Party Politics* 22, no. 3 (2016): 325–38.

Gökçen, Amed. *Osmanlı ve İngiliz arşiv belgelerinde Yezidiler.* Istanbul: Bilgi University, 2012.

Gökçen, Amed. *Ezidiler: Kara Kitap Kara Talih*. Istanbul: Istanbul Bilgi Üniversitesi Yayınları, 2014.

Gökçen, Amed and Caroline Tee. "Notes from the Field: Yezidism: A New Voice and an Evolving Culture in Every Setting." *British Journal of Middle Eastern Studies* 37, no. 3 (2010): 405–27.

Gölbaşı, Edip. "'Heretik' aşiretler ve II. Abdülhamid rejimi: Zorunlu askerlik meselesi ve ihtida siyaseti odağında Yezidiler ve Osmanlı idaresi." *Tarih ve Toplum Yeni Yaklaşımlar* 9 (2009): 87–156.

Gölbaşı, Edip. "Turning the 'Heretics' into Loyal Muslim Subjects: Imperial Anxieties, the Politics of Religious Conversion, and the Yezidis in the Hamidian Era." *The Muslim World* 103 (2013): 3–23.

Goner, Ozlem. *Turkish National Identity and Its Outsiders: Memories of State Violence in Dersim*. New York: Routledge, 2017.

Guest, John S. *The Yezidis: A Study in Survival*. New York: KPI, 1987.

Guest, John S. *Survival among the Kurds: A History of the Yezidis*. Abingdon: Routledge, 1993.

Gülsoy, Ufuk. "Sıradışı bir Dinî Topluluk: Osmanlı Yezidîleri (XIX. ve XX. Yüzyıllar)." *Türk Kültürü İncelemeleri Dergisi* 7 (2002): 129–62.

Gunter, Michael M. "Kurdish Studies in the United States." In *Routledge Handbook on the Kurds*, edited by Michael M. Gunter, 13–22. New York: Routledge, 2018.

Gurses, Mehmet. *Anatomy of a Civil War: Sociopolitical Impacts of the Kurdish Conflict in Turkey*. Michigan: University of Michigan Press, 2018.

Güven, Dilek. *Cumhuriyet dönemi azınlık politikaları bağlamında 6-7 Eylül olayları*. Vol. 149. İstanbul: Tarih Vakfı, 2005.

Hakyemez, Serra. "Margins of the Archive: Torture, Heroism, and the Ordinary Prison No. 5 in Turkey." *Anthropological Quarterly* 90 (2017): 107–38.

Hardi, Choman. *Gendered Experiences of Genocide: Anfal Survivors in Kurdistan-Iraq*. Abingdon: Routledge, 2016.

Harley, John B. "Deconstructing the Map." *Cartographica* 26, no. 2 (1989): 1–20.

Harley, John B., and David Woodward. *The History of Cartography, Volume 1: Cartography in Prehistoric, Ancient, and Medieval Europe and the Mediterranean*. Chicago: University of Chicago Press, 1987.

Hassanpour, Amir. "The Making of Kurdish Identity: Pre-20th Century Historical and Literary Sources." In *Essays on the Origins of Kurdish Nationalism*, edited by Abbas Vali, 106–62. Costa Mesa, California: Mazda Publishers, 2003.

Hechter, Michael. *Containing Nationalism*. Oxford: Oxford University Press. 2000.

Helmreich, Paul C. *From Paris to Sèvres: The Partition of the Ottoman Empire at the Peace Conference of 1979–1920*. Columbus: Ohio State University Press. 1974.

Heper, Metin. *The State and Kurds in Turkey: The Question of Assimilation*. London: Palgrave Macmillan, 2007.

Hobbes, Thomas. *Leviathan*. Edited by Richard Tuck. Cambridge: Cambridge University Press, 1996.

Hobsbawm, Eric J., and Terrence Ranger. *The Invention of Tradition*. Cambridge: Cambridge University Press, 1983.

Hosgor, Ayse Gunduz, and Jeroel Smith. "Intermarriage between Turks and Kurds in Contemporary Turkey: Inter-Ethnic Relations in Urbanizing Environment." *European Sociological Review* 18, no. 4 (2002): 417–32.

House, Edward Mandell, and Charles Seymour. *What Really Happened at Paris, the Story of the Peace Conference 1918-19/by American Delegates*. London, 1921.

Hovannisian, Richard G. "The Armenian Question in the Ottoman Empire." In *The Armenian People from Ancient to Modern Times*, edited by Richard G. Hovannisian, 203–38. New York: St. Martin's Press, 1997.

Hyde, Lewis. *A Primer for Forgetting: Getting Past the Past*. New York: Farrar, Straus and Giroux, 2019.

Hyder, Syed Akbar. *Reliving Karbala: Martyrdom in South Asian Memory*. New York: Oxford University Press, 2006.

Jamison, Kelda. "Hefty Dictionaries in Incomprehensible Tongues: Commensurating Code and Language Community in Turkey." *Anthropological Quarterly* 89, no. 1 (2016): 31–62.

Jejo, Ameen Farhan. *Al-Qawmiyyah al-Ezidiyyah, Jidhuruha, Muqawwmatiha, Mu'anatiha [The Yezidi Nationalism: Its Roots, Constituents and Sufferings]*. Baghdad: Al-Taif Company for Limited Printing, 2010.

Jejo, Ameen Farhan. *Qamus Arabi-Ezidi [A Yezidi- Arabic Dictionary]*. Baghdad: Al-Taif Company for Limited Printing, 2013.

Jejo, Ameen Farhan. *Jidhoor al-lugha al-Ezidiyyah [The Roots of the Yezidi Language]*. Baghdad: Al-Taif Company for Limited Printing, 2014.

Joseph, John. *The Nestorians and Their Muslim Neighbors: A Study of Western Influence on Their Relations*. Princeton, NJ: Princeton University Press, 1961.

Jost, John, Mahzarin Banaji, and Brian Nosek. "A Decade of System Justification Theory: Accumulated Evidence of Conscious and Unconscious Bolstering of the Status Quo." *Political Psychology* 25, no. 6 (2004): 881–919.

Jwaideh, Wadie. *Kürt Milliyetçiliğinin Tarihi: Kökenleri ve Gelişimi*. İstanbul: İletişim Yayınları, 2009.

Imber, Colin. *Ebu's-su'ud: The Islamic Legal Tradition*. Palo Alto: Stanford University Press, 1997.

Kaligian, Dikran. *Armenian Organization and Ideology under Ottoman Rule 1908–1914*. New Brunswick; London: Transaction Publishers, 2009.

Kane, Sean. *Iraq's Disputed Territories: A View of the Political Horizon and Implications for US Policy*. Washington, DC: US Institute of Peace, 2011.

Karakoç, Ekrem. "Ethnicity and Trust in National and International Institutions: Kurdish Attitudes toward Political Institutions in Turkey." *Turkish Studies* 14, no. 1 (2013): 92–114.

Karakoç, Ekrem, and Zeki Sarıgil. "Why Religious People Support Ethnic Insurgency? Kurds, Religion and Support for the PKK." *Politics and Religion* 13, no. 2 (2020): 245–72.

Kaplan, Morgan L. "Foreign Support, Miscalculation, and Conflict Escalation: Iraqi Kurdish Self-determination in Perspective." *Ethnopolitics* 18, no. 1 (2019): 29–45.

Kardam, Ahmet. *Cizre-Botan Beyi Bedirhan: Sürgün Yılları*. Ankara: Dipnot Yayınları, 2013.

Kayhan Pusane, Özlem. "Turkey's Kurdish Opening: Long Awaited Achievements and Failed Expectations." *Turkish Studies* 15, no. 1 (2014): 81–99.

Kelly, Michael J. "The Kurdish Regional Constitutional within the Framework of the Iraqi Federal Constitution: A Struggle for Sovereignty, Oil, Ethnic Identity, and the Prospects for a Reverse Supremacy Clause." *Penn State Law Review* 114, no. 3 (2010): 707–808.

Khani, Ahmed. *Mem and Zin*. Translated by Salah Saadalla. Diyarbakir: Avesta, 2008.

Khenchelaoui, Zaïm. "The Yezidis, People of the Spoken Word in the Midst of People of the Book." *Diogenes* 187, no. 47 (1999): 20–37.

Kizilhan, Jan Ilhan. "PTSD of Rape after IS ('Islamic State') Captivity." *Archives of Women's Mental Wealth* 21, no. 5 (2018): 517–52.

Klein, Janet. "Conflict and Collaboration: Rethinking Kurdish-Armenian Relations in the Hamidian Period, 1876–1909." *International Journal of Turkish Studies* 13, no. 1–2 (2007a): 153–65.

Klein, Janet. "Kurdish Nationalists and Non-Nationalist Kurdists: Rethinking Minority Nationalism and the Dissolution of the Ottoman Empire, 1908–9." *Nations and Nationalism* 13, no. 1 (2007b): 135–53.

Knight, David B. "Territory and People or People and Territory? Thoughts on Postcolonial Self-Determination." *International Political Science Review* 6, no. 2 (1985): 248–72.

Koçunyan, Aylin. "Long Live Sultan Abdülaziz, Long Live the Nation, Long Live the Constitution …." In *Constitutionalism, Legitimacy, and Power : Nineteenth-Century Experiences*, edited by Kelly L. Grotke and Markus J. Prutsch, 189–210. Oxford: Oxford University Press, 2014.

Kreyenbroek, Philip G. *Yezidism—It's Background, Observances and Textual Tradition*. New York: The Edwin Mellen Press, 1995.

Kreyenbroek, Philip G. *Yezidism in Europe: Different Generations Speak about Their Religion*. Vol. 5. Wiesbaden: Otto Harrassowitz Verlag, 2009.

Kreyenbroek, Philip G., and Khali Jindy Rashow. *God and Sheikh Adi Are Perfect: Sacred Poems and Religious Narratives from the Yezidi Tradition*. Wiesbaden: Harrassowitz, 2005.

Kurdo, Qanatê. *Tarixa Edebiyata Kurdi*. Diyarbakır: Wesanen Lîs, 2010.

Lajnat al-Buhuth wa al-dirasat. *Karithat Shangal: Majmuat Bhuth wa Dirasat (3 August 2014)*. Duhok: Hawar, 2016.

Laughlin, Jim Mac. "The Political Geography of 'Nation-Building and Nationalism in Social Sciences: Structural vs. Dialectical Accounts.'" *Political Geography Quarterly* 5, no. 4 (1986): 299–329.

Layard, Austen Henry. *Nineveh and its Remains*. Vol I. London: John Murray, 1850.

Leezenberg, Michiel. "Ehmedê Xanî's Mem û Zîn: The Consecration of a Kurdish National Epic." In *Routledge Handbook of the Kurds*, edited by Michael M. Gunter, 79–89. Abingdon: Routledge, 2019a.

Leezenberg, Michiel. "Nation, Kingship and Language: The Ambiguous Politics of Ehmedê Xani's *Mem û Zîn*." *Kurdish Studies* 7, no. 1 (2019b): 197–216.

Lescot, Robert. *Enquete sur les Yezidis de Syrie et du Djebel Sindjar*. Librarie du Liban: Beyrouth, 1975.

Lie, John. *Modern Peoplehood*. Boston: Harvard University Press, 2004.

Loizides, Neophytos. "Elite Framing and Conflict Transformation in Turkey." *Parliamentary Affairs* 62, no. 2 (2008): 278–97.

Longrigg, Stephen Hemsley. *Four Centuries of Modern Iraq*. London: Oxford University Press, 1925.

Machiavelli, Niccolo. *The Prince and Other Writings*. Translated by Wayne Rebhorn. New York: Barnes and Noble Classics, 2003.

MacLean, Gerald. "British Travelers, the Kurds, and Kurdistan: A Brief Literary History, c.1520–1680." *Kurdish Studies Journal* 7, no. 2 (2019): 113–34.

Macmillan, M. *Peacemakers: The Paris Peace Conference of 1919 and Its Attempt to End War*. London: John Murray, 2002.

Maisel, Sebastian. *Yezidis in Syria: Identity Building among a Double Minority*. Washington DC: Lexington Books, 2016.

Mann, Michael. *The Dark Side of Democracy: Explaining Ethnic Cleansing*. Cambridge; New York: Cambridge University Press, 2004.

Mansfield, Harvey. *Machiavelli's Virtu*. Chicago: University of Chicago Press. 1996.

Masud, Muhammad Khalid, Brinkley Messick, and David S. Powers, ed. *Islamic Legal Interpretation: Muftis and Their Fatwas.* Oxford: University Press, 2005.

Maunsell, Francis R. "Kurdistan." *Geographic Journal* 3, no. 2 (1894): 81–92.

Maunsell, Francis R. *Reconnaissances in Mesopotamia, Kurdistan, North-West Persia, and Luristan from April to October 1888.* Vol. 2. Simla: Intelligence Branch, Quarter Master General's Dept., [114v] (233/312), 1890.

Maxwell, Alexander, and Tim Smith. "Positing 'Not-Yet-Nationalism': Limits to the Impact of Nationalism Theory on Kurdish Historiography." *Nationalities Papers* 43, no. 5 (2015): 771–87.

McDowall, David. *A Modern History of the Kurds.* London: I.B. Tauris, 1996.

McDowall, David. *A Modern History of the Kurds.* 3rd ed. London: I.B. Tauris, 2004.

McGee, Thomas. "Saving the Survivors: Yezidi Women, Islamic State and the German Admissions Programme." *Kurdish Studies* 6, no. 1 (2018): 85–109.

McMurray, Jonathan S. *Distant Ties: Germany, the Ottoman Empire, and the Construction of the Baghdad Railway.* Westport: Praeger Publishers, 2001.

Meiselas, Susan, *Kurdistan: In the Shadow of History.* 2nd ed. Chicago: University of Chicago Press, 2008.

Mem, H. *Üçüncü Öğretmen Xanî.* Istanbul: Kurt Enstitusu Yayinlari, 2005.

Mignan, Robert D. *Winter Journey through Russia, the Caucasian Alps and Georgia: Thence Across Mount Zagros by the Pass of Xenophon and the Ten Thousand Greeks, into Koordistaun.* London: Richard Bentley, 1839.

Mill, John Stuart. *Considerations on Representative Government.* London: Longmans, Green and Co., 1872.

Millingen, Fredrick. *Wild Life among the Koords.* London: Hurst and Blackett, 1870.

Moradi, Fazil. "The Force of Writing in Genocide: On Sexual Violence in the al-Anfāl." In *Gender Violence in Peace and War: States of Complicity*, edited by Victoria Sanford, Katerina Stefatos, and Cecilia M. Salvi. New Brunswick: Rutgers University Press. 2016.

Muhammad, Qadir Muhammad. "Kurds and Kurdistan in the View of British Travellers in the Nineteenth Century." PhD diss., University of Leicester, 2017.

Nalbandian, Louise. *The Armenian Revolutionary Movement.* Berkeley and Los Angeles: University of California Press, 1963.

Nasstrom, Sofia. "The Legitimacy of the People." *Political Theory* 35, no. 5 (2007): 624–58.

Nicolaus, Peter, and Serkan Yuce. "A Look at the Yezidi Journey to Self-Discovery and Ethnic Identity." *Iran and the Caucasus* 23, no. 1 (2019): 87–104.

Nodia, G. "Nationalism and Democracy." In *Nationalism, Ethnic Conflict and Democracy*, edited by L. Diamond and M. Plattner, 3–22. Baltimore: Johns Hopkins University Press, 1994.

Nursi, Bediuzzaman Said. *Ictimai Receteler.* Istanbul: Zehra Yayincilik, 2006.

Nyers, Peter. *Rethinking Refugees: Beyond States of Emergency.* New York: Routledge, 2006.

Oehring, Otmar. *Christians and Yazidis in Iraq: Current Situation and Prospects.* Berlin: Konrad Adenauer Stiftung, 2017.

Olson, Robert. *The Kurdish Nationalist Movement in the 1990s: Its Impact on Turkey and the Middle East.* Lexington: University Press of Kentucky, 1996.

Omarkhali, Khanna. *The Yezidi Religious Textual Tradition: From Oral to Written. Categories, Transmission, Scripturalisation and Canonisation of the Yezidi Oral Religious Texts.* Wiesbaden: Harrassowitz, 2017.

Oran, Baskın. *Türkiye'de azınlıklar: kavramlar, teori, Lozan, iç mevzuat, içtihat, uygulama.* İstanbul: İletişim Yayınları, 2013.

O'Shea, Maria. T. *Trapped between the Map and Reality: Geography and Perceptions of Kurdistan.* London: Routledge, 2004.

Ozkirimli, Umut. *Theories of Nationalism: A Critical Introduction*. London: Palgrave/ Macmillan, 2010.

Özok-Gündoğan, Nilay. "Ruling the Periphery, Governing the Land: The Making of the Modern Ottoman State in Kurdistan, 1840–70." *Comparative Studies of South Asia, Africa and the Middle East* 34, no. 1 (2014): 160–75.

Özoğlu, Hakan. *Kurdish Notables and the Ottoman State: Evolving Identities, Competing Loyalties, and Shifting Boundaries*. Albany: State University of New York Press, 2004.

Parry, Oswald H. *Six Months in a Syrian Monastery*. London: Horace Cox, 1895.

Pettigrew, Thomas. "The Contact Hypothesis Revisited." In *Contact and Conflict in Intergroup Encounters*, edited by Miles Hewstone and Rupert Brown, 169–95. Oxford, UK: Basil Blackwell, 1986.

Pettigrew, Thomas. "Generalized Intergroup Effect on Prejudice." *Personality and Social Psychology Bulletin* 23, no. 2 (1997): 173–86.

Pinker, Steven. *The Better Angels of Our Nature: Why Violence Has Declined*. New York: Viking, 2011.

Pratto, Felicia, Jim Sidanius, and Shana Levin. "Social Dominance Theory and the Dynamics of Intergroup Relations: Taking Stock and Looking Forward." *European Review of Social Psychology* 17, no. 1 (2006): 271–320.

Pratto, Felicia, Jim Sidanius, Lisa Stallworth, and Bertram Malle. "Social Dominance Orientation: A Personality Variable Predicting Social and Political Attitudes." *Journal of Personality and Social Psychology* 67, no. 4 (1994): 741–63.

Randall, Jonathan. *After Such Knowledge What Forgiveness?: My Encounters with Kurdistan*. New York: Farrar, Strauss & Giroux, 1997.

Rawlinson, Major. "Notes on a March from Zohab, at the Foot of Zagros, along the Mountains of Khuzistan (Susiana), and from Thence through the Province of Luristan to Kirmanshah, in the Year 1836." *Journal of the Royal Geographical Society of London* 9 (1839): 26–116.

Rich, Claudius James. *Narrative of a Residence in Koordistan, and on the Site of Ancient Nineveh*. Cambridge: Cambridge University Press, 1836.

Roe, Paul. "Securitization and Minority rights: Conditions of Desecuritization." *Security Dialogue* 35, no. 3 (2004): 279–94.

Romano, David. *The Kurdish Nationalist Movement: Opportunity, Mobilization and Identity*. Cambridge, New York: Cambridge University Press, 2006.

Said, Edward. *Culture and Imperialism*. London: Vintage, 1994.

Sakallioglu, Umit Cizre. "Kurdish Nationalism from an Islamist Perspective: The Discourses of Turkish Islamist Writers." *Journal of Muslim Minority Affairs* 18, no. 1 (1998): 73–89.

Saraçoğlu, Cenk. *Kurds of Modern Turkey: Migration, Neoliberalism and Exclusion in Turkish Society*. New York: I.B. Tauris, 2010.

Sarıgil, Zeki. *Ethnic Boundaries in Turkish Politics: The Secular Kurdish Movement and Islam*. New York: New York University Press, 2018.

Sarıgil, Zeki, and Ekrem Karakoç. "Inter-ethnic (In)tolerance between Turks and Kurds: Implications for Turkish Democratisation." *South European Society & Politics* 22, no. 2 (2016a): 197–216.

Sarıgil, Zeki, and Ekrem Karakoç. "Who Supports Secession? The Determinants of Secessionist Attitudes among Turkey's Kurds." *Nations and Nationalism* 22, no. 2 (2016b): 325–46.

Sasson, Jean. *The Iraqi Refugees: The New Crisis in the Middle East*. London: Bloomsbury Publishing. 2009.

Savelsberg, Eva, Siamend Hajo, and Irene Dulz. "Effectively Urbanized. Yezidis in the Collective Towns of Sheikhan and Sinjar." *Études Rurales* 186 (2010): 101–16.

Scalbert-Yücel, Clémence, and Marie Le Ray. "Knowledge, Ideology and Power. Deconstructing Kurdish Studies." *European Journal of Turkish Studies* 5 (2006).

Schumpeter, Joseph A. *Capitalism, Socialism and Democracy.* 5th ed. London: Routledge, 1976.

Scott, James. *The Art of Not Being Governed: An Anarchist History of Upland Southeast Asia.* New Haven: Yale University Press, 2009.

Şem'î. *Terceme-i Tevârîh-i Şeref Hân*, edited by Adnan Oktay. Istanbul: Nûbihar, [1682] 2016.

Şerif, Ahmet. *Anadolu'da Tanîn.* Ankara: Türk Tarih Kurumu Basımevi, 1999.

Sezgin, Dilara, and Melissa A. Wall. "Constructing the Kurds in the Turkish Press: A Case Study of Hürriyet Newspaper." *Media, Culture & Society* 27, no. 5 (2005): 787–98.

Shakely, Farhad. *Kurdish Nationalism in Mam û Zîn of Ahmadî Khanî.* Brussels: Kurdish Institute of Brussels, 1992.

Sharaf Khān. *Sharafnāma.* MS. Elliott 332, Bodleian Library, Oxford, 1597.

Sidanius, James, and Felicia Pratto. "The Inevitability of Oppression and the Dynamics of Social Dominance." In *Prejudice and Politics in American Society*, edited by Paul Sniderman and Philip Tetlock, 173–211. Stanford, CA: Stanford University Press, 1991.

Sidanius, James, and Felicia Pratto. *Social Dominance: An Intergroup Theory of Social Hierarchy and Oppression.* New York: Cambridge University Press, 2001.

Sidaway, James D. "Postcolonial Geographies: An Exploratory Essay." *Progress in Human Geography* 24, no. 4 (2000): 591–612.

Sılan, Necmeddin Sahir. *Doğu Anadolu'da toplumsal mühendislik, Dersim-Sason.* İstanbul: Tarih Vakfı Yurt Yayınları, 2010.

Six-Hohenbalken, Maria. "The 72nd *Firman* of the Yezidis: A 'Hidden Genocide' during World War I?" *Genocide Studies International* 13, no. 1 (2019): 52–76.

Smith, Anthony D. *The Antiquity of Nations.* Cambridge: Polity, 2004.

Smith, Page. "From Masses to Peoplehood." *Reflexions Historiques* 1, no. 1 (1974): 115–38.

Soleimani, Kamal, and Ahmad Mohammadpour. "Can Non-Persians Speak? The Sovereign's Narration of 'Iranian Identity'." *Ethnicities* 19, no. 5 (2019): 925–47.

Somer, Murat, and Evangelos G. Liaras. 2010. "Turkey's New Kurdish Opening: Religious Versus Secular Values." *Middle East Policy* 17, no. 2 (2010): 152–65.

Somer, Murat, and Gitta Glüpker-Kesebir. "Is Islam the Solution? Comparing Turkish Islamic and Secular Thinking toward Ethnic and Religious Minorities." *Journal of Church and State* 58, no. 3 (2016): 529–55.

Spät, Estzer. *The Yezidis.* London: Saqi, 2005.

Spät, Estzer. "Yezidi Identity Politics and Political Ambitions in the Wake of the ISIS Attack." *Journal of Balkan and Near Eastern Studies* 20, no. 5 (2018): 420–38.

Strohmeier, Martin. *Crucial Images in the Presentation of a Kurdish National Identity: Heroes and Patriots, Traitors and Foes.* Leiden: Brill, 2003.

Sykes, Mark. *Dar-ul-Islam*, London: Draft Publishers Ltd, 1904.

Sykes, Mark. "The Kurdish Tribes of the Ottoman Empire." *The Journal of the Royal Anthropological Institute of Great Britain and Ireland* 38 (1908): 451–86.

Szanto, Edith. "'Zoroaster Was a Kurd!': Neo-Zoroastrianism among the Iraqi Kurds." *Iran and the Caucasus* 22, no. 1 (2018): 96–110.

Taylor, Charles. "The Politics of Recognition." In *Multiculturalism: Examining the Politics of Recognition*, edited by Amy Gutmann, 25–86. Princeton: Princeton University Press, 1994.

Tek, Ayhan. "Yanlis Yorumlarin Golgesindeki Ehmedê Xanî'ye Sahih Bir Yaklasim." In *Kurt Tarihi ve Siyasetinden Portreler*, edited by Yalçın Çakmak and Tuncay Şur, 415–23. Istanbul: Iletisim Yayinlari, 2018.

Ter Minassian, Anahide Ter. *Ermeni Devrimci Hareketi'nde Milliyetçilik ve Sosyalizm, 1887–1912*, 1. basım., Cep üniversitesi 95. Cağaloğlu, İstanbul: İletişim Yayınları, 1992.

Tezcür, Güneş Murat. "When Democratization Radicalizes: The Kurdish Nationalist Movement in Turkey." *Journal of Peace Research* 47, no. 6 (2010): 775–89.

Tezcür, Güneş Murat. "The Ebb and Flow of Armed Conflict in Turkey: An Elusive Peace." In *Conflict, Democratization, and the Kurds in the Middle East*, edited by David Romano and Mehmet Gurses, 171–88. New York: Palgrave, 2014.

Tezcür, Güneş Murat. "Ordinary People, Extraordinary Risks: Participation in an Ethnic Rebellion." *American Political Science Review* 110, no. 2 (2016): 247–64.

Tezcür, Güneş Murat. "A Path Out of Patriarchy? Political Agency and Social Identity of Women Fighters." *Perspectives on Politics* (2019a). https://doi.org/10.1017/S1537592719000288.

Tezcür, Güneş Murat. "A Century of the Kurdish Question: Organizational Rivalries, Diplomacy, and Cross-Ethnic Coalitions." *Ethnopolitics* 18, no. 1 (2019b): 1–12.

Tilly, Charles. "States and Nationalism in Europe 1492–1992." *Theory and Society* 23, no. 1 (1994): 131–46.

Torî. *Bir Kürt Düşüncesi: Yezidilik ve Yezidiler*. Istanbul: Berfin Yayınları, 2000.

Tripp, Charles. *A History of Iraq*. 2nd ed. New York: Cambridge University Press, 2002.

Türkmen, Gülay. "Negotiating Symbolic Boundaries in Conflict Resolution: Religion and Ethnicity in Turkey's Kurdish Conflict." *Qualitative Sociology* 41, no. 4 (2018): 569–91.

Türkyılmaz, Yektan. *Rethinking Genocide: Violence and Victimhood in Eastern Anatolia, 1913–1915*. PhD diss., Duke University, 2011.

Tyner, Judith A. "Persuasive Cartography." *Journal of Geography* 82, no. 4 (1982): 140–4.

Uluğ, Özden Melis, and J. Christopher Cohrs. "An Exploration of Lay People's Kurdish Conflict Frames in Turkey." *Peace Conflict: Journal of Peace Psychology* 22, no. 2 (2016): 109–19.

Ünlü, Barış. "The Kurdish Struggle and the Crisis of the Turkishness Contract." *Philosophy & Social Criticism* 42, no. 4–5 (2016): 397–405.

Vali, Abbas. *Essays on the Origins of Kurdish Nationalism*. Costa Meza, California: Mazda Publishers, 2003.

van Bruinessen, Martin. "17. Yüzyılda Kürtler ve Dilleri: Kürt Lehçeleri Üzerine Evliya Çelebi'nin Notları." *Studia Kurdica* 1–3 (1985): 13–37.

van Bruinessen, Martin. *Agha, Shaikh and the State: The Social and Political Structures of Kurdistan*. New Jersey: Zed, 1992.

van Bruinessen, Martin. "Nationalisme Kurde et Ethnicités Intra-kurdes." *Peuples Méditerranéens* 68–69 (1994): 11–37.

van Bruinessen, Martin. "Kurdistan in the 16th and 17th Centuries, as Reflected in Evliya Çelebi's *Seyahatname*." *The Journal of Kurdish Studies* 3 (2000): 1–11.

van Bruinessen, Martin. "Ehmedê Xanî's *Mem û Zîn* and Its Role in the Emergence of Kurdish National Awareness." In *Essays on the Origins of Kurdish Nationalism*, edited by Abbas Vali, 40–57. California: Mazda Publishers, 2003.

van Bruinessen, Martin. "Kurdish Paths to Nation." In *The Kurds: Nationalism and Politics*, edited by Faleh A. Jabarand Hosham Dawod, 21–48. London, San Francisco, Beirut: Saqi Books, 2006.

van Bruinessen, Martin, and Hendrik Boeschoten, *Evliya Çelebi in Diyarbekir*: The Relevant Section of the Seyhatname. New York: E.J. Brill, 1988.

Weiss, Matthew. "From Constructive Engagement to Renewed Estrangement? Securitization and Turkey's Deteriorating Relations with Its Kurdish Minority." *Turkish Studies* 17, no. 4 (2016): 567–98.

Whelan, Anthony. "Wilsonian Self-Determination and the Versailles Settlement." *International and Comparative Law Quarterly* 43 (1994): 99–115.

Wimmer, Andreas. *Nationalist Exclusion and Ethnic Conflict: Shadows of Modernity.* Cambridge: Cambridge University Press, 2002.

Wimmer, Andreas. "Elementary Strategies of Ethnic Boundary Making." *Ethnic and Racial Studies* 31, no. 6 (2008): 1025–55.

Wintle, Michael. "Renaissance Maps and the Construction of the Idea of Europe." *Journal of Historical Geography* 25, no. 2 (1999): 137–65.

Xanî, Ehmedê. *Memozîn.* Stockholm: Nefel, 2004.

Xanî, Ehmedê. *Mem û Zîn.* Istanbul: Nûbihar, 2010.

Xanî, Ehmedê. *Ehmedê Xanî: Hemû Berhem.* Diyarbakir: Weşanen Lis, 2019.

Yadırgı, Veli. *The Political Economy of the Kurds of Turkey: From the Ottoman Empire to the Turkish Republic.* Cambridge: Cambridge University Press, 2017.

Yeğen, Mesut. "Türkiye Solu ve Kürt Sorunu." In *Modern Türkiye'de Siyasi Düşünce: Sol,* edited by Tanil Bora and Murat Gültekingil, 1208–36. Istanbul: Iletisim Yayınları, 2007.

Yeğen, Mesut. "'Prospective-Turks' or 'Pseudo-Citizens': Kurds in Turkey." *The Middle East Journal* 63, no. 4 (2009): 597–615.

Yeğen, Mesut. "The Turkish Left and the Kurdish Question." *Journal of Balkan and Near Eastern Studies* 18, no. 2 (2016): 157–76.

Yiftachel, Oren. *Ethnocracy: Land and Identity Politics in Israel/Palestine.* Pennsylvania: University of Pennsylvania Press, 2006.

Yıldırım, Kadri. *Ehmedê Xanî'nin Fikir Dünyası.* Ağrı: Ağrı Kültür ve Yardımlaşma Derneği Yayını, 2011.

Yılmaz, Arzu. *Atruş'tan Maxmur'a: Kürt Mülteciler ve Kimliğin Yeniden İnşası.* Istanbul: İletişim Yayınları, 2016.

Yılmaz, Arzu. "Gegeneinander, miteinander: Die KDP und die PKK in Sindschar." In *Die Kurden im Irak und in Syrien nach dem Ende der Territorialherrschaft des "Islamischen Staates,"* edited by Günter Seufert, 46–57. Berlin: Stiftung Wissenschaft und Politik, 2018.

Zaller, John. *The Nature and Origins of Mass Opinion.* Cambridge: Cambridge University Press, 1992.

Zaza, Nurettin. *Memê Alan.* Damascus: Wesanen Orfeus, 1996.

Zeydanlıoğlu, Welat. "Turkey's Kurdish Language Policy." *International Journal of the Sociology of Language* 217 (2012): 99–125.

Zolberg, Aristotle, A. Shurke, and S. Aguayo, *Escape from Violence: Conflict and the Refugee Crisis in the Developing World.* New York: Oxford University Press, 1989.

Reports

Armenian Church. *Teghekagir Hoghayin Grawmants' Handznazhoghovoy I.* K. Polis: Tpagr. T. Tōghramachean, 1910.

Armenian Church. *Teghekagir Hoghayin Grawmants' Handznazhoghovoy II.* K. Polis: Tpagr. T. Tōghramachean, 1911.

Armenian Church. *Teghekagir Hoghayin Grawmants' Handznazhoghovoy III.* K. Polis: Tpagr. T. Tōghramachean, 1912a.

Armenian Church. *Teghekagir Hoghayin Grawmants' Handznazhoghovoy IV*. K. Polis: Tpagr. T. Tōghramachean, 1912b.

Black, Jeremy. *Maps and Politics*. London: University of Chicago Press, 2000.

Board of Relief and Humanitarian Affairs (BRHA). "IDPS and Refugees in Duhok Governate: Profile and General Information," Annual Report, 2016. Duhok: Duhok Governate, 2017

Bor, Güley. "Response to and Reparations for Conflict-Related Sexual Violence in Iraq: The Case of Shi'a Turkmen in Tel Afar." *LSE Middle East Centre Reports*, London, 2019. http://eprints.lse.ac.uk/102145/.

Danish Immigration Service. "Security and Human Rights Issues in Kurdistan Region of Iraq (KRI), and South/Central Iraq (S/C Iraq)." Copenhagen, 2009: 38–9. https://www.nyidanmark.dk/NR/rdonlyres/5EAE4A3C-B13E-4D7F-99D6-8F62EA3B2888/0/Iraqreport09FINAL.pdf

"The Deterioration of Economic, Social, and Cultural Rights." *Geneva International Centre for Justice*. Geneva, 2015. https://tbinternet.ohchr.org/Treaties/CESCR/Shared%20Documents/IRQ/INT_CESCR_CSS_IRQ_21658_E.pdf.

General Directorate Yezidi Affairs in the Ministry of Endowments and Religious Affairs, KRG; Duhok Governorate, Board of Relief and Humanitarian Affairs (BRHA), Executive Directorate, IDPs and Refugees in Duhok Governorate: Profile and General Information, 2016.

Human Rights Watch (HRW). "Turkey: Turkey's Failed Policy to Aid the Forcibly Displaced in the Southeast." 1996. https://www.hrw.org/reports/1996/Turkey2.htm.

Human Right Watch (HRW). "World Report 2008." 2008. https://www.hrw.org/world-report/2008.

Human Rights Watch (HRW). "On Vulnerable Ground: Violence against Minority Communities in Nineveh Province's Disputed Territories." 2009. https://www.hrw.org/report/2009/11/10/vulnerable-ground/violence-against-minority-communities-nineveh-provinces-disputed.

Human Rights Watch (HRW). "Flawed Justice: Accountability for ISIS Crimes in Iraq." 2017. https://www.hrw.org/report/2017/12/05/flawed-justice/accountability-isis-crimes-iraq.

"Humanitarian Situation of the Kurdish Refugees and Displaced Persons in South-East Turkey and North Iraq Report No. 8131." Committee on Migration, Refugees and Demography, Parliamentary Assembly, May 3, 1998.

Ibn-I Nuh. *Van Tarihi*. Translated by Zeki Tekin. Van: Ahenk Yayinevi, 2003.

IDPs and Refugees in Duhok Governorate Profile and General Information, KRG Board of Relief and Humanitarian Affairs, B.R.H.A., Executive Directorate, February 2016.

IDPs and Refugees in Duhok Governorate Profile and General Information, KRG Board of Relief and Humanitarian Affairs, B.R.H.A., Executive Directorate, February 2017.

International Crisis Group. "Iraq's New Battlefront: The Struggle over Ninewa." 2009.

International Crisis Group. "Winning the Post-ISIS Battle for Iraq in Sinjar. Middle East report No. 183." 2018. https://www.crisisgroup.org/middle-east-north-africa/gulf-and-arabian-peninsula/iraq/183-winning-post-isis-battle-iraq-sinjar.

Jefferson, LaShawn. "In War as in Peace: Sexual Violence and Women's Status." *Human Rights Watch*. 2004. https://www.hrw.org/news/2004/01/25/war-peace-sexual-violence-and-womens-status

League of Nations. "Question of the Frontier between Turkey and Iraq. Report submitted to the Council by the Commission instituted by the Council Resolution of September 30th, 1924 (1925)."

Maisel, Sebastian. "Social Change amidst Terror and Discrimination: Yezidis in the New Iraq." *The Middle East Institute Policy Brief 18*, 2008.

"Memorandum on the Claims of the Kurd People." Kurdish Delegation to the Peace Conference. Paris, 2019.

Office of the United High Commissioner for Human Rights (OCHR). "They Came to Destroy: ISIS Crimes against the Yazidis." 2016. https://www.ohchr.org/Documents/HRBodies/HRCouncil/CoISyria/A_HRC_32_CRP.2_en.pdf.

"PAX for Peace: After ISIS: Perspectives of Displaced Communities from Ninewa on Return to Iraq's Disputed Territory." Colophon. 2015. https://www.paxforpeace.nl/media/files/pax-iraq-report-after-isis.pdf

RSHID International e.V, Yazda, and Endangered Archaeology in the Middle East and North Africa (EAMENA). "Destroying the Soul of the Yezidis: Cultural Heritage Destruction during the Islamic State's Genocide against the Yezidis." 2019. https://docs.wixstatic.com/ugd/92f016_b5b37c3356754ba8b30e0f266e5b58d4.pdf

Salloum, Saad, Saad Salah, and Majid Hassan. "Political Participation of Minorities in Iraq." Baghdad: *Heartland Alliance International & MCMD*, 2015. http://masaratiraq.org/wp-content/uploads/2016/02/POLITICAL-PARTICIPATION-OF.pdf.

Smith, Crispin, and Vartan Shadarevian. "Wilting in the Kurdish Sun: The Hopes and Fears of Religious Minorities in Northern Iraq." *United States Commission on International Religious Freedom*, 2017.

TEVDA. "The Founding Statement of the Preparatory Committee, the Free Yezidi Democratic Movement." January 2, 2004a.

TEVDA. "The Final Statement of the Free Yezidi Democratic Movement." March 18–20, 2004b.

Turshen, Meredeth. "The Political Economy of Rape: An Analysis of Systematic Rape and Sexual Abuse of Women during Armed Conflict in Africa." In *Victors, Perpetrators or Actors: Gender, Armed Conflict and Political Violence*, edited by C. Moser and F. Clarke, 55–68. London: Zed Books, 2001.

UK House of Commons, Foreign Affairs Committee. "Kurdish Aspirations and the Interests of the UK." Third Report of Session 2017–19, 2018.

United Nations Assistance Mission for Iraq (UNAMI). "District Analysis Summary. Sinjar District and Qahtaniya Sub-District." 2009.

United Nations High Commissioner for Refugees (UNHCR). "Background Information on the Situation of Non-Muslim Religious Minorities in Iraq." 2005. https://www.refworld.org/pdfid/4371cf5b4.pdf.

United Nations Human Settlements Programme in Iraq (UNHABITAT). "Emerging Land Tenure Issues among Displaced Yazidis from Sinjar, Iraq." 2015. https://unhabitat.org/wp-content/uploads/2015/12/Emerging%20Land%20Tenure%20Issues%20among%20Displaced%20Yazidis%20from%20Sinjar%20Iraq.pdf.

United States Institute of Peace (USIP). "Iraq's Disputed Territories: A View of the Political Horizon and Implications for U.S. Policy." 2011. https://www.usip.org/publications/2011/04/iraqs-disputed-territories.

Newspaper Articles and Online News Sources

Ahmado, Nisan. "Uncertain Future Awaits Displaced Syrian Yazidis in Lebanon." *Voa News*. May 12, 2019. https://www.voanews.com/extremism-watch/uncertain-future-awaits-displaced-syrian-yazidis-lebanon.

Altuğ, Seda. "The Armenian Genocide, Sheikh Said Revolt, and Armenians in Syrian-Jazira." *The Armenian Weekly, Hairenik Association Eastern Region* USA. May 8, 2010.

https://armenians-1915.blogspot.com/2010/05/3085-armenian-genocide-sheikh-said.
html.

"Assessing Kurdish Militancy in Armenia—So Far, Not Too Much (telegram)." *WikiLeaks*.
October 24, 2006. https://wikileaks.org/plusd/cables/06YEREVAN1484_a.html.

"Atrosh Camp: Facts of the Cause and Practices of PKK." *Brayeti Press*, 1999.

Barber, Matthew. "The KRG's Relationship with the Yezidi Minority and the Future of the
Yezidis in Shingal." *Joshua Landis.com*. January 31, 2017. https://www.joshualandis.
com/blog/krgs-relationship-yazidi-minority-future-yazidis-shingal-sinjar/.

"Barzanî: Kurdên êzîdî nasnameya netewî ya kurdî parastine." *Rudaw*. August 3, 2015.
https://www.rudaw.net/kurmanci/kurdistan/0308201516.

"BM Göçe El Attı." *Özgür Ülke*. May 28, 1994.

"BM'den Kürt Göçmenlere Güvenli Bölge." *Özgür Ülke*. May 18, 1994.

"Christian Women Kidnapped by IS Reunited with Father after Four Years." *Kurdistan
24*. April 5, 2018. https://www.kurdistan24.net/en/news/987a77c3-56c3-44b7-a8f9-
e6a8d63d0e00.

"Dağ'a Çıkarız." *Milliyet*. February 12, 1997.

Eziden Weltweit EWW [Initiative for Yezidis around the World]. February 7, 2015. http://
ezidis.org/.

"Êzîdxan - Ezidi Anthem." *ÊzîdîPress*. January 22, 2017. https://www.youtube.com/
watch?v=ZniTg73Xwgs.

"The Failed Crusade." *Dabiq*. October 11, 2014, 4.

"Göçenler Güney'de de Hedef." *Özgür Ülke*. June 21, 1994.

Haratch, June 9, 1909, 3.

Haratch, June 12, 1909, 4.

Haratch, July 3, 1909, 10.

Haratch, November 10, 1909, 47.

Haratch, December 18, 1909, 58.

Ibrahim, Shivan. "US Wants Kurdish Groups to Reconcile in Eastern Syria." *Al-Monitor*.
July 17, 2019. https://www.al-monitor.com/pulse/originals/2019/07/syria-kurdish-
national-council-dispute-us-france-initiative.html.

"Iraq Voters Back New Constitution." *British Broadcasting Corporation (BBC)*. October 25,
2005. http://news.bbc.co.uk/2/hi/middle_east/4374822.stm.

Iris, June 1, 1911, 6.

Iris, June 15, 1911, 7.

"Ji Mîre Êzidiyên Cîhanê banga referandûmê." *Rudaw*. September 23, 2017. https://www.
rudaw.net/kurmanci/kurdistan/230920175.

"KRG Divided: Special Advisor Krajeski Discusses Corruption, Media Freedom, and
Minority Issues with Kurdish and Yezidi Leaders, Part I." *WikiLeaks*. December 1,
2008. https://wikileaks.org/plusd/cables/08BAGHDAD3776_a.html.

"Kürt Göçmenler Eylemde." *Özgür Ülke*. June 14, 1994.

"Kürtleri Sınırdışı Etmek Cinayettir." *Özgür Gündem*. March 25, 1994.

"Kuzey Irak'a Göç." *Milliyet*. July 19, 1994.

"Lone Yezidi Parliamentarian Criticizes Kurdish Treatment of Minorities." *WikiLeaks*.
March 7, 2006. https://wikileaks.org/plusd/cables/06BAGHDAD736_a.html.

Metzadurian, K. "The Boons of the Constitution." *Antranik*. May 23, 1909, 19.

"Mülteci Cumhuriyeti." *Milliyet*. December 26, 1996.

"Obama Allows Limited Airstrikes on ISIS." *The New York Times*. August 7, 2014. https://
www.nytimes.com/2014/08/08/world/middleeast/obama-weighs-military-strikes-to-
aid-trapped-iraqis-officials-say.html.

Pet, M. "The Situation of Bulanık." *Haratch*. August 21, 1909, 24.

"PKK'nın yeni adı KADEK." *Radikal*, April 17, 2002. http://www.radikal.com.tr/turkiye/pkknin-yeni-adi-kadek-629948.

"PM Barzani Pledges Continued Support for Yezidis on Genocide Anniversary." *Rudaw.* August 3, 2018. https://www.rudaw.net/english/kurdistan/030820182.

"Rebellious Yezidis Are Subdued in Iraq." *The New York Times.* October 26, 1935.

Salloum, Saad. "Will Iraq's Minorities Return to Their Homelands Post-IS?" *Al-Monitor.* August 14, 2016. https://www.al-monitor.com/pulse/originals/2016/08/minorities-nineveh-iraq-kurdistan.html#ixzz5yjz7E9Ai.

"Statement on the Occasion of the Day of Ezidkhan National Flag." *Xabercom: Independent Iraqi Newspaper.* September 4, 2015. http://xebercom.com/2015/09/ب‌ن‌اي-بهمن‌اس‌بق-إلا-اهي‌أ-ن‌اخدي‌ز ي‌إ-مل‌ع-موي.

Tezcür, Güneş Murat. "Three Years Ago, the Islamic State Massacred Yazidis in Iraq. Why?" *The Monkey Cage Blog of the Washington Post.* August 15, 2017. https://www.washingtonpost.com/news/monkey-cage/wp/2017/08/15/three-years-ago-the-islamic-state-massacred-yazidis-in-iraq-why/.

"Türkiye Göçmenler için Güney'e Heyet Gönderdi." *Özgür Ülke*, March 17, 1997.

Turshen, Meredeth. "The Political Economy of Rape: An Analysis of Systematic Rape and Sexual Abuse of Women during Armed Conflict in Africa." In *Victors, Perpetrators or Actors: Gender, Armed Conflict and Political Violence*, edited by C. Moser and F. Clarke, 55–68. London: Zed Books, 2001.

Tutuncian, Arshak. "Hınıs: Educational Situation." *Haratch*, August 25, 1909, 25.

"Press Release." *Yazda.* May 15, 2016. https://www.facebook.com/yazda.organization/posts/yazda-press-releasea-statement-about-recent-political-developments-in-shingal-si/484781928398425/.

"Yezidi Protest at Embassy." *WikiLeaks.* April 27, 2007. https://wikileaks.org/plusd/cables/07YEREVAN528_a.html.

Yilmaz, Algin. "Die Eziden aber bezeichnen ihre Sprache als 'zyman e ezda' (die Sprache der Eziden)." *ÊzîdîPress.* September 12, 2018. http://www.ezidipress.com/blog/ezdiki-die-sprache-der-eziden/.

Official Documents

"Al-Waqa'I' al-Iraqiyya [The Official Gazette of Iraq]." September 19, 1972, 2184. http://gjpi.org/wp-content/uploads/2009/02/iraqstatuteengtrans.pdf; http://wiki.dorar-aliraq.net/iraqilaws/law/5663.html.

Devlet Arşivleri Başkanlığı (Directorate of State Archives of the Republic of Turkey). A. {DVNS.MHM.d., 2/319, 27 R. 963 (March 10, 1556), A. (DVNS.MHM.d., 2/320, 27 R. 963 (March 10, 1556).

"The Kingdom of Iraq and Its Minorities," Memorandum (n.d.), Foreign Office 371/15316, in: Rush, Alan de Lacy, and Jane Priestland, eds. 2001. Records of Iraq, 1914–1966, Vol. 6: 1930–1932: Mandate to Treaty (Slough: Archive Editions, 2001).

Law No.1, 1982, An Amendment to the Religious Cult Patronage Law: The Religious Cults Officially Recognized in Iraq, No.32 of 1981. Al-Waqa'I' al-Iraqiyya, Vol. 2867, dated January 18, 1982.

UN Security Council. "Security Council Resolution 688, S/RES/688." April 5, 1991. http://www.refworld.org/docid/3b00f1598.html.

Selected Interviews and Personal Communication

Interview with Abdulaziz Tayyib, Former Governor of Duhok, Duhok, March 6, 2011.
Interview with M. A. Misirik, KRI (Kurdistan Region of Iraq), March 16, 2011.
Interview with Osman Öcalan, Koya, KRI, July 11, 2011.
Interview with R. K., Misirik, KRI, February 1, 2012.
Interview with M. A., Gregewre, KRI, February 5, 2012.
Interview with M. C., Mele Berwan, KRI, February 15, 2012.
Interview with L. Y., Hassaniye, KRI, March 1, 2012.
Interview with M. F., Gregewre, KRI, March 12, 2012.
Interview with B. A., Hassaniye, KRI, March 22, 2012.
Interview with Süleyman Hasso, Semel, KRI, April 17, 2012.
Interview with M. Z., Maxmur Camp, Iraq, May 13, 2012.
Interview with H. A., Maxmur Camp, May 18, 2012.
Interview with M. H., Maxmur Camp, May 23, 2012.
Interview with H. R., Maxmur Camp, May 26, 2012.
Interview with S. H., Maxmur Camp, May 26, 2012.
Interview with S. T., Maxmur Camp, May 26, 2012.
Interview with R. K., Maxmur Camp, May 26, 2012.
Interview with M. Ş., Maxmur Camp, May 27, 2012.
Interview with R. O., Maxmur Camp, May 28, 2012.
Interview with Osman Öcalan, Koya, KRI, May 28, 2012.
Interview with Abdurrahman Belaf, former Governor of Maxmur district, Erbil, June 15, 2012.
Interview with Murat Karayılan, Qandil, KRI, May 25, 2013.
Interview with L. I., Maxmur Camp, Iraq, May 27, 2013.
Interview with S. A., Hassaniye, KRI, June 21, 2012.
Interview with Nizamettin Taş, Erbil, KRI, September 29, 2014.
Interview with a Yezidi religious authority, Sheikhan, September 27, 2017.
Conversations with Yezidi community members, Duhok, December 2017 and May 2018.
Interview with a Yezidi IDP, Duhok, April 20, 2018.
Conversations with members of Yezidi community, Duhok, May 2018.
Interview with a Yezidi faculty member, Duhok, May 28, 2018.
Interview with a Yezidi IDP, Duhok, May 26, 2018.
Interview with Khidir Domle, Duhok, May 28, 2018.
Interview with a Yezidi female humanitarian NGO staff, Duhok, May 29, 2018.
Interview with Prince Hassan, Prince's House in Sheikhan, May 29, 2018.
Interview with a Yezidi politician affiliated with a Kurdish party, Duhok, May 31, 2018.
Interview with two Yezidi sexual violence survivors, Sharya camp, Duhok, May 31, 2018.
Interview with a Yezidi originally from Sinjar (Skype), October 4, 2018.
Interview with a Yezidi refugee living in the United States (Skype), November 27, 2018.
Interview with Hussein Kuro Ibrahim, Duhok, August 12, 2019.

INDEX